A COUNTRY OF WORDS

Abdel Bari Atwan

A Country of Words

A Palestinian Journey from the
Refugee Camp to the Front Page

SAQI

London   San Francisco   Beirut

ISBN: 978-0-86356-621-9

A full CIP record for this book is available from the British Library.
A full CIP record for this book is available from the Library of Congress.

Manufactured in Lebanon

SAQI
26 Westbourne Grove, London W2 5RH
825 Page Street, Suite 203, Berkeley, California 94710
Tabet Building, Mneimneh Street, Hamra, Beirut
www.saqibooks.com

To refugee children all over the world, especially those in Palestine and the diaspora.

To Mai Ghoussoub

We Travel Like Other People

We travel like other people, but we return to nowhere ...
We have a country of words. Speak speak so I can put my road on the
    stone of a stone.
We have a country of words. Speak speak so we may know the end of
    this travel.

Mahmoud Darwish
from *Victims of a Map*, Saqi , 2005

Contents

Acknowledgments

I am especially grateful to Susan de Muth who helped me with researching and writing this book. Also to Said Aburish, who found the time, despite ill health, to revise some of the chapters and give me his observations which I greatly appreciated.

Without the late Mai Ghoussoub's persistence and persuasion this book would not have come into existence. It is a matter of deep regret that she did not live to see the manuscript. André Gaspard, the publisher of this volume, took over where Mai left off and it was his encouraging comments and support that gave me the impetus to finish the project.

I must also thank my family, Basima, Khalid, Nada and Kareem, not only for starring in several episodes in my memoir, but because they were so patient when writing this book impinged on the very little free time I have to spend with them. Khalid and Nada read the manuscript and were my harshest critics; I eventually saw the light and accepted their censorship for which I am grateful.

Preface

When my late, and very dear, friend Mai Ghoussoub first suggested that I write this memoir I admit that I hesitated. Mai, however, was of the opinion that my journey from the refugee camps of the Gaza Strip to a fairly elevated position in the international media was not only intriguing but 'inspirational'. The latter is my goal: if my experiences can encourage other people in difficult circumstances to persevere and go after their dearest wish, despite all the obstacles fate may throw in their path, then I will be content and Mai's faith in the project will not have been in vain.

Another aspect of this memoir that I hope will have a lasting impact is my first-hand account of life in the occupied territories of Palestine. The level of suffering and poverty in Gaza has not improved; in fact it is now worse than ever, and I hope, through telling my story, to bring this blighted part of the globe to my readers' attention. Not that this is a sombre tome. Far from it. There have been tragic moments in my life, of course, but many more that are amusing.

I have lived in London for thirty years with one foot firmly in the West and with the other in the turbulent Middle East. This has given me an unusual perspective and objective standpoint on a narrative of people, events and politics in both worlds which I hope is represented in these pages.

As the founding editor of one of the Arab world's first truly independent newspapers, *al-Quds al-Arabi*, and as a regular contributor to al-Jazeera and many Western media outlets, I am well placed to comment on the Arab media and to reflect on the Western media's representation of the Middle East.

In short, I hope that this book will reach a wide audience and that the reader will find much in these pages that is new, informative, amusing and challenging.

A. B. Atwan
London, February 2008

I

Thorns in our Feet

In Palestine, there is a forty-day period from late December when the nights are long and icy cold and nobody ventures out. My earliest memories are set in this winter darkness, in Deir al-Balah refugee camp in the Gaza Strip. We children used to sit on the floor round the fire, huddled against each other for warmth, our faces illuminated by the glowing logs as our mother told us stories. The roof above us was made of sticks and branches, the walls of mud, but this little house was luxury compared with the tent we had initially been given by the UN.

My mother, Zarifa Atwan, was illiterate but, like most women of her generation, knew hundreds of narratives by heart; some were traditional folk tales, others sprang from her imagination, and all were rich in detail and observation. She terrified us with supernatural tales of ghosts and djinns and fuelled our blossoming imaginations with strange legends and fabulous creatures of her own invention. It was the stories from her past, though, that affected us most deeply and we loved to hear about Isdud, the small Mediterranean village she and my father lived in until the *Nakba* or catastrophe befell the Palestinian people in 1948.

In those days Isdud was home to fewer than 5,000 Palestinian people. Under Israeli occupation, it was renamed Ashdod and became their largest seaport with a population of 204,000. My mother often talked about the idyllic life she and my father had enjoyed there, farming land that had been in the family for generations; we knew every detail of the house, the colourful rugs and mattresses on the floor, the shady courtyard which was the centre of domestic life, shared with sheep and chickens and ducks. My mother made it seem as if it had all been a wonderful dream, revisiting it in her mind's eye as she gazed into the firelight. 'There was fruit growing in the courtyard,' she told us. 'You could pick the figs and eat them straight from the trees.'

We knew what was coming next: 'And the berries, Yamma? Tell us about the berries!'

'You have never seen such berries!' Her eyes used to widen as if she was seeing them again. 'We used to wait until evening when they were just about to burst and pick them right at the last minute and eat them all up!' She would mime scooping handfuls of juicy berries into her mouth, making us laugh. 'Delicious!' she'd sigh, 'But gone now. All gone ...' Her smile would fade but we'd clamour for another glimpse of that lost paradise.

She'd tell us then about a time when there was no money because there was no need for it. 'Our village produced wheat and peas and okra that we stitched onto strings to dry. We stored what we needed for the winter and anything left over was bartered or exchanged. We couldn't grow olives because the land wasn't dry enough by the sea but traders used to come from Nablus and Tulkarm and trade olive oil for our grain. It was a simple time, we hadn't learned to fear strangers then.'

If foreigners were passing through they would be entertained by the village men in a guest house owned by the wealthiest family, with food and accommodation freely offered. Should they want to stay, they would be absorbed into a traditional, tribal society. Palestinian villages and towns often contained several tribes and each would have its own quarter. The newcomers, according to my mother, would be 'distributed equally' between the tribes because nobody wanted to miss out. Once assimilated, they were protected and enjoyed full citizenship.

Occupation

Jewish migration to Palestine started in 1882 following the formation of the Zionist movement in Europe and in response to widespread pogroms in Russia the previous year. At the time, few Palestinian villagers would have suspected that the trickle of strangers fleeing persecution in the West would ultimately become their mortal enemies. Indeed, they welcomed them and extended the hospitality Arabs offer all visitors. In the 1920s and 1930s the number of Jewish settlers increased due to the rise of anti-Semitism in Europe, and Zionist agencies started to purchase land. The three primary Jewish land companies, whose names are revealing, were the Palestine Jewish Colonization Association (PICA), the Palestine Land Development Company and the Jewish National Fund. Over 50 percent of land settled by Jews was purchased from absentee landlords, replacing Arab tenants with European Jewish settlers. Other major landowners, such as the churches and foreign companies, were enticed into selling their land for sizeable profits, seemingly without any thought for the political and geographical implications of their actions. Indigenous smallholders were also approached, including my grandfather who owned a strip of land by the sea adjoining a new Jewish settlement. He refused, and my father told me that he had lectured the whole neighbourhood on the dangers of selling their land which was the only source of an independent livelihood.

In the aftermath of the First World War, Palestine had been mandated to Britain at the 1920 San Remo conference and remained under heavy-handed British administration until 1948, a situation that created a great deal of resentment, several uprisings and numerous employment opportunities. In 1940, my newly married father was tempted into abandoning the family fields and his principles for lucrative building work at the British army barracks; for one day's work a man could earn as much as he could reap from the land in a month. He omitted to tell my grandfather, and when he came back after the first week was greeted with an axe. 'If you go back to work for the British I will kill you,' my grandfather said. 'Imagine the shame we will bring on ourselves if we sacrifice our pride and dignity for a few coins. Imagine the betrayal of future generations if we abandon the land that we love and that feeds us to the Zionists.' My father obeyed his father, and often told us this story. Whenever I have been tempted to compromise my beliefs in order to have security, be it financial or otherwise, it comes to mind.

My parents' young family expanded as they continued with their pleasant existence on the Mediterranean coast, as my mother used to recall on those cold nights around the fire in the refugee camp. She explained to us how hard people worked:

> As soon as I woke, I would go and clean up under the cows, taking the manure for fertilizer in the fields. Nothing was wasted. Then I came back into the house, woke the children up – there were four already – and gave them some breakfast. The older ones went off to school and I'd go to the fields with your father, to help with weeding or harvesting depending on the time of year. We women used to take the younger children with us, the babies in slings which we'd hang from a bough or a nail in the wall. At lunchtime I'd make food for everyone, and so it went on, from dawn to sunset everyday. The women helped with the threshing too. Sometimes your father would sleep on the threshing floor – which the whole village used – to make sure our grain didn't get mixed up with anyone else's. We made butter and clay cooking pots, and fetched water. There was always something that had to be done. It was hard work but everything was satisfying; you felt you were on God's earth for a purpose.

My mother wore traditional Palestinian costume – the *thoub* – for the whole of her life. This full, long-sleeved garment had evolved over the centuries to be at once practical for work and modest; my mother's generation could never have anticipated the strong political and nationalistic associations the *thoub* has acquired in more recent times. Women in Gaza refugee camps, for example, commemorated the outbreak of the al-Aqsa intifada in 2000 with a *thoub* made of Palestinian flags and embroidered with pictures of the Dome of the Rock. My mother taught us how to recognize which part of Palestine a woman came from by the intricately embroidered panels on the chest, sides, sleeves and hem of her *thoub*. The panels were embroidered separately, she explained, and then pieced together with fabric. The number of pieces was a further indicator of origin: the *thoub* from Bethlehem was made of twenty-five sections, for example, while a Gazan dress contained just fourteen. This tradition has continued to the present day – even in the diaspora communities of exiled Palestinians, women have developed their own style of traditional dress as a statement of their identity: I encountered one such group on a trip to Sydney in 2007.

My parents had to work hard in their Isdud days, but there were plenty of occasions for festivities and we loved hearing about the villagers' parties and celebrations. Weddings lasted a week with day after day of music and dancing – some people were too poor to own musical instruments but, according to my mother, every family had at least one great singer who made up for the lack of flutes and drums with his or her vocal power. Circumcision, the return of a pilgrim from the *Hajj* to Mecca, Eid, and the first reading of the Qur'an in its entirety by a young boy, were all reasons for the community to come together. There were even parties when the roof was completed on a new house, and the village would collectively put on a feast, giving the head mason a robe or coat in celebration.

Marriages were arranged by family discussion, witnessed by the local religious Sheikh and *mukhtar* (head of the village). 'Will you marry my daughter?' 'I accept your daughter as my wife.' That was it. Nothing was registered, not even births and deaths. Few Arabs of that generation know when they were born. My mother would tell us how people's birthdays were recorded in public memory, according to a significant event: my father, for example, was born 'before the severe heat wave'. We were particularly struck by the idea that one of my uncles was born 'on the day the British soldier fell from the sky with his parachute'. This remarkable event happened towards the end of the Second World War, and it was a great day for that part of the village because 'everybody got new silk trousers'.

The closeness of these communities also meant there was little petty crime. 'In a village everybody knows your business,' she pointed out. 'The shame would be so great that a criminal would have to leave and never come back.' Where there were disputes, she said that an elder or a tribal leader would be consulted. The two sides would be brought together to work out a compromise. In some villages even murders were dealt with in this way, with *diya* (blood money) paid in cash or cows.

This simple lifestyle was totally uprooted and destroyed in the months following the Declaration of the Independent State of Israel on Palestinian land on 14 May 1948. My story is linked to that of my family's, which in turn is entwined with the tragedy of Palestine's recent history.

Despite the fact that I have British nationality, as a Palestinian I still harbour some resentment towards my host nation for the role it played in the downfall of my people, and their long-standing interference in Arab affairs in general. The infamous Balfour Declaration of 1917, in which the

British government backed 'the establishment in Palestine of a homeland for the Jewish people', was born of just such meddling. The British had only been able to invade Palestine, which was then part of the Ottoman Empire, on the back of a pan-Arab uprising against the Ottomans, led by Hussein bin Ali who was born in what is now Saudi Arabia. In order to encourage the Arab uprising, the British had promised Hussein that he would head a large independent Arab state with Syria at its heart. At the same time, Syria had been allocated to the French as part of the intended post-war partition of the region outlined in the Anglo-French Sykes–Picot agreement of 1916. The British had also assured Chaim Weizmann and the Zionists that Palestine would be the new Jewish homeland, totally disregarding the fact that it was already home to at least 1.5 million Palestinians. Hussein bin Ali's son, Faisal, proclaimed himself king of Syria in 1918 with full British support. He then entered the 1919 Faisal–Weizmann Agreement, backing the Jewish state with the proviso that they would support his wider ambitions in the region. When the French took Syria in 1920 and expelled Faisal he fled to London where it was decided to make him king of Iraq instead.

The British army facilitated the Jewish occupation of Palestine in the early years. In 1929, the British reneged on their promise of parity for the Palestinians in a proposed Legislative Council – already a bitter enough pill for the Palestinians, who made up 90 percent of the population, to swallow – and widespread riots ensued. From 1936–9, there was a further sustained attempt by the Palestinians, known as the 'Great Uprising', to oust the occupiers but this was put down, often brutally, by the British army who had 100,000 troops stationed in Palestine – more than they then had in India. Yet after aiding the Jewish occupiers, the British government temporarily halted further immigration from Europe, stopping many from escaping Nazism and its horrors. By now the British were courting Arab support in their war with Hitler and needed troops that were tied up in Palestine to fight in Europe. Even after the war, Jews attempting to illegally enter Palestine in 1946–7, using small boats, were captured at sea by the British who put them in camps in Cyprus.

The United Nations (UN) intervened in 1947. The suffering of the Jewish population in the Holocaust had understandably created international sympathy for the idea of a Jewish state, but now the Palestinians were to suffer instead. A partition plan was proposed, giving more than half of Palestine to the Jews for an independent state, even though they owned only 6 percent of the land and constituted only 32 percent of the population. It was opposed by the Palestinians, surrounding Arab states and extremist Zionist groups such as the Irgun (at one point led by Menachem Begin, later Israeli prime minister) who wanted even more territory, including Jerusalem. It was the Irgun who, in July 1946, had blown up the King David Hotel in Jerusalem killing ninety-two Britons, Arabs and Jews in an attack that British Prime Minister Clement Atlee described as 'one of the most dastardly and cowardly crimes in recorded history'. The partition plan, contained in UN resolution 181, was adopted in November 1947 and British troops began to withdraw, leaving Palestine in chaos with Jews and Arabs in bloody conflict. On the evening of 14 May 1948 the Zionists declared the establishment of the state of Israel and full-scale war erupted between them and their five Arab neighbours. In just thirty years the political, social and psychological make-up of a once peaceful and stable nation had been thrown into a nightmarish maelstrom that endures to this day. The *Nakba*, which is still lamented every 15 May on the streets of Palestine, had well and truly begun.

Dispossession

Rumours of the massacres spread by word of mouth. There were no radios and few newspapers in the remote Palestinian villages. The Zionist strategy was to use fear to suppress the Palestinians and prevent them from becoming a violent enemy within. It is one of history's strangest ironies that those who had been the victims of persecution and genocide should now become perpetrators of such horrors themselves. My parents told us how news of the April 1948 Deir Yassin massacre had been brought to Isdud by a neighbour who had been to the market on his donkey. The paramilitary group, Haganah, which had several brigades, aided by elements from the Irgun and Stern gangs, had slaughtered and mutilated 254 innocent villagers; to ensure maximum terror they had bayoneted the bellies of twenty-five pregnant women and maimed fifty-two children in front of their petrified parents before beheading them.

Menachem Begin later disclosed that Deir Yassin was selected because it was on high ground between Tel Aviv and Jerusalem, and that the future state of Israel would need to build an airport landing strip there. Houses were dynamited and Israeli bulldozers destroyed the cemetery. The few survivors of the massacre fled for their lives, spared perhaps only to ensure that the news would be spread among the rest of the Palestinian population. By September, the village had been rebuilt and repopulated by Orthodox Jews, newly arrived from Poland, Romania and Slovenia. Deir Yassin was the first in a series of such land grabs and was the template for things to come.

From April 1948 onwards, a campaign of ethnic cleansing along the coastal region saw 400 Palestinian villages systematically wiped out. This bloody work was facilitated by the sinister 'village files' sponsored by the Jewish National Fund (JNF) which contained aerial photographs and detailed information concerning access routes and levels of 'hostility' among the populace towards the Zionist project. According to Ilan Pappe who has written at length about this in his book, *The Ethnic Cleansing of Palestine*, individuals who had participated in the 1936 uprising were identified in each village and later singled out for execution.

Utilizing the topographical information contained in the 'village files', the Alexandroni Brigade, part of Haganah, developed a chilling method whereby villages were surrounded on three sides, with the population put to flight through the fourth. In the case of Tantura, a large village of around 1,500 inhabitants, the Israelis decided to surround it on all sides and capture most of the villagers. Forced onto the beach, the women and children were sent off in lorries to Fureidis, a nearby village, while all the men under fifty-five were shot dead. When the Arab–Israeli War began in May 1948 it was against this backdrop of terror and intimidation which continues to this day.

Another well-documented attack, on the Palestinian village of Dawayma, took place in October 1948. This one, in which 100 people died, was notorious for the way in which the terrorists dispatched infants: by fracturing their skulls with heavy sticks. Some years later, convinced of the efficacy of a policy of terror, Ben-Gurion established Commando Unit 101, the Zahal, dedicated to this task alone and staffed entirely by volunteers. Its commander was Ariel Sharon, who would later become the Israeli leader. Unit 101 went into action on 14 October 1953 in a village on the Jordanian border called Kibya. Seventy-five Arabs were slaughtered and having run out of humans to shoot at, the unit turned its fire on the cows.

Like many men in our village, my father had managed to scrape together enough money to buy a gun, in his case by selling silver and gold that had been in our family for generations. But the weapon was to prove of little use to him when the Israelis came to Isdud on 28 October 1948.

My mother always wept when she spoke of the day her life changed forever. 'It was a cold day, like today', she told us.

> People were frightened by the stories of the massacre at Deir Yassin and feared that the Zionist terrorist groups would now come for them. Many villagers had already left for Gaza because people were saying this was the only safe place to go. It was so sad to see men, women, old people and children hurrying away, carrying everything they could manage in handcarts or cloth bundles. Your father insisted that we stay; he refused to be intimidated out of his family home. Suddenly, we heard a lot of trucks coming into the village and the sound of shots being fired into the air. We could hear loudspeakers and we rushed to the village square to see what was going on. It was the Israelis and they were saying in Arabic, 'Leave your houses and go to Gaza where you will be safe. If you don't leave we will kill you.' People started to panic. Nobody knew what to do [my mother told us, the tears brimming in her eyes]. Your father looked at me. He started to tell me not to worry, that the Arab armies would eventually be victorious and kick these invaders out of our country. Then we heard the gunshots – the Israelis had killed two men from our village at point-blank range. They were lying dead on the ground in a pool of blood and their women and children were hysterical. The villagers were herded into the Israeli trucks like cattle, the killings had made them silent and obedient, everyone was in a state of complete shock. We got in the trucks too. We didn't have time to pack, all we had were the clothes we were wearing, and all around us was the sound of women wailing and the explosions of Israeli mortar fire.

My parents, like thousands of others, believed they were leaving their village for a short time, until the combined Arab armies vanquished the Israelis or the world intervened. The minority educated middle class fled to oil-rich countries where they found good jobs, but most of the newly created refugees were poor, uneducated people who were strangers to hatred and had no experience of war and conflict. They were unprepared for what happened to them and for years accepted the situation passively. After the great uprising of 1936–9, many Palestinian resistance leaders had been killed or exiled, leaving the population with no organized means of defending themselves, and many from the older generation tried to prevent their children from becoming politicized for fear of retaliation.

My father was not the type to be a passive victim of history but in reality there was little he could do without getting shot for his trouble. He managed to revisit the house in Isdud just twice. The first time, he was able to collect a few possessions, including his gun which he had hidden in the roof. The second time, about two months after they had been expelled, he was heartbroken to discover that the house had been demolished and Israeli settlers had taken the land. I don't think he got over this assault on his dignity and pride. He developed a stomach ulcer and suffered ill health for the rest of his life.

Home Birth, Palestinian Style

When the villagers arrived in Deir al-Balah refugee camp they found that the UN had already established huge cities under canvas, with the tents arranged in such a way that people from one place could all be neighbours. My parents at this point had three sons and a daughter, and the whole family had to share one large tent with my three aunties, grandparents and two uncles. God knows how, but I was conceived in this tent.

I was born in February 1950. The date on my birth certificate is 19 February, but that is the date I was registered; usually nobody got around to registering a newborn for a few days and in my case there was good reason for the delay. Just as my mother went into labour my father collapsed and had been taken by my uncle to the British-run hospital in Gaza City, some forty kilometres away. He was put into intensive care immediately; my uncle sat and waited in the reception area. After several hours, an English doctor in a white coat came out and handed my uncle a form, indicating that a signature was needed. Since he didn't understand English my uncle had no idea what the doctor was saying; furthermore he was illiterate and the only documents he had ever seen that needed a signature were birth and death certificates. He therefore assumed that my father was dead and offered his thumb for a print to be taken, making his mark on the place the doctor pointed at. Grieving and in shock, he headed back for the refugee camp having resolved not to tell my mother the terrible news until she was stronger after the birth.

Meanwhile, I had been safely delivered by the village midwife and my uncle agreed to my mother's suggestion that I would be named Abdel Bari, meaning 'servant of the healer' – she was praying that God would spare my father whom she still believed to be ill in hospital. My uncle then went to the United Nations Relief and Works Agency for Palestine Refugees (UNRWA) office to register the birth.

The next day, an ambulance pulled up near our tent. My uncle thought they were delivering my father's corpse and almost fainted when the back opened and the man himself got out, weak, but alive. The document my uncle had signed was not a death certificate but one that gave his permission for an operation, which had been successful. Having been shown the new baby, the first thing my father said was, 'We will call the boy Sayeed' ('happy' in Arabic) 'in honour of my recovery.'

'But we've already named him Abdel Bari', my mother told him. 'In honour of your recovery.'

'That's a terrible name,' he replied. 'Listen, I survived and the boy was born. This is a happy time.' They all agreed and so I have the name Abdel Bari on my birth certificate, but everyone in my family calls me Sayeed.

We all got accustomed to the ritual of birth because my mother was always either nursing a baby or expecting one. I was number five of an eventual ten. The midwife in the camp was an old lady called Um Muhammad. She had no formal qualifications but had learned all that she knew from the even older lady who was her predecessor. Um Muhammad had delivered all my family's babies in Isdud, and afterwards in the camps. Once she appeared with her gasoline stove and started boiling water we knew that we would soon hear the wailing of a newborn infant.

After she had given birth, a neighbour would make my mother something to eat because she was so exhausted. If she was lucky this would be two fried eggs, a luxury to compensate her for her suffering. But she wouldn't be able to rest for longer than a few hours since the house was full of children who all needed something from her. She was a remarkable woman.

Resolution 194

After a few months in the refugee camp, my parents started to realize that this disaster was going to last longer than they had first anticipated. Our house was no more and our village had been occupied by Israelis. The first Israeli Prime Minister, David Ben-Gurion, was personally supervising a policy of 'memoricide' which saw all the Arabic names for our mountains, valleys, springs and roads replaced with Hebrew ones. The combined Arab forces were losing the war with Israel whose army was well equipped, having been stockpiling weapons from the West since 1946, and increasingly numerous as Jewish immigrants poured into Palestine at a rate of over 10,000 per month. The Israeli fighting force comprised members of Irgun, Stern and Haganah, supplemented by a variety of fighters, including men who had fought in the British army during the Second World War. Their combined numbers increased from 29,677 at the beginning of hostilities to 108,300 by the end in July 1949.

In the course of the conflict, the UN sent a mediator, Count Bernadotte, to the region. He proposed a three-point plan: the unconditional repatriation of the refugees, the internationalizing of Jerusalem and the partitioning of the land according to the distribution of the two populations. He was assassinated by Zionist terrorists in September 1948. This did not, however, prevent the UN welcoming Israel as a member in April 1949.

In December 1948, the UN General Assembly passed Resolution 194, which made the right of return for Palestinian refugees a prerequisite for a general peace agreement, with compensation payable to any who did not choose to exercise it. This has been reaffirmed by the General Assembly every year since, and is further endorsed by Article 13 of the 1948 Universal Declaration of Human Rights which states: 'Everyone has the right to leave any country, including his own, and to return to his country.' Sadly, the provisions for solving the refugee problem described in Resolution 194 continue to be ignored by Israel.

Deir al-Balah

Deir al-Balah was the smallest of the Gaza Strip refugee camps hastily established by UNRWA, initially accommodating 9,000 people. The camp was located beside the sea, next to the town of Deir al-Balah which, as its name (literally 'monastery of dates') suggests, was famous for its abundant palm groves. The tents were slowly replaced by mud-brick houses but there was neither a sewerage system nor running water. My mother and the other women used to collect water from the well in clay pots carried on their heads. UNRWA provided schooling but it was hard for us children to keep up with homework since there was no electricity and the only source of light was kerosene lamps.

Like many of the men, my father felt an overwhelming anger and frustration. They had been the heads of families, the providers, who had status within their own community. Now everything had been snatched from under their noses and they were reduced to living on handouts from UNRWA. Many broke down under the strain and, to this day, there is a higher incidence of mental illness in the Palestinian refugee camps than anywhere else in the Arab world.

There was little work in the area, and widespread unemployment compounded an already crushing sense of impotence and humiliation. My father had managed to bring a small sum of money with him to the camp and this he now put to good use, striking a deal with a local landowner whereby he would farm some of his land and share the produce with him. We moved into a mud house on the edge of the camp, in a field surrounded by tall cacti to keep out intruders. The house had a roof made of sticks which was home to a variety of fascinating animals and insects. It wasn't uncommon for scorpions to drop onto us as we slept, and we'd hear snakes and rats scuttling around. The roof wasn't waterproof so the little rain we did have usually found its way onto our ancient cotton mattresses too.

So my parents started their life of toil again. 'We were better off than most,' my mother insisted. 'Yes, we worked hard and yes, we were still poor, but at least we had salvaged some pride.' Compared with the neighbouring town of Deir al-Balah with its brick houses and roads, we were living in primitive conditions but many of our fellow refugees were still in tents at this time and envied us enormously. My father always managed to provide for us despite the adverse circumstances and I admire him for that.

I had never known anything but the refugee camp, so for me, everything was normal. As I remember, I had many happy times in my childhood. Perhaps my enduring socialist tendencies stem from those early days, equality refined through poverty: when sardines came into shore, we all ate sardines; in summer, we all ate grapes; we were all given equally inappropriate and ill-fitting second-hand clothes; and in illness too, no one was better or worse off – we all got flu or tummy bugs in equal measure, with no medicines to help us out. Everyone was angry and everyone was starving!

I started primary school at the age of six and immediately loved it; especially the first day of the academic year when everything was new. We'd be given notebooks, and sharp pencils that smelt of fresh wood shavings. The barber came on that day and shaved the boys' heads which were inevitably crawling with lice. I was a good student but was always late, which resulted in a beating. The teachers all carried sticks and would hit you on the hand. We used to differentiate between them according to how hard they beat you, hating the hard-hitters and loving the more gentle ones. All the teachers were male and some of them were not particularly well educated themselves but they were devoted to their task. I suppose they could see that it was only through academic achievement that we would have a chance of getting out of the refugee camps. No sooner had I started school, however, than a new set of calamities occurred and put a halt to my education.

Intimidation

The Gaza Strip had been under Egyptian military administration since that country had signed an armistice with Israel on 24 February 1949. As a result, Israeli soldiers rarely ventured into the camps and in my imagination they had an almost mythical status like the ghosts and owls my parents used to scare us with. The Egyptian authorities were frightening enough: every town and village had a hakim (military ruler) who had the power to arrest, beat and torture anyone they wanted to, with or without good reason. These hakims had been issued with ancient black Volkswagen

Beetles for some reason and their arrival was always heralded by the sound of a backfiring engine.

The status quo was rocked in February 1955, when Israeli soldiers attacked the Egyptian military outposts in Gaza, killing thirty-nine people. The Israelis claimed they were being attacked from the Gaza Strip and that the Egyptians were supporting guerrilla activity. Although Palestinian fedayeen had initiated some token resistance against the Israelis between 1949–56 most people thought the problem would be solved by other means and did not, in general, support violence. In fact, the Israelis were looking for an excuse to invade the Gaza Strip, which they did on 29 October 1956, along with the Sinai (as prearranged with the British and French) and as a prelude to the Suez Campaign. They announced their arrival with a series of massacres that even the Israeli press could not stomach. The Israeli daily, *Kol Haam*, reported the massacre at Kafr Kassim on its front page on 19 December 1956, under the headline 'How 49 inhabitants of Kafr Kassim were Slaughtered' (See Appendix for the report in full.)

Worse was to follow. Israeli regiments would storm into refugee camps and round up all the men aged between seventeen and fifty-five; the lucky ones were arrested, but many were lined up against the walls and shot dead. The Israelis claimed they were 'screening' for men with weapons but their real aim was to quash any potential for armed uprising. On 3 November 1956, the Israelis went into the Khan Younis refugee camp and butchered at least 275; on 12 November 111 were killed in the Rafah refugee camp; sixty-six others died at the hands of the Israelis in other refugee camps between 1 and 21 November. (These figures come from the UNRWA report[1] for the period as the most impartial statistical source, although Palestinian accounts claim the numbers were larger.)

I was six years old when the Israeli tanks rolled into Deir al-Balah on 14 November 1956. My mother recognized the sinister sound and screamed at us to stay in the house. The refugees in Deir al-Balah had heard about the massacres in Khan Younis and Rafah, and were paralysed with fear. We could hear the commotion outside as tanks and jeeps came to a halt in the middle of the camp.

Ignoring my mother's whispered begging and her gentle attempts to

---

1. http://domino.un.org/unispal.nsf/0/6558f61d3db6bd4505256593006b06be?Op
enDocument

restrain him, my father took down his handgun from the roof. We children stared at it in awe as he opened the bullet chamber; it was empty and he put it down on the table and went to a cupboard to fetch bullets. At that moment the door burst open and five heavily armed Israeli soldiers marched in. Realizing that if they saw the gun my father would be killed, my mother managed to cover it with a basket.

It was one of the most nightmarish experiences of my life to witness those Israeli soldiers beating my father and being just a little boy unable to intervene or defend him. They hit him with their gun butts until he nearly fell, then they told him to get out of the house, pushing him with their rifles. We were all screaming and crying and we followed them, emerging into bright sunlight and a terrifying scene: my father, together with the rest of the men from the camp, being kicked and shoved towards the empty bit of wasteland where we usually played football. Then the soldiers ordered all the men to stop. 'Put your hands above your heads,' they barked in Arabic. The women were wailing and sobbing, some were on their knees pleading for mercy; they knew what had happened at other camps and that this was the end for their men.

Out of nowhere, an Israeli jeep arrived at incredible speed and came to a screeching halt right by the firing squad. A young colonel got out and started talking to them. To our amazement the firing squad saluted, put their guns over their shoulders, clambered back into their tanks and jeeps and left the way they had come. We stood and watched them disappear, and remained in stunned silence until the clouds of dust from their vehicles had settled. It dawned on us that the men had been spared and we started talking, quietly at first. We raced over to my father, clinging to him and jumping up and down for joy that he had been spared.

Meanwhile, the young colonel started talking to my people in perfect Arabic, asking for Abu Muhammad and his family. After a while, Abu Muhammad came forward out of the crowd of traumatized men and identified himself. The Israeli murmured something to him, at which point Abu Muhammad grabbed the colonel by his arms, staring into his face, then ran off, returning with his wife and children who started embracing the colonel, crying and laughing all at once. People watched in wonder at the sight of this much-feared Israeli soldier celebrating with one of our poorest families, bringing out packets of olives and cheese from the jeep which he pressed into their hands.

After the colonel drove off everyone gathered round Abu Muhammad who told them the incredible story behind their escape from certain death: in the chaos of their eviction from the village of al-Nabi Robeen in 1948, the family had become separated from one of their sons, the then twelve-year-old Muhammad. We were told he had been left behind as the others fled, lost, alone and afraid. Among the Israelis who commandeered the village was a family who found him hiding in his father's house and took pity on him. They adopted him and brought him up as one of their own and when he was an adult, he joined the Israeli army. He had recently found out that all the refugees from al-Nabi Robeen were in the Deir al-Balah refugee camp and when he heard the Israeli army was on its way there and for what purpose, he raced to find his family – whom he still remembered with vivid clarity – before it was too late. Some time later, when the Israelis withdrew from Gaza, Colonel Muhammad returned to the camp and asked Abu Muhammad and the rest of the family to move to Israel with him. They accepted, never to see their friends and relatives again.

The period following the Israeli invasion of the Gaza Strip was disastrous for refugee families. All the UNRWA schools were closed while the Israelis 'screened' the teachers and the Egyptian curriculum for subversive elements. They removed the animals and farm equipment from the Agricultural Training Centre (which deprived the young men of their only realistic employment opportunity) and forced a change in legal tender from the Egyptian to the Israeli pound, imposing an exchange rate that was far lower than it should have been. At the same time, the British government was persuaded to hand the Israelis control of several bank accounts bulging with the accumulated taxation revenue of the Palestinian population from the Mandate years, thus completing the total dispossession of the Palestinians. Unemployment soared to new heights as UNRWA operations diminished and Egyptian administrative posts became redundant.

Meanwhile, all eyes were on Egypt, which had been invaded by Israeli, British and French troops on 5 November 1956. The Palestinians felt that their future was inextricably linked with the outcome of this confrontation. Thankfully, we were not in suspense for long. The attempt to regain the Suez Canal and topple Nasser failed after he put up a robust resistance and sank every foreign ship in the Suez Canal. Under pressure from the UN, the aggressors withdrew on 29 November 1956. The Israelis refused to relinquish the Gaza Strip, however, and maintained their presence there until 7 March 1957 when the Egyptians took over again. Nasser banned Israeli shipping from the Suez Canal on 15 March and there were great scenes of jubilation among the Palestinians. He was our champion and he had dealt a final blow to the bullies who were oppressing us. I was such a fan of Nasser that I wrote him an admiring letter but then realized I didn't know his address. So I just put 'General Nasser, Cairo' on the envelope and took it to the post office.

The Power of the Written Word

Our school was reopened and I appreciated it all the more for having been deprived of it for several months, though I had yet to make any friends. I was seven years old by now, well behaved and diligent, afraid of getting into trouble because the teachers used to beat miscreants. So when the newly appointed headmaster and four of his colleagues, all bearing sticks, came into the class one day, and I heard them say my name to the teacher, I was terrified and started racking my brains for possible misdemeanours I might have inadvertently committed. The headmaster looked at me with a serious expression. 'Are you Abdel Bari Atwan?' he asked

'Yes, sir,' I replied, my voice trembling with fear.

'How do you know General Nasser?' he asked. I was astonished. What a question!

'Er ... from the radio, sir,' I ventured. We didn't have television or newspapers in those days but our neighbours had a radio and I used to listen to it whenever I could. The headmaster snapped his fingers at one of the teachers who accompanied him and the man produced a large brown envelope.

'Well, this came for you in the post,' said the headmaster and all the children in the class strained to look at this miraculous apparition; letters were a rarity, and for a seven-year-old to get one was unheard of. I took it and scrutinized the package. The address read, 'Abdel Bari Atwan, Deir al-Balah refugee primary school, Gaza Strip', and it had an Egyptian postage stamp. It had been opened and stuck back down again.

'Well, open it then,' the headmaster urged and I tore the envelope apart. It was a letter from General Nasser, thanking me for mine and asking me to accept the books and photographs of himself that he enclosed.

The news spread like wildfire and the incident was the talk of the refugee camp. I and many others loved Nasser even more for this act of personal generosity and kindness. My family were bombarded with questions and I became a star overnight. It was the first time I benefited from writing.

Survival

From that day on, everyone wanted to be my friend and I was soon part of a close-knit gang who did everything together, in and out of school. My three best friends were Ali, a daring boy with an anti-authoritarian attitude, Hamza, a dreamer, and Muhammad, who was a fantastic footballer. We became friends at the age of seven and are still in touch today.

The school was segregated and there was no uniform but we had to be neat and clean with an inspection every morning before lessons began. I had inherited the family's only pair of shoes from my brother but they were far too tight, and it was agony to wear them. I can still feel the pain, like having burning boulders crushing my feet. I used to put them on for the duration of the inspection and then spend the rest of the day barefoot like everyone else. There were lots of cacti in and around the camp and we were always getting thorns in our feet – the most popular boys were those who could be relied on to have a needle at hand for getting them out. Ali used to have one stuck in his trouser waistband.

Clothes were provided by UNRWA once a year and were a cause of mortification, humiliation and hilarity. Each family would get a bundle of second-hand garments wrapped in a blanket and it was pot luck. Sometimes a family would have lots of sons and get a bundle with only girls' clothes in it. In winter you'd see an old man with a moustache wearing a tight-waisted woman's coat, or a teenage boy in a girl's slacks. Many families were so poor they'd have to sell whatever clothes they got just to buy basics like tea. It was a tragic situation.

There was never enough to eat; not only was there nothing to buy but nobody had any money or the means of earning any. We were literally starving and I have had anaemia all my life as a result of my childhood diet. The meagre rations that somehow sustained us came from UNRWA. I was recently shown UNRWA statistics for the 1960s and saw my childhood and family life mapped out in grim figures and stark financial detail. The UNRWA food budget provided $13 a year per capita; just enough to provide us with rations of flour, sugar, rice, pulses and oil, never any meat or fresh vegetables or fruit. Each family had a plastic-coated card detailing how many mouths there were to feed. This further served as their proof of identity, since we were all now officially 'stateless persons'.

Rations were handed out once a month at an UNRWA depot three kilometres from the camp. I remember going with my father to collect ours and the festive atmosphere that accompanied the trip. The majority of refugees went on foot, carrying sacks of provisions home on their backs but, because my father was working the land, we had the luxury of a donkey, the equivalent of a Rolls-Royce in Deir al-Balah. Sometimes the UNRWA workers would hand out dates as a special treat, the nearest thing to sweets we ever knew. When we had dates on board, my hand would sneak into the bag containing them all the way home, extracting one at a time as the donkey stomped along. By the time we got back, I would have consumed much more than my fair share and often got a beating from my father on this account.

We had some relatives who tried to fiddle the system by claiming they had lost their identity card and procuring another. On the basis of this, they got double their share for a while, but the camp was so small and faces became so familiar that they were quickly found out. Fortunately, it was a fellow Palestinian, working for UNRWA, who caught them rather than one of the European supervisors. Getting a job at UNRWA was the dream of every refugee, offering security and a good salary, and those lucky enough to have one were envied.

One day, when I was eight or nine, I was walking through the camp with my friends and we were grumbling about how we always felt hungry, jokingly counting our protruding ribs. Ali looked thoughtful and said, 'Come with me!' He took us to the edges of the camp and pointed out the fields that lay beyond its fences; fields that were full of crops or vegetables. The nearest one had cucumbers in it. 'I'd love to eat one of those,' said Hamza.

'Who do they belong to?' I asked, wary that Ali was about to get us into trouble.

'Farmers from the town,' he replied. 'My brother works for one of them. I reckon that if we just popped over the fence we could take a few cucumbers and no one would ever know.'

'What if they see us?' I asked, hesitant but dying to taste a cool, refreshing cucumber.

'We'll have to run!' said Muhammad, who could run incredibly fast.

'Let's do it,' said Ali, organizing his ranks. 'Muhammad, you stand guard because you're the tallest and you'll see if anyone's coming. Let's go!' And we scrambled under the barbed-wire fence and raced to the edge of the field, laughing and panting, fuelled by adrenalin and excitement. On this occasion nobody saw us and we took our spoils down to the beach and enjoyed them at our leisure.

Emboldened by this display of initiative we soon developed other means of satisfying our hunger. We used to spend hours trying to trap gulls on the beach and when we did catch a thrashing, feathery bundle it was always Muhammad's task to cut its neck and gut it, since he was the only one who possessed a knife. Then we would roast it on a fire made of driftwood and that bird would give all four of us the luxury of a few mouthfuls of tough, salty meat.

As I have already mentioned, Deir al-Balah was famous for its dates and we soon developed a scheme for stealing some of these wonderful, plump fruits. Date palms grow very tall and it was a more serious matter to shin up one of these monsters than to carry out a grab-and-run operation in a cucumber field. My friends discovered that I was agile and strong enough to get to the top quickly, and so I was the one persuaded to risk life and limb.

'Go on Abdel Bari, you're like a lizard,' Ali told me as we stood gazing up at the distant fruit with its leafy canopy. Ali looked left and right in case one of the guards employed by the owner of the palm grove came along, and smiled at me. 'Get up there now while no one's looking, then give it a good shake and we'll catch the dates,' he commanded. 'We'll keep an eye out for guards and collect your share for you.' I climbed up and when I finally got to the top waved in triumph at my friends beneath. They looked tiny with their grinning face upturned towards me, cheering me on. I started to shake the palm and dates began to rain down, scooped up by my partners in crime. I sought out the heaviest laden parts and shook again, but as I went to watch them tumble down I saw my friends turn heel and run. I scanned the earth beneath and recognized, with a sinking heart, the white-robed figure of the guard; he had a knotted stave with him which he now brandished at me.

The guard and I remained in stalemate for maybe an hour with neither of us moving. Then a cat-and-mouse game began: my enemy would pretend to wander off, at which point I would start my descent. As I neared the bottom, the guard would thunder back cursing and shouting and waving his stave and I would have to scoot back up out of reach. I decided patience was the only policy that would work. It was a siege mentality and I knew I would win. I resolved to stay up that tree all night if necessary.

It was a hot day and after a while I realized I hadn't heard my enemy moving for some time. I focused my hearing to determine his whereabouts and nearly whooped for joy when I caught the faint but unmistakable sound of snoring. I left him slumbering for a good ten minutes before I decided to risk a tentative descent. Coming down slowly and silently, my heart beat so loudly I feared it would give me away. Halfway down I scanned beneath me to see where he was – my persecutor had propped himself up against the bottom of the trunk to make sure I couldn't escape without waking him. I gingerly wound myself down the back of the palm, landing on my feet like a cat and sped off leaving him sound asleep in the baking sun. I didn't dare make a sound until I'd reached our house but as I burst through the door I started roaring with laughter.

We spent a lot of time on the beach; whenever we weren't at school we'd be there playing football or swimming, nibbling on grapes or figs stolen from some unlucky local farmer. The beaches were dazzling, luminous pale sand and clear, bright blue waters. Like an advertisement for a tropical paradise, no one would know that this was actually part of an open-air prison, the de facto jail that the Gaza Strip was turning into. Hamza was enthralled by the sea and he'd sit on the sand staring out at the horizon. 'What is at the other side of the sea?' was his favourite question. We once got hold of an atlas at school to arm ourselves for the next time he asked us and astonished him with a chorus of 'Greece! Turkey! Italy!' Then he promised us, 'I'm going to go across the sea when I grow up.'

Many years later, Hamza did indeed cross the seas and ended up teaching in an Islamic school in Malta where he married a local woman and had a child, Yusuf. I met him in London, in 1991, quite by chance in Shepherd's Bush. We stared at each other, first in astonishment and then in delight, and after much embracing embarked on several hours of reminiscence over cups of coffee. Hamza's wife had a clothes shop and he was in London to buy stock. But he told me he was disenchanted with life in Europe. 'It's too sophisticated and Malta is too small,' he explained. 'To tell you the truth I long to return to Gaza, despite those damned Israelis.'

We were always naked on the beach because we didn't have any swimming costumes or beachwear and were lucky if we had any clothes that fitted us at all. Even the fishermen who worked from the shore or in small boats were naked. Nobody taught us how to swim, we just learned naturally.

The beach provided much in the way of drama. I remember one day, we were overjoyed to see ten camels in the waters being washed by Bedouin, who were taking them to market in Gaza. Then there were the fishermen who were busy mending their nets or repairing their boats when they weren't fishing.

The fishermen had two main methods of catching fish: nets and dynamite. If there were a lot of fish, nets would suffice, but if there was one fleeting shoal they would pursue it in their boats and then light sticks of dynamite, tossing them into the midst of the shoal. The explosion would kill the fish and they'd plummet to the ocean floor. The fishermen would then dive in and scoop up as many as they could. One day we were sitting watching this spectacle when Ali had an idea: 'We could offer to dive for the fish,' he said. 'Look at them. Some of them are ancient – they can't hold their breath for long. I bet we could get loads more than them.' When the fishermen returned to shore, Ali bargained with them and five minutes later we had a job! The deal was that we would get a third of whatever we amassed.

Two days later the fishermen beckoned to us as they pushed their boats out into the sea. Whooping with joy, we raced down and jumped into the boats. Muhammad and I in one with a man called Abu Jenna, Ali in another with the unofficial leader of the fishermen, Salman. Then they were off, rowing over the choppy water at great speed, the spray in our faces. Suddenly, there was a shout as one of the fishermen spotted the shoal they were chasing. 'Quick,' said Abu Jenna, and he lit a stick of dynamite and threw it out into the sea where it exploded with a great bang, water spouting up into the blue sky. 'Jump!' he shouted. Muhammad and I looked at each other, and jumped, swivelling over as we entered the water to dive downwards. The sea smelt of dynamite and was murky from the explosion. Sand and air bubbles were all we could see for awhile and then we made out the fish corpses, drifting downwards, glassy-eyed.

The fishermen were pleased with our performance and we had a feast on the beach with the proceeds of our hard work. Each of us had at least four or five fish to eat and we fed some friends too. Dynamite fishing became a regular sport until one day I was in the boat about to dive in when I saw some ominous looking fins gliding through the water towards us. 'Jump!' shouted Abu Jenna, eager for his catch. 'What are those?' I yelled, pointing at the fins. 'Sharks!' he said. 'Then no!' I shouted, wrapping my arms round myself and standing stubbornly rooted to the boat's wooden floor. The next thing I knew I hit the water with a splash – Abu Jenna had pushed me in. 'Dive!' he ordered. I looked around and saw with relief that the shore was not that far away. Gulping for air, I headed for the beach as fast as I could, hoping that the sharks wouldn't decide they'd rather have a boy than dead fish for their supper.

That was my last outing with the fishermen but afterwards I noticed that a few of them had an arm or hand missing. Shark bites, it seems, were part of the job. The sharks were attracted by the smell of blood when the fish were blown up and in the subsequent turmoil and turbulence they couldn't differentiate between a fish and a human arm or leg.

That's Entertainment

UNRWA sometimes organized safer leisure pursuits for the children of the refugee camps. Every so often a travelling funfair would arrive and set up a dazzling display of lights, music and mechanical rides, transforming the dusty wasteland into something magical and exciting. UNRWA would give us tokens for the rides; there were roundabouts and wild swings and all sorts of haggling among the children. Ali usually managed to find a gullible soul to swap his tokens for some worthless item, such as a chewed pencil stub or a rotting orange. He had what the Irish call 'the gift of the gab' in abundance. Ali was so useless academically that his father pulled him out of school when he was thirteen and got him an apprenticeship with a car mechanic in the town of Deir al-Balah. This man also sold second-hand motors and Ali became a genius at palming off old bangers, for which he was rewarded with his cut of the profit.

My favourite treat, provided by UNRWA, was the cinema, and my first experience of the movies was sitting in the dust by a half-demolished house with the film projected onto the only intact wall. The whole camp would turn out and people played drums and got completely involved in the story, shouting at the characters, laughing and crying. I once saw a man who became so convinced that the film was real that he leaped to his feet, offering to fight a villain. When we were older we used to go into Gaza City to see a movie in the real cinema. We liked action films best and these were rated according to how bloody they were. If there was only one shootout we'd feel cheated and complain; if the entire scenario was a bloodbath we'd come out satisfied that we'd had our money's worth.

The other great event was our monthly visit to the *hammam* (public baths). UNRWA used to give us one piece of soap to share. I often think about this when I run a bath at home in London, and it saddens me to think that our poverty was so severe that just one little sliver of soap seemed such a great luxury to us in the refugee camp.

One day we found a small scruffy-haired brown dog outside our house. Dogs are not treated well in Arab countries; in fact they are considered unclean and usually shooed away unless they can be put to good use, hunting or guarding. There was something endearing about him and we children clamoured to be allowed to keep him. My mother reluctantly agreed and we called him 'dog' – as I said, we Arabs are not used to having pets. We fed him scraps and he became a great playmate and later revealed his talent as rat-catcher which improved his status in the camp. When we moved to another refugee camp, we had to leave 'dog' behind with some relatives and after a few months we heard that he had pined away through missing us.

Larger than Life

I can't remember when we first noticed an extraordinary boy called Salah, who would become the final member of our gang. I must have been nine or ten years old. Once we spotted him he became a constant source of conversation among us. We envied him because he didn't go to school, but spent all day roaming the dunes, fields and beaches. He carried knives that he was very proud of, throwing them with great precision into the bark of date palms and sometimes spearing fish in the water. Salah really was a wild boy and used to sleep in the little hollows in the sand dunes, his parents displaying absolute indifference to his whereabouts. He had long shaggy hair and a hirsute body, but the most amazing thing for us was that he had six fingers and six toes.

Ali, in particular, was fascinated by Salah and hung around him all the time, borrowing his knives and flattering him. When he did become part of our gang, he distinguished himself with his bravery during our raids on fields, vineyards and orchards. Unfortunately, he was generally the one to get into trouble because – since we were barefoot – there was no disguising his distinctive six-toed footprints.

I lost touch with Salah after we moved from Deir al-Balah to Rafah refugee camp, but in 1974 I read in the newspaper that a guerrilla fighter had been killed in the course of bombing an Israeli patrol. The paper reported that the attacker's remains had six fingers and toes and it seemed quite likely to me that Salah would have died in such a way.

By the time I was twelve, the focus of my interests had shifted a little and while I was still crazy about football and the beach, I was becoming vaguely interested in the opposite sex. I was absurdly shy and had never dared so much as talk to a girl my own age, but there was a flamboyant female character in the camp who captivated all of us, called Mabrouka. Although she was married and lived with her husband and children, Mabrouka, who must have been in her late thirties, walked about the camp all dressed up with kohl around her eyes, wearing red lipstick and leaving a cloud of heavy perfume behind her. This was cheap Egyptian perfume more usually associated with death since it was used to anoint corpses to mask the smell of decomposition.

Mabrouka wasn't beautiful but she knew how to show off her assets to their best advantage. She was tall and haughty, a white embroidered scarf bouncing loosely on her thick black hair and she cast the most seductive looks at every man between the ages of sixteen and sixty. Gossip about her was rife and people said that men used to visit her to 'have fun'. At our age we had little idea what this meant but it was sufficiently intriguing for us to spend a lot of time loitering around her house, which was conveniently placed next to the school, on the edge of the refugee camp by the sea.

It was rumoured that a man would take Mabrouka a present – a kilo of sugar or some tea – and knock at her door. If she liked the look of him, she would accept the present and invite him in. We never managed to catch anyone at her door but we overheard one of my neighbours, Sami, whispering to a friend that he had managed to 'visit' her. We already admired this neighbour because he was a rebellious teenager who had failed all his exams and been kicked out of school, and this only added to his appeal. We clamoured around him: 'Tell us about Mabrouka! Did you "have fun"? What did you do when you got inside her house?' Sami narrowed his eyes at us and told us to go away. We persisted and he rewarded us with a long smile as if recalling every moment of his visit and drawled, 'I will only say that I had a very good time.'

We were desperate to know what was going on. Women were the ultimate mystery to us and now we were on a mission, constantly on watch outside Mabrouka's door. Our reward came sooner than we expected. A few days into our surveillance, seven Palestinian policemen came rushing towards the house; five of them surrounded it while the two others kicked the door down. They dragged out a naked man and Mabrouka, who was fully clothed. We gaped in astonishment at the man, not only because he was naked but because we recognized him: he was one of the policemen who patrolled the camp! His uniformed comrades forced him and Mabrouka to walk in a parade of shame all the way through the refugee camp and into the town to the police station, two kilometres away. Crowds gathered and lined their route shouting insults and throwing sand and gravel at them. The policeman was humiliated, repeatedly trying to cover his private parts, but Mabrouka held her head up and strolled along as if she was walking to market. We children were skipping beside them, laughing. It was like a carnival for us. 'You bastard!' the crowds shouted at the naked policeman, 'You devil!' Mabrouka was released from jail two days later and carried on as if nothing had happened. The policeman was never seen again.

During the First Intifada,[1] I was sitting in my office at *al-Quds al-Arabi*

---

1. The First Intifada known as the 'intifada of stones' lasted from 1987–93. The word intifada literally means 'shaking off' and consisted of widespread rioting

talking with a colleague and she asked me who was the most memorable woman I had met. I expect she thought I'd say Margaret Thatcher or Indira Gandhi but I replied in jest, 'Mabrouka', and told her a little about that lady. 'I love larger than life characters,' I said. 'It doesn't matter whether I approve of them or not – I just enjoy them.'

A few days later the same colleague was looking at the news as it came in on the wires. She tore off a story and came over to me. 'Abdel Bari!' she said, scanning the paper rapidly. 'You remember you were telling me about Mabrouka – was her surname X?' (I cannot disclose her real identity for obvious reasons.) I confirmed that it was.

'Look at this wire,' she said. 'Mabrouka X was killed by Palestinian guerrillas when they discovered that she had been informing on them to the Israelis.'

'I am sure it's her,' I said. 'Mabrouka and loyalty were strangers; she never believed in patriotism or nationalism. She only believed in keeping in with the authorities whether Israeli, Egyptian or Palestinian. She looked to them for protection and it didn't matter who they were. "The King is dead. Long live the King." That's the way it was with her.'

Some years later, I heard from colleagues on the ground that Mabrouka's eldest son had been killed fighting against the Israelis in the intifada and that one of her grandsons too had died a martyr. In this way they managed to redeem their family's honour.

My Father

My father was called Muhammad and I never saw him smile. I inherited two things from him: my stomach ulcer and the number eleven etched deeply

---

against the Israeli occupation. The first riots occurred in the Gaza refugee camp of Jabalaya when an eighteen-year-old boy, Hatem al-Sisi, was killed by the IDF after he threw a stone at their truck. Rioting spread throughout Gaza, the West Bank, and Jerusalem and became a full-scale uprising against Israeli brutality and repression manifested over the decades in massacres, murders, mass detentions, house demolitions, crop destruction, the spread of illegal settlements, and the continued Israeli military occupation of Palestinian territories. The Intifada was also born of a stagnated political situation where the PLO had made little headway in their attempts to establish a Palestinian state, and erstwhile allies (such as Egypt and Jordan) had gone decidedly silent on the international stage.

into the centre of my forehead (some people call these 'frown lines'). He always wore a *keffiyeh* and had lost two of his front teeth; primitive gold ones stood in their place. Despite everything that had happened to him, he remained resilient and strong to the end. His grimness was almost military, as though to smile or laugh would be undisciplined.

As if he hadn't endured enough in the *Nakba* when he lost everything and became a refugee, 1959 brought him worse troubles. A spy had told the Egyptian authorities that my father possessed a gun and the Palestinian police were quick to pay him a visit. Miriam, a Bedouin lady, was visiting, drinking tea and gossiping with my parents when a boy came running to our house to warn us that the police were on their way.

'Your gun!' my mother hissed at my father who was wearing the weapon, as he always did, in a holster on his trouser belt. He took it out of the holster and gave it to Miriam who stuffed it down the front of her dress and got up. Just at that moment, four policemen barged through the entrance. Miriam screamed and pretended to swoon with fear. The policemen gestured at her to leave and she ran out, her hand over her mouth.

'Muhammad Atwan', said the senior policeman. 'We have reason to believe you are in possession of a firearm.' My father denied this.

'What is that then?' the policeman asked pointing at the empty holster.

'And what are these?' added another policeman who had been foraging about among the mattresses on the floor and found several handgun magazines.

'I wear the holster because I like to pretend I have a gun,' my father said, trying to sound convincing. 'And the kids brought those magazines in. I don't know where they found them.'

The policemen arrested my father and took him away. We didn't see him for six months during which time, we learned afterwards, he was tortured every day in an effort to force a confession. He was hung by his feet from the ceiling, and was beaten and punched in the face. He knew that if he confessed he would be jailed for fifteen years and somehow he managed to withstand the pain and maintain his innocence to the end. When they finally gave up and let him go he had changed forever; he walked with a stoop and was more distant and bitter than before, seething with rage and humiliation. He suffered from backaches and was tormented by nightmares for the remainder of his life.

By 1965, we were a family of ten children, and my parents seemed intent on breaking all records for the production of babies when my father's health started to fail. He had always been physically and mentally resilient and I found it disturbing to witness this decline. He invested his hopes for the future in his children and was strict with us in the belief that only discipline, and self-discipline above all, could mould us to achieve what we were capable of. I was closest to him and he often repeated his wish that I would do well and be strong, for myself and for others. My mother told me, years later, that on his deathbed my father had told her, 'Of all your children this one, Sayeed, will do something special.'

He was only forty-two years old but now looked much older. He had lost a lot of weight and complained of pain in his upper abdomen that sometimes got so bad he would be doubled over. One of his cousins, Hussein (who worked for UNRWA), knew something about medicine; he took one look at my father and insisted he go to the hospital. This was not an easy matter – the hospital was forty kilometres away – but Hussein hired a car in Deir al-Balah and took him there himself.

The next day, my mother and aunts went with Hussein to the hospital to visit my father. They returned with his body on a stretcher, covered in a shroud. He had suffered a burst stomach ulcer which resulted in a fatal haemorrhage. My mother broke down; they had survived so much together and he had been everything to all of us.

Islamic tradition and practicality dictate a speedy burial – there are no chilly morgues in a refugee camp – but they kept my father's body in the house for a few hours to say goodbye. I stayed outside. I was in total shock and couldn't bear to see the corpse; I didn't have the courage. Eventually, we took my father to the cemetery and buried him. We felt completely bereft.

My two older brothers were away: Abdel Fatah was studying in Egypt and Kamal was working as a teacher in Saudi Arabia. At fifteen, I was the oldest boy left at home and even as I wept for my father I understood that I was now going to have to be the head of the family, the man of the house. I comforted my mother and my elder sister; I looked after my four younger brothers and two younger sisters; I arranged the mourning reception and stood at the head of the line to receive family and friends, to reply to their condolences, to offer them coffee. It was difficult for me to adopt this new role at such a time but I forced myself through it and I think I changed a lot at this point in my life. I realized that the limits we impose on ourselves are not real and can always be expanded; that we grow stronger in response to our experiences, not as a matter of course.

After the mourning reception, I had one final task to perform; my mother had been obliged to pay a deposit for the stretcher and this money, which we couldn't afford to lose, was only refundable when it was returned to the hospital. I managed to get a space in one of the communal taxis bound for Gaza City. These taxis would habitually cram twelve people into a vehicle meant for six at the most. I was squashed up against the door with the window wide open, the bottom of the stretcher on the floor between my knees, the rest jutting up through the window, wrestling with the wind above the car. It was comical but I didn't feel like laughing. At the edge of Gaza City the taxi disgorged its occupants and I continued on foot to the hospital, which was another three kilometres away. When the few coins were tipped into my hands by a nurse I resolved to make enough money to save my mother from this kind of desperation as soon as I could.

My mother, Zarifa, was young at thirty-eight and despite having ten children was still considered desirable. She was beautiful, with blue eyes and long dark hair – all my siblings inherited her looks, I am the only one who took after my father. From the outset of her widowhood she was besieged by suitors, including one of her own cousins, but she refused them all. 'I am married to my children,' she told them. 'I am devoting myself to their welfare and upbringing and there's no room for anything else.' We decided that we should leave Deir al-Balah and go to Rafah refugee camp instead. My grandmother was living there, as were my uncles who, according to our family tradition, would protect us now that our father was dead. Protection was necessary – the Gaza Strip is a rough part of the world. My eldest sister, Souad, was seventeen, while at the other end of the line my little brother Bashir was only three years old. Bashir doesn't have any recollection of our father and this has marred his life in many ways.

When I received death threats from the Ku Klux Klan, my main concern was that if I died my son Kareem, who was only one at the time, would never have known his father and might become angry and bitter like Bashir. My abiding prayer to God is that He won't let me die before Kareem has had enough years with his father.

Rafah Refugee Camp

My father had left a small amount of money which enabled us to secure a modest house at the edge of the Rafah camp, next door to our grandmother's; this unfortunate old lady couldn't walk due to crippling arthritis in her hips. There were no wheelchairs available at that time – they were far too expensive – and the only way my granny could move was to crawl about like a baby. She needed a lot of looking after and my aunts were pleased that my mother had come to help them wash and feed her. One of my cousins lived with my grandmother; Abdullah was a serious youth who came and went secretly and rarely said anything to anyone.

We managed to establish a comfortable home with the help of family and neighbours, and with the few pounds we had left my mother bought some chickens and ducks, which she bred to sell along with their eggs. She also kept pigeons which we fattened with grain and berries to eat as a rare special treat. I had to organize new schools for my brothers and sisters, meet the head teachers and generally act in loco parentis. I continued my own studies at one of the several UNRWA secondary schools. Rafah was the biggest and most densely populated of all the camps in the Gaza Strip; situated on the Egyptian border it was then home to around 50,000 refugees, although that number has doubled since. From my point of view it was much better; there were lots of teenagers, and lots of girls!

When we arrived all the boys my age had formed groups of friends and at first I felt isolated and left out. Perhaps because I had just lost my father, I didn't have much social confidence. After a week or so I made more of an effort and got chatting to a young man of around sixteen called Zaki. He was witty and I enjoyed his company. Zaki was quite a ladies' man despite his youth and taught me how to put Vaseline in my hair and comb it back. He also pointed out that long trousers were de rigueur as no girl would be interested in a boy in shorts. I made some awkward attempts at being charming but I was tall, skinny and gawky: hopeless beside Zaki. There was a custom in Rafah at that time that if a girl liked the look of a young man she would send him a handkerchief with perfume dabbed on it. The popular men had several such handkerchiefs tucked into their pockets. Zaki himself had five and I was dying to start my own collection.

At one point, I thought I had attracted the interest of a girl called Soraya, in that our eyes met once or twice and she giggled and blushed when I said hello. In total desperation, I penned a florid, romantic poem that I pressed into her hand the next time we met. Some of its lines remain etched in my memory, presenting myself as the 'moon in the east' and the object of my affections as the 'sun in the west', before moving on to speculate where the two would meet. The next time I saw Soraya I greeted her and she ignored me. I caught her eye and was met with the most steely gaze I had ever encountered. I had been 'dumped' before I'd even begun. This experience put me off versifying for life and I have never attempted this literary form again, despite many of my friends being accomplished poets.

In 2002, I went to the United Arab Emirates to give a lecture. The hall was packed with people and after the event several came to greet me, asking for an autograph or to have their photo taken with me. The last in line was an elderly chap, as I thought, smart and well dressed with a well-oiled head. 'You don't recognize me do you, Abdel Bari?' he laughed. It was Zaki. He invited me to his home in Fujairah and I discovered he was married, with nine kids, and worked as a bus driver.

Being teenagers we were obsessed with romance and often discussed how our parents had met. A boy called Ismael's parents had a particularly interesting story: like me, his family came from Isdud and his father, Muhammad, regularly travelled to Jaffa by donkey to sell wheat and barley. It was common for such villagers to take advantage of the many entertainments on offer in the big city, and they'd often spend nearly all the proceeds from their sales on going to nightclubs and listening to music. 'One night in Jaffa, my father met a beautiful girl,' Ismael told me, 'he fell in love at first sight and decided to marry her. The family were against it, the whole village was against it ... they were up in arms! Marry someone from outside the village! Unthinkable!' Ismael laughed. 'Well, my father was determined and soon he brought her to the village to visit. The women were amazed by her city clothes – remember at that time the only acceptable outfit was the *thoub* – and one thing more than anything else scandalized them – she was wearing shoes! Nobody wore shoes in those days. Everyone went barefoot. There was an uproar!' We were all laughing so hard it hurt.

'It was a social earthquake!' I chipped in.

'And then,' Ismael continued, 'when the family sat down to eat, she asked for a knife and fork!' More laughter at this, and then he would always become serious as he related the details of a marriage born of deep mutual love which, I have to admit, was obvious even twenty years on.

One day, in May 1967, we were all sitting in the shade outside Ismael's house, propped up against the wall, when we saw a strange group of people approaching. They were Israelis but not the frightening, military ones we were used to; these were civilians and one of them was a rabbi. We jumped to our feet, not at all sure what to do, and Ismael ran into the house to tell his father. 'Good afternoon,' said the rabbi. 'Is this the house of the Daoud?' Muhammad now emerged from the shadowy doorway, wiping his hands nervously on his *jalabiya*. 'It is,' he said.

'We are looking for your wife,' said the rabbi.

'Why? What is wrong with her?' asked Muhammad, looking around to see if any neighbours were watching. He insisted we all go inside and the following conversation ensued:

'We have come to take her back,' said the rabbi. 'She is Jewish and we want to offer you the opportunity to come and live in Israel. You can become Israelis, and your children too are Jews ...' He didn't get to finish his sentence because Muhammad reached into his *jalabiya* and pulled out a dagger: 'Please leave,' he said, in a low voice that trembled with emotion. 'I have kept this secret for twenty years. My wife converted to Islam years ago and I never want this mentioned again.' The Israelis left, shaking their heads in disbelief and Ismael and I were sworn to secrecy. Some time later Ismael asked his mother if she would ever have considered moving to Israel and she slapped his face for his trouble.

Meanwhile, another friend, a bright-eyed boy called Ibrahim, initiated me into something quite different: radical politics. He had read Marx and was in favour of the fedayeen, considering any form of violent uprising against occupation and oppression legitimate. It was the first time I had heard anyone talk about 'martyrdom'. 'I want to die a martyr,' he used to say, his eyes blazing. 'And I will take as many of those Israeli bastards with me as I can.'

In pursuit of this wish Ibrahim left Gaza for Jordan in 1967, where he joined Fatah. He lost his life in 1968 along with 120 of his comrades in the Battle of Karameh and whenever I was drawn towards sadness over his death I reminded myself that martyrdom was what he wanted.

Like Deir al-Balah, Rafah refugee camp also had its share of characters.

One man, in particular, sticks in my memory, and this was Sheikh Muhammad. In our culture, if somebody is disabled in any way, we call them Sheikh as an indication of our respect, as a sign of our acceptance that God meant this person to be this way, that it is neither his fault nor is it a mistake. Sheikh Muhammad was mentally handicapped and deaf and dumb. He had an alarming habit of wearing a *jalabiya* but no underwear and whenever he encountered a member of the opposite sex, he would whisk up his *jalabiya* and expose himself. Despite being shocked, the women used to laugh and talk about Sheikh Muhammad's reproductive equipment that was, by any standards, enormous.

Sheikh Muhammad was great friends with an elderly widow called Um Khalil, who had her own house and took care of him. He used to carry buckets of water for her from the well to the house, and then he'd go inside. After about an hour Sheikh Muhammad would emerge, scrubbed and brushed and looking extremely satisfied and content. This occasioned much gossip in the camp but nobody knew for sure what happened inside the widow's house and, being unable to communicate, Sheikh Muhammad couldn't tell us anything himself.

Slaughter

I had been in Rafah little more than a year when the Six-Day War erupted on 5 June 1967. The Israelis occupied the Gaza Strip bringing back such awful memories for my mother that her knees buckled and she nearly fainted when she recognized the rumble of tanks and jeeps. My brothers and sisters crowded around me, terrified.

'Just keep very quiet,' I told them as calmly as possible, locking the door. 'We're just going to stay in here until they've gone, alright? Nobody is to go outside or near the door.' My mother was crying. I put my arm round her. 'Come on, Yamma,' I said. 'It'll be okay.'

'What if they take the men again?' she sobbed. 'Like they did in Deir al-Balah. What if they take you outside? I couldn't bear to lose you as well ...' I didn't have time to reply because the tense silence was broken by the sound of Israeli voices shouting followed by machine-gun fire, just by our house. My mother stifled a scream.

'Nobody move,' I hissed. 'We're not going out until they've gone.'

A grotesque sight greeted our eyes when we finally crept out of our house more than an hour later. My grandmother's door was shot to bits and inside she was lying dead in a pool of blood. We later pieced together what had happened: Abdullah had been involved with the fedayeen and the Israelis had come to look for him at my grandmother's house. They banged on the door and my grandmother must have started to crawl towards it to open it. Suspicious of the length of time it was taking for the door to be opened, yet hearing someone moving about inside, the Israelis thought Abdullah was escaping and opened fire through the door riddling my grandmother with bullets. The terrible irony was that Abdullah had not, in fact, been at this house for some time, having decided his presence was jeopardizing my grandmother's safety.

Because it was too dangerous to go out, we decided to bury my grandmother inside her house, digging a grave in the mud floor. We moved her a few days later to another grave in her courtyard but couldn't bury her properly in the cemetery for almost a month.

Nor did the bloodshed end with the war. The Israelis imposed a curfew and one night we again heard shouting followed by gunshots. In the morning we found Sheikh Muhammad face down in the dust; he hadn't understood what a curfew was and had been on his way to visit Um Khalil as usual when the Israelis ordered him to stop. Being deaf and dumb he was oblivious to their commands and carried on ... they shot him in the back. By the end of June 1967, twenty-three refugees had been killed in Rafah and my family were forced into making the decision that would change my life for ever.

2

Sleeping on the Roof

Leaving Gaza was the only realistic option. The Israeli occupation resulted in my school being shut down at the beginning of what should have been my last year of secondary education and employment opportunities were almost non-existent. Work was available on the other side of the Green Line that demarcated Israeli and Palestinian territory, but only for those who surrendered their last vestiges of pride and dignity. I will never forget the sight, one morning at sunrise, of hundreds of Palestinian men in search of a day's labour, crammed together in what looked like animal pens on the other side of an Israeli checkpoint. As soon as an Israeli factory or farm truck turned up, the pens were opened by soldiers and the men started pushing and shoving each other, falling over their own and each other's feet, as they raced to scramble into the vehicle desperate for this chance to earn a day's wages. Israeli bosses who hired workers in this way jokingly referred to 'the slave markets' and the situation was reproduced on the outskirts of every main city in Gaza and the West Bank.

My mother's greatest fear was that the Israelis would come to Rafah, as they had done back in 1956, and massacre all the young men. I must have subconsciously absorbed this anxiety since it was at this time that I started sleepwalking. According to my mother, I would get up in the night and walk around the house with my eyes wide open. It was only when someone tried to talk to me that they realized I was completely unconscious. This latest development only added to my poor mother's concerns. 'Please, Sayeed,' she begged. 'Promise me that you will never live in a high building. I am worried that you might come to some harm with this sleepwalking.'

By September we had all come to terms with the fact that I would have to leave Palestine by either choice or coercion. The Israelis had implemented a policy of forced migration and had already managed to expel more than 325,000 Palestinians from Gaza and the West Bank in the period directly after the Six-Day War. Many Palestinians had already left their homeland voluntarily. As early as the 1950s, accepting the improbability of regaining their lands, many middle-class families had moved to the Gulf States to establish new enterprises with what remained of their capital.

Another significant group of emigrants was composed of unemployed workers, who left to look for work in the Gulf countries. Disparaged by their countrymen for choosing personal wealth over national unity and resistance, these Palestinian exiles were also unpopular with their hosts, as they tended to be militant and vociferous in their demands for workers' rights. Palestinians were active, for example, in a series of strikes in the Saudi Aramco refineries in the 1950s: the Saudis responded with legislation imposing a two-year prison sentence on anyone found guilty of organizing industrial action.

Another wave of migration occurred when the guerrilla movement started to gain strength and momentum after the Six-Day War, and the Israelis came looking for their leaders, often killing or injuring innocent civilians in the process. My father-in-law, Abdel Khalek Abu Atwan, took up arms in the wake of the Arab defeat in 1967, and joined one of the independent guerrilla groups that sprang up spontaneously at the time. He was involved in several raids across the border and the Israelis put a price of $3,000 on his head, a large amount of money at the time. A teacher by profession, he went on the run and slept in a chicken coup outside an aunt's house until he was smuggled out to Jordan where he was joined by his family.

Regardless of who or what they were before the Israeli occupation, most Palestinian refugees were forced to contend with a complete loss of status after it, whether at home or in other Arab countries. Even those in possession of good qualifications struggled to find a job in neighbouring countries: in Lebanon government quotas initially limited the employment of Palestinians and later banned them from working at all; in Jordan discrimination in both attitude and legislation meant that many professional Palestinians were unable to work at a level that reflected their qualifications, even though that country continued to absorb the largest numbers of Palestinian refugees, who now constitute 55 percent of its population (to be fair, there were some notable exceptions, such as Tahir al-Masri who briefly became Prime Minister and Speaker in parliament). In Lebanon, refugees were prohibited by law from buying arable land and most property. During this period, in the Middle East, the most common work available to immigrants was in either the construction or service industries. Palestinians stoically accepted this fate, saving money and sending it home with the stipulation that, once the family was fed, education was the priority; they saw this, rightly, as the only escape route from the camps for the next generation.

Taking the Plunge

Since the death of my father, my brother Kamal had been sending my mother money from Saudi Arabia, sparing us from destitution and starvation. He also supported Abdel Fatah in his studies in Egypt.

My uncle Ibrahim, who lived in Rafah, also took care of us and helped us in any way he could. He came around regularly and had a special bond with me; he always hoped that I would marry his daughter Yusra at some point, but she died of an unidentified illness at the age of 19. Medical care for refugees was almost non-existent – UNRWA spent less than $4 a year per person on healthcare in the camps at the time.

Ibrahim was a witty man who could make us laugh even under the most dire circumstances. In the emerging culture of the refugee camps, sons – especially ones with brains – were weighed up in terms of their earning potential. Ibrahim was quick to identify my market value: 'Zarifa, look at this one,' he joked one evening, putting his arm round my shoulder. 'This is a good asset. We will invest in his education to fatten his brain, and then put him to work. What shall he be? A doctor?'

'Or an architect,' my younger brother Ziad butted in. 'Architects earn thousands of dollars.'

'But I want to be a journalist,' I said.

'Journalist!' Ibrahim laughed. 'There's no money in that. You've got to think of your mum now, Sayeed,' he said, patting my arm with a sympathetic friendliness.

The consensus was that I would leave Palestine forthwith and finish my secondary education in Jordan (which offered the advantage of an internationally recognized passport to all Palestinian refugees), before moving to Egypt where I would go to university. 'Then you can consider how best to help the family finances,' Ibrahim concluded.

I started to make preparations for my journey and was mystified when I couldn't find my only pair of shoes; only ever worn on special occasions, these were essential for my travels. I asked my mother where they were, suspicious that one of my brothers had decided to keep them for the Atwan family communal shoe collection when I left.

'You will see,' she said. 'They will be here tomorrow.'

The next day, Ibrahim arrived with a brown paper package from the cobbler's under his arm. He and my mother conferred in low voices.

'What's going on?' I asked them, feeling irritated. 'Are those my shoes? They didn't need mending. I've hardly worn them.' I took the bundle from my uncle and opened it. There were my shoes, exactly the same as the last time I saw them. My mother and Ibrahim exchanged glances. He nodded at her, laughing.

'Here is a riddle for you, Sayeed,' he said. 'Your fortune is in these shoes.' I was baffled and after everyone had had a guess at what he could mean and failed – I think the most unwelcome suggestion was from my sister, Fatima, who suggested I could walk to Jordan to save the bus fare – my mother took the shoes and tapped the heels. 'Your uncle has taken all his savings,' she said, 'and had the cobbler hide it in your shoes.' Objections were useless and I hugged and thanked him, insisting that I would pay him back as soon as I could. Later, I carefully prised off the heels and counted the 30 Egyptian pounds he had managed to scrape together through those years of hardship. In today's money this would be worth about £10 sterling. It was his entire fortune.

The day for my departure came and at dawn I said goodbye to my family. We didn't know what would happen to me or how safe they would be in Rafah now that the Israelis had occupied Gaza. I worried for my siblings and vowed that I would provide for them and help them to better their lives. Ibrahim accompanied me to the bus station: I would travel first to the West Bank and from there to Amman in Jordan.

Waving goodbye to my uncle through the bus window as it pulled out onto the dusty highway I felt that I was well and truly on my own with my whole life ahead of me to make of what I would. It was exciting and daunting at the same time. My reveries about the future were interrupted by five or six Israeli soldiers, who banged on the windows and doors of the bus with their rifle butts at the checkpoint on the way out of Gaza. They scanned the passengers' anxious faces and I was among those whom they ordered out of the bus. I was petrified and my hands were shaking so much that I could hardly comply with the orders they barked in heavily accented Arabic.

'Papers!' said one, holding out his hand. The only ID I had was my student card; I worried that this would not suffice, that my journey would end here and that I'd be sent back defeated to the camp. The soldier beckoned another, taller, one over and they looked at my card. The tall one laughed.

'Where are you going?' he asked me.

'Amman,' I managed to stammer.

'We'll see,' the soldier said, using his gun to herd a group of women and children over beside me. He started interrogating one woman who had been my neighbour on the bus. She had four children with her and told the soldiers she was on her way to Kuwait to join her husband who had got a job out there. Yet another soldier joined us now with a sheaf of papers in his hand.

'Sign this!' said the tall one, writing our names on them before handing us one each. My neighbour whispered to me, 'What is it?' and I realized that she couldn't read. I scanned the short document. It was a sworn guarantee that once we had left the Occupied Territories we would never try to return. I explained this to her in Arabic and she started to cry. The tall one strode forward and asked, 'Do you want to go or not?'

'Yes,' she whispered.

'Then sign,' he said.

'She can't write,' I managed to get out. He wrenched her right hand out in front of her and put her thumb on an ink pad. 'Just make your mark above your name,' he said. 'That'll do.' I too had to sign or face God knows what consequences; once we had all complied we were waved through and I realized that all they really cared about was getting rid of as many of us as possible, in whatever way they could.

By the time the bus entered Hebron in the West Bank, I had regained enough composure to take in the sights; it was all new to me for this was my first glimpse of urban society. Here were streets and markets, shops and cars. Not only was Gaza poorer but it was also more conservative. In Hebron, young men were dressed in Western-style clothes and the women walked around with their heads uncovered displaying chic haircuts, an unimaginable luxury in Rafah. I had to ask my neighbour if these were really Palestinians, for the only ones I had encountered were impoverished waifs in Gazan refugee camps.

Amman

I had two relatives in Amman – one, Hussein, who was the dean at Amman University and lived in a smart house in a bourgeois area. Every other week someone from our peasant family in Gaza would turn up at his door with a bunch of thyme and expect to stay for a month. Hussein was at his wits' end because he couldn't say no to these strays, but his elegant and sophisticated Jordanian wife was threatening to divorce him because of the never-ending stream of rough-mannered visitors. I had taken pity on him and decided instead to throw my lot in with my cousin, Salah.

Salah was there to greet me and the first thing I noticed was his ridiculous shoes. Not only were they far too long and disproportionately wide but they were also a vivid shade of green. Salah suffered from flat feet and had difficulty finding any shoes to fit him. It was the bane of his life and he so was grateful to find any that could accommodate his malformed extremities that he had long since ceased caring what they looked like.

The last time I had seen Salah, he had been a slight young man; now he was twice his former self – in every direction – and had become extremely hairy. This big hulking gorilla emerged from the crowd and greeted me with great enthusiasm, kissing and hugging me, and slapping me on the back. He took my bag and was asking hundreds of questions about Palestine and our family as we walked through the thronging streets. I had assumed he would be taking me to his home and was surprised when we stopped in front of a hotel with a sign that read, *al-Arabi*. I felt embarrassed because the only money I possessed in the entire world was a tiny sum: the 10 Egyptian pounds my mother had pressed into my hand when I left and the 30 pounds in my shoes. Salah must have understood my expression

'Don't worry Sayeed,' he reassured me. 'This is not a hotel.'

'But it *is* a hotel,' I said pointing at it. 'I can see it's a hotel. Why are you telling me it's not?'

'For us Palestinians, this is not a hotel. It is the cheapest accommodation in the whole city,' he said. 'Come on, you will see.' And he took my hand and we walked through a side door of the hotel and started climbing the stairs.

We climbed one storey after another. I was beginning to think my cousin had either gone insane or become enormously wealthy without telling anyone, though his threadbare clothing and down-at-heel shoes did not suggest this.

'Are we going to the penthouse?' I asked him and he started to laugh.

'Not exactly,' he said, stopping at a rusty door at the very top. He pushed the door with his shoulder and we found ourselves on the roof.

There were rows of beds on one side and rows of bare mattresses on the other; scores of men, sitting or lying down, were smoking, chatting or eating under the blazing blue sky. Salah was well known and people greeted him in a friendly manner. He introduced me and an endless round of handshaking and kisses began. 'Welcome to your new home!' said Salah, indicating one of the beds in the row nearest the edge of the roof, which had no safety railings whatsoever. I imagined my mother's reaction if she could see where I, the somnambulist, was meant to sleep and decided I would have to invent some kind of safety system for myself to keep me from falling to my death in the night. I thanked Salah for his thoughtfulness in providing me with accommodation and we sat on the bed chatting.

'I am working like a dog,' he said. 'Imagine, I want to do my degree in mathematics, but here I am, slaving on a building site for a few piastres a day. Even so,' he said, looking around the motley collection of rooftop dwellers, 'I am luckier than most of these, who cannot find any work at all. They'll have to go back to the camps and live on UNRWA handouts, poor bastards. What about you?' he asked me. 'What kind of work are you looking for?'

'Oh, I'm not looking for work,' I replied airily. 'I'm going to finish my high-school education and then go to university in Egypt like my brother Abdel Fatah.' Salah started to laugh. 'Did you know you have to pay for schools here?' he asked me. 'Have you got any money?' I looked around. It was probably not a good idea to advertise the little I had, still concealed in my shoes, in front of all these desperate, hungry people. I managed to communicate that I had just over 40 Egyptian pounds. 'That's nothing,' he informed me. 'It wouldn't even pay for a term and then you've got to eat and have a roof over your head, or under it in this case,' he joked. 'I'm sorry Sayeed, but your money is worthless.' I tried to put a brave face on it but the idea that my uncle's lifetime savings were 'worthless' almost made me want to cry. 'You'll have to get a job', he said, 'and that is easier said than done.'

And so my first day in Jordan ended with the realization that all my plans were unrealistic and I was going to have to work extremely hard to get what I wanted. Night fell and Salah went off to his mattress on the other side of the roof. I lay down on the bed, looking up at the stars and the wisps of cigarette smoke spiralling up to them, listening to the hum of men's voices. I had nearly nodded off to sleep when I remembered my sleepwalking predicament. I sat up with a start and began racking my brains for a solution. I had few possessions and none of them appeared to offer any salvation except, perhaps, the cotton *keffiyeh* I had brought with me. I knotted one corner around my ankle and tied another end firmly to the bedpost. Testing the strength of this voluntary restraint, I decided it would prevent me from going far in the night.

I lived on the roof for more than a month and soon got used to such novel accommodation. Our bird's-eye view took in other buildings and sometimes we were rewarded with the glimpse of a woman's thigh as she washed, believing herself unobserved on her own rooftop. I am sure the sunsets were beautiful too but we were not looking for scenery but survival. There was a *hammam* on the roof where you could enjoy the luxury of a hot bath for a few *fils* on a Friday.

I remember the man who was my neighbour on the roof. He was a curious character who told the same strange story, night after night in the dark, as if he was trying to exorcise himself of some demon. He had been a policeman in Gaza and one night a young woman's body was brought to the police station while he was on duty. She had been found on the beach, the victim of an 'honour killing'. He was left alone with the corpse to guard it as it lay on a table beside him.

'It was raining and freezing cold outside,' he used to tell us. 'I couldn't have gone out even if I had wanted to. But I didn't want to – I was irresistibly drawn to the young woman. As the night wore on I found myself wrestling with a horrible desire to look at her body and until dawn I was tortured with conflicting desires and emotions.' Each night he would go over this repugnant fantasy, embroidering it with more and more detail, encouraged by our curiosity and disgust.

An Uneasy Relationship

The Jordanian regime has long had an uneasy relationship with the Palestinian people. Under the British Mandate following the First World War, 80 percent of the area termed 'Palestine' was east of the River Jordan and some of the Palestine Liberation Organization's (PLO) founders maintained a claim to this land. The province of Transjordan was created at the 1921 Cairo conference presided over by British Colonial Secretary, Winston Churchill, who installed the Hashemite Prince Abdullah as Emir. Hailing from the Hijaz (part of what is now Saudi Arabia), Abdullah was seen as a safe pair of hands for what was essentially to be a buffer between Balfour's Zionist agenda in Palestine and the rest of the Arab world. The modern independent kingdom of Jordan was established in 1946.

King Abdullah was shot dead on 20 July 1951 by Mustapha Shukri Usho, a Palestinian seeking revenge for the regime's actions in the wake of the *Nakba*, when Lebanon and Jordan started negotiating a separate peace deal with Israel. King Hussein was on the throne when I arrived in 1967 and was already ill at ease with the large number of Palestinians now living in the kingdom which he perceived, realistically, as a threat to his power. Salah pointed out, however, that the Jordanians should be grateful to their resident Palestinian businessmen and entrepreneurs because much of the progress and comparative prosperity the kingdom enjoyed was due to them. Prior to this, the Hashemite Kingdom had been a dusty Bedouin backwater.

Hard Work

The little work that was available for Amman's refugees was fiercely fought over. Among those who had held jobs, the consensus was that a sympathetic Palestinian boss or the municipal authority were the most desirable employers. In the short time I was in Amman I managed to work for both.

My first job was in a tomato canning factory. Housed in a compound behind imposing iron gates, there were three hangars: one contained the machinery which transformed sheet metal into cans; the second was dominated by a vast vat in which tons of tomatoes bubbled before being deposited, by machine, into the cans which were then machine sealed and ejected at an alarming rate onto a platform; the third was the warehouse where the finished product was stored and distributed.

I started in the warehouse, carrying crates to the lorries and loading them for delivery. It was back-breaking work, especially for such a bony youngster: I was over six feet tall but weighed just 55 kilos as a result of the malnutrition that had overshadowed my formative years. Being mindful, though, of the widespread unemployment among my compatriots, I was grateful to be working at all and applied myself with vigour.

Our Palestinian boss, Mr Hijazi, was from a well-known Hebron family. He was in his forties and because his family had fled Palestine before the Israelis could confiscate their assets they had remained comparatively wealthy. Mr Hijazi took a liking to me and saw that I was exhausting myself with all this heavy lifting. He moved me to the second hangar where I was tasked with transferring the filled cans from the platform to crates.

The air was thick with steam and the stench of rotten fruit that had been discarded underneath the vat. The problem with this new job was that the tomatoes were still boiling hot when they were canned. As the factory bosses didn't provide gloves, my hands were soon blistered and sore; each can I touched was absolute torture. Apologetically, I approached Mr Hijazi and showed him my hands.

'They'll soon toughen up,' he said, slapping me on the back. 'How do you think the others manage?'

'Would you allow me to move just once more?' I pleaded. 'I won't ask you again. I will put up with hell rather than ask another favour.'

'Alright,' he said. 'But only because we are brother Palestinians. So don't let me down.' And he gave me a new position in the can-making factory.

This was the most hazardous of all my occupations before or since, and I include my perilous journeys through the Middle East in search of newsworthy stories, even going to Tora Bóra to meet Osama bin Laden. My new job entailed thrusting the half-made cans into a machine where a bottom was clamped onto it. The noise was unbearable, nothing but banging, clanking, screeching and squealing, from dawn to dusk. All day long my head was throbbing. But that was nothing compared to the machine's apparent desire to hammer my hands at the same time as it clamped on the lids. I still have a large scar on my right hand from a two-inch cut this infernal creation inflicted on me. On another occasion, a sheet of metal, left upright on the floor, performed the function of a razor-sharp sword on my foot when I accidentally walked onto it. Both times I was rushed to hospital in a bloody mess. The factory supervisors were more concerned with when I would be getting back to work than preventing such accidents happening again by introducing safety measures. I received neither apologies nor – unthinkable – compensation.

They paid me the equivalent of 30 pence a day for a twelve-hour shift; overtime was sometimes available at 5 pence per hour. Mr Hijazi started to pay the Palestinian workers an additional 10 pence a day as a gesture of solidarity and I got to know him quite well. True to my word, I didn't moan or complain about my new job but he soon moved me onto a kinder machine, where I had a couple of underlings, one the age of my father, and my first experience as a boss.

Not all the management staff were as sympathetic to Palestinians as Mr Hijazi. We had a supervisor called Hamouda who had only the thumb and little finger on his right hand as a result of an accident he'd had in the quarry where he worked previously. The torturous work of breaking up boulders begged for short cuts and he had jumped at the chance of using some dynamite; unfortunately, he had blown up his own hand and the rocks remained intact. Perhaps it was this accident that caused him to be

so embittered but we didn't care about the psychology behind his relentless persecution of us. He kept all the Palestinian workers under constant
surveillance, appearing from behind stacks of cans where he'd been spying
and searching us on our way out of work, openly accusing us of stealing. In
short, he made our lives hell. One day, he didn't turn up for work and we
later found out he had been sacked for stealing solder from the factory. We
were delighted at this news and it kept us cheerful for days, repeating the
few details we knew and inventing those we didn't, further embellishing
the story each time we recounted it.

At this time, Kamal was supporting Abdel Fatah in his studies and I was
the main breadwinner for the family back in Rafah, a responsibility I was
always mindful of. The memory of the grinding poverty and deprivation
of the camps was still fresh in my mind. Soon after my arrival in Amman
I discovered that the rooftop mattresses were cheaper than the beds and
I saved a few pence by swapping over – the hazard of sleepwalking now
avoided by tying my ankles together. It was considered fashionable to smoke
and most young men dangled a casual cigarette from their lips or fingers
but I decided not to embark on this expensive habit, nor did I join my
co-workers on their jaunts to restaurants. I religiously saved every penny
that I did not need for basic survival to send back home – with no bank
accounts or other means of transferring money at our disposal we relied
on the honesty and good will of Palestinians who were passing through on
their way back to Gaza to deliver the funds in person. As for the £30 my
uncle had given me, I exchanged £10 into Jordanian dinars to tide me over
when I first arrived but sent the rest back to my mother. My mother used the
money I sent to buy fresh vegetables for the children and, very occasionally,
a piece of tripe or sheep's head, the only meat she could afford.

One day, one of the older workers called Moosa called me over to him.
Moosa spent most of his time either chain-smoking or playing practical
jokes so I was a bit wary as I went up to him. He pulled a roll of papers
out of his pocket and unfurled them under my nose. I blushed and stam-
mered and felt embarrassed but also fascinated. Moosa's pictures were of
naked women and I had never seen such a thing in my life. He laughed
and slapped his thighs as he observed my reaction, but thankfully didn't
broadcast my discomfort to the rest of the workforce. There were only two
real-life women in the factory, an elderly lady and her daughter, who had

a glass eye. Although they were not very attractive, a lot of the men used to find a reason to talk and even flirt with them.

The least popular job in the whole operation was loading the cans onto the lorry in the warehouse for delivery. It was tiring and difficult and all the workers used to run off and start doing something else the minute it was obvious this task was next. Mr Hijazi had excused me from this duty because of my weak build but once he asked me, 'How can I stop the men disappearing when I want them to load up the truck?' I soon came up with a solution: 'Put the old lady and her daughter to work in the warehouse; that way they'll all be vying to show the young woman who is the strongest and who has the biggest muscles.' It worked a treat and the truck was now loaded in minutes rather than hours.

My best friend at the factory was a Palestinian teenager called Muhammad Rashidi. He was from Jaffa and seemed incredibly urbane to me. His family were middle class and he spoke with a different accent from my peasant dialect. Like me, Muhammad's father had died young; he had three brothers and they were all working, providing a decent standard of living for their mother and two sisters who had accompanied them to Jordan. The first time he invited me to his house I was impressed – it was a proper villa in a good area of Amman. As I entered, a wave of stirring, passionate music engulfed me. A woman's voice, deep, powerful and so emotionally charged she sometimes seemed to be weeping, undulated over a small orchestra of *oud*, drums and violins. We walked into their living room and I discovered the source of this wonderful music was an electric record player! I hadn't encountered one before and was amazed. The singer was Umm Kulthoum, the great Egyptian diva. To me, all of this was paradise. I used to go to their house every Friday and Muhammad's mother would cook traditional food from the Jaffa region for us and then we would go to the cinema where you could watch three old movies in one go. Whenever the family purchased a new record they would invite me over and it would be played over and over, while we discussed its merits. Later they bought a television and the first time I watched this fantastic invention my hero, Jamal Abdel Nasser, was giving a speech which made the occasion all the more memorable.

I am still friends with the Rashidi family and visit Muhammad when I am in Jordan. He has a shop selling women's accessories, lots of children, and a house in a pleasant area. The last time I saw him was in 2001: he invited all the neighbours around to meet me, because I was often on the television and he wanted to show me off. They all had their photographs taken with me and asked for my autograph as if I were a famous pop star. I enjoyed these festivities because everyone was happy. Though I had arrived in a taxi and was staying in a five-star hotel, whose threshold we wouldn't have dared approach when we worked in the factory, I still felt more at home with Muhammad and his friends.

Room for Improvement

The nights were getting colder and I decided that my rooftop existence would have to end. I asked around and heard about a room in a flat in an upmarket area of Amman that, to my surprise, was within my budget. I found out why when I went to see it: the room was about four square metres and completely taken up by four narrow camp beds. I would be sharing it with three other Palestinians, all working either in factories or as scaffolders on building sites; Ayman and Saad were about my age and then there was Abu Mustafa who was approaching forty. He was a bad-tempered man who moaned ceaselessly. He moaned about the fact he was a widower, and what his wife had been like when she was alive, he moaned about his kids, and about his job. Because he was older than us, we used to tell Abu Mustafa all our problems and then he'd moan about them for us, which saved us the effort.

Abu Mustafa was fussy, almost effeminate, and made his bed each morning, keeping everything tidy. My sliver of the room on the other hand was dedicated to chaos: I couldn't see the point of making the bed when you were only going to get back in it later and make it all messy again. The bed and the floor around and under it were piled high with old newspapers and magazines. This occasioned regular, low-level nagging and muttering, but that was nothing compared to his reaction over the savings incident.

I had been in the habit of saving a one-dinar note on alternate weeks as a contingency against losing my job. Having no faith in banks, I had cut a hole in the cover of my mattress and, when everyone else was out, used to stuff the money into its woolly insides as far as my arm could go. After a couple of months, I was seized with the paranoid notion that my dinars had been stolen. Alone in the room, I knelt down, inserted my arm into the mattress and wiggled my fingers around. I felt nothing! I tried again, this time extracting some of the filling to make my search easier. After about ten minutes, I was surrounded by a range of woolly mountains and my mattress was nearly empty. Looming above one of the peaks, his arms folded, was Abu Mustafa. He was not amused.

'Look at this mess!' he boomed. 'What are you doing, you mad man?'

'My money's gone,' I said hysterically. Abu Mustafa cast his fiery glance around and fished out several crumpled notes from the debris, dashing them to the floor beside me. He stamped his foot and like a lone volcano in the midst of those white peaks, threw back his head and erupted; all Abu Mustafa's pent-up ire was spent on me.

Meanwhile we had become increasingly intrigued by our downstairs neighbours. For weeks we had heard the sound of female voices below and they were always laughing raucously, teasing each other, or having fierce quarrels. It seemed that these young women used to sleep all day and then go out until the early hours, usually returning with male company. The reason we knew all this was that, with the exception of Abu Mustafa, we all spent hours with our ears pressed to the ground, listening to this real-life soap opera and exchanging observations. One day Ayman – who had been doing a night shift – burst into the room excitedly just as the rest of us were getting ready to go to work. It was 5 AM. 'I've seen them!' he announced.

'Who?' we asked blearily.

'The bad girls!' he said, for that's what we had started calling them. He showed us a window halfway down the stairwell; the curtain had been drawn back and now we could get a bird's-eye view into their living room. There they were, three pretty, wicked-looking girls, wearing a lot of make-up, short skirts and high heels, chatting and laughing as they handed out drinks to some men.

Naturally, we took to peeping in on the bad girls every time we passed by (which was fairly often), until one evening they all turned around and looked up at us, waving and giggling, and beckoning us to come in. This was embarrassing. We were shy, bumbling young men who were intoxicated by the mysteries of womankind, but this was too much. After running for the shelter of our room, we never looked in that direction again. I even considered placing a curtain over the outside of the window so that we wouldn't be tempted.

Driving Force

On Fridays, five or six of us would gather in a café in the centre of Amman, where we'd spend much of the day nursing one cup of coffee apiece, playing cards and chatting, much to the irritation of the owner. We used to bring in second-hand newspapers, magazines, and novels that we'd bought from street sellers and swap them – when these had done the rounds we'd sell them back again for slightly less than we'd paid. It was in Amman that I first started reading seriously, guided in my choice of literature by my brother, Abdel Fatah. I read European classics translated into Arabic: Shakespeare, Hugo's *Les Misérables* and several works by Camus and Beckett. I enjoyed Dickens and Dostoevsky. Reading became a means of escaping poverty and depression and in my imagination I travelled the world with the characters in these books. Reading gave me a sense of the universal nature of much of human existence and this in turn contributed to the confidence I later needed to function outside the Arab world and, eventually, to live in London.

When we weren't reading we'd talk. The conversation would inevitably turn to politics and a quarrel would ensue. Our youth meant that we were fiercely competitive and even though we were all left-wing we discovered various shades of red and were quick to hurl insults such as 'imperialist agent', 'America lover', and 'Zionist' at each other. After one such quarrel, everyone rose to their feet and stormed out leaving just me, Salah and the bill. I had been feeling down for some time and was glad of this opportunity to talk things over with my cousin in private. 'I've been at the tomato factory for a year now,' I told him, 'and I don't feel any nearer to achieving my goals. I'm living from hand to mouth and feeling trapped.' Salah looked troubled but his face suddenly brightened. 'I know!' he said. 'There's a job going as a driver at the municipal council and it's much better paid.'

'But I can't drive,' I reminded him.

'That doesn't matter,' he said. 'It won't take long to learn. Just come here next Friday at 10 AM and you'll see.'

The next Friday, Salah was at our usual table with a man I'd never met before. Sam – short for Samir – was the Arab equivalent of a 'wide boy'. He was a taxi driver on the Amman-Beirut route and a born raconteur. He told us tall stories about the Beirut nightclubs and belly-dancers and his scrapes with the police. It was impossible to separate fact from fiction but it didn't really matter. I enjoyed his flamboyance and casual attitude to money. Knowing that I couldn't afford driving lessons, Sam undertook to teach me himself. His Mercedes was outside. 'Yallah!' he said. 'Let's go.'

About three hours later, Sam had shown me all the basics: how to start the car, put it in gear and move forward, reverse and indicate, and we had had a brief but bone-shaking tour around the block with me at the wheel. As I wrenched the hand-brake on with a screech outside the café, he patted me on the back and said, 'That's it. You're ready to take your test. I am confident you will pass.' And he was right. It seemed that you only had to be able to get a vehicle to move, however jerkily, to obtain a licence in Jordan at that time.

Barely able to drive a car, I soon found myself behind the wheel of a tractor, working for the municipal council. While I drove the tractor through the city centre, four men stood on the back spraying insecticide from red cans in an attempt to deal with the cockroaches, mosquitoes and other bugs that threatened to overrun the streets of Amman. Although these cans were clearly marked with a skull and crossbones, indicating the toxic nature of their contents, not one of us was furnished with a mask or any kind of protection. We were expected to purchase such things for ourselves if we were worried about our health but nobody could afford that luxury. My other complaint about the job was the ponderous pace of the tractor; now that I was a driver I would have preferred something speedier.

Throughout my life, I have been blessed with older people taking an interest in me and offering a helping hand. My mentor at the council was an engineer called Hassan, also Palestinian and in charge of the department. One day, I came in after driving the tractor with my eyes and nose streaming. Hassan looked at me and shook his head.

'Why are you doing this job, Abdel Bari? It's making you ill.'

'I don't have any choice, Hassan,' I said, punctuating my words with a sniff. 'I am grateful for the work and can't afford to be picky.'

'It's a job for old people who don't mind dying,' he said. 'Can't you feel the effect of those chemicals? They could kill you,' he said, taking out a ledger and flicking through the pages. 'Listen, I need someone on the rubbish lorries. Do you think you could drive a truck?'

The smell was unbearable, especially in the heat of a Jordanian summer, but the money was better and being the driver I didn't have to work as hard as my co-workers, the dustmen. These muscular and grimy heroes had to cling precariously to the back of the truck, leaping down every other minute to empty some foul bin or other onto the stinking mountain in the back. I was happy sitting perched up high, driving around the different districts of Jordan and dreaming of the elusive future I was planning for myself. My compatriots used to scour the rubbish for anything they could take home with them. They used to prefer the days when we toured the more affluent districts of Amman for here were richer pickings, sometimes fruit or vegetables, and even items of furniture that they would show me triumphantly through the window.

After a couple of weeks, I realized I could afford to rent a room of my own and found lodgings with a family in the Marka district of Amman: a rundown but lively area, both overcrowded and friendly. The family consisted of a widowed mother and her six unmarried daughters. They treated me like a prince, washing my clothes and feeding me until I could hardly move. Then, when they had finished with me, the neighbours (who had three unmarried daughters) would take over, inviting me for coffee and cakes and pampering me in every conceivable way. Fierce competition broke out between the two families. I was viewed as quite a catch – I had a job, an income, and worked for the municipal council – and nobody seemed to notice that I was usually accompanied by a whiff of the refuse cart. I couldn't move without meeting one of those nine pairs of melting brown eyes, which would instantly be modestly lowered.

One of the girls was called Salwa and she had heard me complaining about the cold as winter drew in. She suggested that, if I would buy the wool, she would knit me a sweater. This labour of love lasted several months and it was only as I was leaving Jordan for Egypt with winter long behind us, that she presented me with the finished article, wrapped in some tissue paper. I didn't open the parcel until I got to Alexandria, revealing a fine piece of handiwork. On closer inspection, I saw that she had knitted some of her own hair into the sweater, as a token of her feelings for me. This charming, romantic gesture was my first such experience but I had long ago decided against any sort of relationship because for me such a connection would mean marriage.

It was around this time that my mother came to visit me in Amman for ten days. She got off the bus and I noticed that she was carrying a saucepan, the lid tied on with string.

'What have you got there, Yamma?' I asked after we had greeted each other.

'Real Palestinian food for you, Sayeed,' she said proudly. She had cooked this meal for me in Gaza and brought it all the way to Amman, clutching it protectively on her lap for the entire ten-hour journey. Prepared with so much love and delivered with such determination, those stuffed courgettes and roasted chicken were the best meal I had ever eaten. I was able to reciprocate a few days later when I fulfilled one of her lifelong desires by taking her to eat in a kebab restaurant.

Early on in her visit, we went for a walk around Amman. She hadn't ever been to a city and was entranced by the tall buildings; in the middle of Amman there was a ten-storey one that stopped her in her tracks. After five minutes of her sky-gazing I was getting impatient.

'Come on, Yamma, let's go,' I said, tugging at her sleeve.

'No, no,' she replied. 'I must have a good look at King Hussein's house.' I started laughing: 'That's not his house, Yamma – '

'Of course it must be,' she insisted. 'It's the biggest one and he is the most important man in Jordan.'

'He lives in a palace Yamma,' I said. 'This is an office building and it's in the centre of town. King Hussein lives outside the city on top of his own mountain, and there is a huge entrance and driveway, and bodyguards everywhere you look.' My mother took a lot of convincing on this matter and when I later interviewed King Hussein, I told him the story of how my mother assumed he would live in the biggest building in the city centre. He laughed and asked, 'Where is she now?'

'She is in Gaza,' I replied.

'Next time please bring her to see me. I would love to meet her and show her the royal court.'

Unfortunately, my mother was unable to leave Gaza again for a long time, but when I met the king again, some five years later, he hadn't forgotten and asked after her.

Meanwhile, I was having problems at work. If the tractor had been slow at least it worked. The rubbish truck broke down with infuriating regularity, often leaving us stranded for hours in the boiling sun until Hassan came to our rescue in his car. If he couldn't fix it on the spot, another lorry would be dispatched and the truck, spilling its filthy contents, would be towed back to the depot to the shouts and hoots of derision of the local population. I decided to pull a few strings and next time I found myself alone with Hassan I broached the possibility of another change.

'You are fed up with that dreadful old truck,' he said. 'You would like to drive a better car, a proper one? Yes?'

'Yes,' I said, surprised by this encouraging response.

'I have just the thing!' he announced. 'From now on you will be driving a brand new car. The newest car in the whole municipal council.' He put his arm around my shoulder. 'Come with me,' he said. 'I will show you.'

As we walked to the garages he outlined the advantages of my new position. 'The salary is better than you are getting now,' he said. 'We will give you four pounds more.'

'Four pounds a year? Great!' I said, beaming.

'No, not a year, a month!' he grinned. 'I know you have brothers and sisters who rely on you now,' he said, unlocking one of the garages. 'Take a look at that my friend!' and he opened the door to reveal a brand new, gleaming, black hearse.

'Oh,' I said, taking a few steps back. 'I don't know. I'm scared of dead bodies. I didn't even see my father.'

'Think of the tips!' Hassan urged. 'Usually it is only rich people who have funerals. They have a lot of money and they are bound to be generous at such a moment.'

But I couldn't be persuaded. The idea of driving with a corpse behind me was sickening. 'I'd crash the car,' I told Hassan. 'I'd panic! I really can't do it.'

'Everybody wants this job,' he said, pained and offended. 'I offer it to you and you turn it down.'

'I am sorry,' I said, 'and grateful too, but I have to say no. Let my family starve. I will have nightmares every night if I drive that hearse. Please let me stick with the rubbish truck.'

A few months later, I was offered another job by a rich Syrian businessman who owned a sweet factory. I became a van driver for his firm, Nashid Brothers, and sat behind the wheel of a normal vehicle for the first time, delivering Turkish Delight to shops and restaurants all over the city. I had an assistant, Mahmoud, who raced in with the cartons at every drop-off point. Mahmoud was a short, stocky man with some sparse wisps of ginger hair on his head. He wasn't bright but you could tell from his appearance that he would have liked to have been a bureaucrat; despite the manual nature of his employment he dressed like a clerk and had a clean shirt every other day.

This was a much better job, and decidedly sweeter smelling. I was briefly addicted to Turkish Delight and couldn't resist sampling each day's batch. Eating all those sweets coupled with the vast amounts of food that my landlady, her daughters, their neighbour and her daughters were constantly plying me with began to have an impact on my figure. For the first time in my life my bones were concealed under a comfortable padding of flesh and I could only just do up the waistband of my trousers. After a few months, however, I went off Turkish Delight and eventually the smell of any kind of sweets made me feel nauseous. To this day, I hate sweets, something my children find incomprehensible.

At night, the innocuous-looking Nashid Brothers sweet factory was transformed into something entirely different. I had noticed that most of the Palestinian workers stayed behind after work and I was soon let into the secret of what went on when everyone else had clocked out. As the machines were turned off and left to cool, the shutters rolled down on the fading light of the Amman skyline and groups of men gathered in the shadows, talking and smoking. After about half an hour, the fluorescent lights buzzed into life again and an air of anticipation and excitement filled the space. The side doors were flung open and in strode the leaders of the Palestinian guerrilla movement, the Democratic Front for the Liberation of Palestine (DFLP). These were dramatic figures dressed in khaki and camouflage, wearing heavy boots, and with rifles and machine guns slung across their shoulders. The sweet factory, like scores of other workplaces in the city, was used to recruit and train fighters for armed struggle against the Israeli occupation.

In the period between 1967–70, Amman was a haven for guerrillas: the spirit of pan-Arabism had been rekindled in the wake of the Six-Day War, and the Jordanian capital became an Arab version of Hanoi. It was a fascinating phase of the Palestinian struggle and it seemed as though people got together every day to declare the establishment of yet another guerrilla group. It was a critical period not only in the evolution of the resistance movement but also in the radicalization of the Arab world in general. Palestinian politics are complex but since they are, and have been, pivotal to my life it is useful to look at what the main guerrilla factions stood for at the time.

Fatah was the oldest and largest resistance group, established on 10 October 1959 at a meeting in a house in Kuwait attended by a small group, most of whom had met at university in Cairo. Among them were men who would later become world-famous freedom fighters and politicians: Yasser Arafat, Salah Khalaf and Khalil al-Wazir (Abu Jihad). Mahmoud Abbas (Abu Mazen), who would become the first Palestinian prime minister in 2003, then based in Qatar, was also one of Fatah's founding members.

Initially an ideological movement, Fatah became involved in armed struggle with the birth of its military wing, al-Asifa ('the storm'), in 1965. Local Fatah commanders encouraged popular resistance and gave West Bank villagers rudimentary military training. The Israelis responded to the resulting, modest, guerrilla attacks with great force: more than 1,000 Palestinians had been jailed without trial by the end of 1967; the homes of suspected sympathizers were demolished and draconian curfews were imposed. Arafat and other Fatah leaders now regrouped in Jordan, establishing their headquarters in Karameh, 40 kilometres outside Ammam.

Fatah started paying people a wage to join them when I was in Amman. I remember this because they were offering 15 dinars a month, which was what I was earning as a truck driver. I didn't approve of this financial incentive, as I felt it compromised an essential ideological commitment to our national cause.

Nevertheless, the fact that they were taking action rather than just talking about doing so ensured a steady growth in Fatah's popularity among the Palestinians. Having chased them out of the West Bank, Israel now sought to extinguish Fatah once and for all by launching a lightning strike on their base in Karameh. Fortunately, Jordanian intelligence got wind of this, informed the Fatah leaders and advised them to flee. When Fatah made it clear they would stand and fight, the Jordanians assured them that they could rely on military back-up from their army. On 21 March 1968, Fatah's headquarters were attacked by a force of 15,000 Israeli soldiers, in tanks and helicopters, armed with all the latest weaponry and intent on destruction. Greatly outnumbered, the fedayeen fought back and were soon reinforced, as promised, by local Jordanian army units. Surprised by the level of resistance, the Israelis quickly retreated, leaving 150 Fatah fighters, 20 Jordanian soldiers and 28 Israelis dead. After the humiliation of the Arab armies' 1967 defeat, this was an important victory and Amman erupted in celebration. I joined the jubilant crowd of thousands on the streets as they shouted, drummed and danced, distributing sweets and shooting guns into the air.

Captured Israeli tanks and armoured vehicles were paraded in Amman's main Hashemia Square and people came from all over Jordan to look at them, the more daring scaling their flanks to be photographed by friends and photo-journalists. The Battle of Karameh is etched in the collective memory of the Palestinian people, and fittingly the town's name, Karameh, is Arabic for 'dignity'. The sacrifice of Fatah's brave fighters inspired 5,000 new recruits to join up in the ensuing forty-eight hours. Karameh also brought Yasser Arafat into the international spotlight for the first time: *Time* magazine carried a blow-by-blow account of the battle in its 13 December 1968 issue and the Fatah leader's face filled the front cover.

Fatah was fêted by Arab leaders who provided much-needed finance; the organization also attracted logistical support from the Chinese government and its leaders were in direct contact with the North Koreans and the Vietcong. By 1969, it dominated the PLO, which had been founded in May 1964 as an umbrella group for the Palestinian guerrilla movement. Although I admired the military successes of Fatah, their politics seemed suspect to me: right of centre, funded by the Gulf States, and opposed to Nasserite pan-Arabism.

For me, George Habash's Popular Front for the Liberation of Palestine (PFLP) was far more appealing. I admired Habash who had been expelled from his hometown of Lydda in the 1948 *Nakba* and afterwards completed his medical training in Beirut. The PFLP was the result of a November 1967 merger of several guerrilla outfits, and the group's first public statement resonated with many of the dispossessed when it said, 'The only weapon left in the hands of the people is revolutionary violence.' Most of the PFLP members were intellectuals with a pan-Arab, socialist agenda.

The PFLP carried out some dramatic actions including hijackings and counted among their numbers the famous female guerrilla, Leila Khaled. Like Che Guevara, she is freeze-framed in the public consciousness in a single iconic image, a gun-wielding beauty with blazing eyes. I didn't meet her until 2005, but the middle-aged woman who strode into my office still exuded the charisma and forceful challenge of the true revolutionary.

This was the era of legends and George Habash was admired by the Palestinians for his 1968 jail break in Syria, where he had been imprisoned for sabotaging the Trans-Arabian Pipeline. While he was in jail, Nayef Hawatma, a member of his group, issued a statement labelling Nasser's government a 'petty-bourgeois regime'. The Egyptian leader was so incensed that he cut off all aid to them. By February 1969, Hawatma and Habash had fallen out so completely that the former left the PFLP to form the DFLP. My boss, the Syrian, supported Hawatma in this split and thus the DFLP's activities were based in his factory. Actually, he could hardly have objected unless he wanted to be branded a traitor – in the radical, left-wing political climate that prevailed among the Palestinian community in Amman the bourgeoisie had to be very careful what they said and did, and had to choose one or other guerrilla outfit to support.

I often stayed on after work to meet the DFLP trainers and observed their activities with interest, sometimes joining in. I was no stranger to handling a gun – at school in Gaza target practice using old Enfield rifles loaded with blanks was part of the curriculum. Now we were taught how to dismantle, clean, load and shoot a Kalashnikov with live ammunition.

I was also connected to the PFLP group in Amman through a relative, Hassan, who was one of their trainers; Hassan used to take me to a stretch of wasteland in the suburbs to practise shooting. I had no aptitude for this despite my best efforts and Hassan was lucky I didn't shoot him instead of the old cans and bottles we lined up as targets. There were many cases of accidental shootings by inept individuals intent on guerrilla action, who under normal circumstances would never have had anything to do with a gun in the course of their lives. I respected Hassan, who later joined the

PFLP general command and was sent to man their office in Iraq. He married a Palestinian woman there and had a large family before being killed during the sanctions era in mysterious circumstances.

Although I was radical and hot-headed in those days, I resisted all attempts to recruit me into any guerrilla group. My mind was focused on the fact that my mother and my younger brothers and sisters relied on me. If I died they would starve, it was as simple as that. I must admit that I have some regrets about this and I envied friends like Ibrahim, who lived the guerrilla experience and died for his beliefs. By way of compensation for my reluctance to fight, I told my trainers that I intended to marry a good Palestinian woman and add to the future generation of our people.

In reality nothing was further from my mind than finding a wife. I was enjoying my freedom after years in a refugee camp. Mahmoud, however, was behaving strangely, gazing absentmindedly out of the van window as we travelled round Amman and humming romantic songs such as Abdel Halim Hafez's 'Yes, My Love' and 'The Empty Pillow', with a smile on his face. One day, he asked me to take a detour from our usual route saying he had to visit someone at the hospital. I waited outside, reading a newspaper I had salvaged from the boss's office, while Mahmoud ran into the hospital. After about ten minutes, I began to worry that we would be late on our round and get into trouble. I started scanning the hospital entrance for signs of Mahmoud and was astonished to see him emerging with a nurse in full uniform. This unlikely pair headed straight for the van and I started the engine up, anxious to be on the move. Mahmoud opened the passenger side door and shouted over the throbbing engine:

'Abdel Bari, this is Sana, a friend of mine, and I want to give her a lift home.' Sana was blonde, with a small yet curvaceous build, quick-witted and always laughing. When I first saw Barbara Windsor I was shocked because she was identical to Sana. I couldn't watch *EastEnders* without thinking of her and this made me laugh, much to the irritation of my wife and children, who had no idea why the appearance of Peggy Mitchell had such an effect on me.

Having established that Sana lived on the other side of the city, I pointed out that she would have to wait until we had finished our round to be deposited back at her front door. Mahmoud smiled broadly, 'I know,'

he said. 'She will just have to sit in the cab with us for the next two hours.'
Sana climbed in, followed by Mahmoud.

We must have looked a strange sight in the front of the van, with the
petite blonde nurse squashed between Mahmoud on one side – staring at
her, a crazed smile fixed on his lips as he tried (in vain) to make conversation – and me on the other, trying (unsuccessfully) to avoid brushing her
thigh whenever I changed gear.

From then on, we picked Sana up nearly every day to 'give her a lift home'
and Mahmoud grew obsessed with her. The problem was that he was hopeless at making conversation and hardly opened his mouth except to make
comments about the traffic or the pieces of Turkish Delight he constantly
offered her: 'This piece has too many almonds in it,' he would observe. 'I
think there may be something wrong with the mixing machine.'

Sana was a Palestinian widow whose husband had been killed in the
1967 invasion of Gaza. From the outset we had a lot in common and talked
about Palestine and the resistance. Mahmoud looked anxious during our
conversations and would send me reproachful looks over Sana's shoulder as
she leaned towards me, eager to hear what I had to say. It became obvious
that Sana did not reciprocate Mahmoud's grand passion and I found myself
in an embarrassing situation because it appeared she actually preferred me,
even though I was only a teenager. Since I had no intention of marrying,
this was an untenable state of affairs and I asked Mahmoud not to give
her lifts anymore. When I returned to Amman many years later, I heard
through the grapevine that Sana and Mahmoud married some time later
but that it had ended in an acrimonious divorce.

In the summer of 1969, my eldest brother, Abdel Fatah, graduated from
Cairo University. Fully qualified as an engineer, he turned up in Amman
hoping to find a good job. He shared my room and we spent many hours
discussing our plans for the future. Abdel Fatah was the only person in my
family who approved of my ambition to become a journalist and was always
very encouraging. While he was looking for work I supported him with my
salary from the sweet factory, which was quite a burden on a young man of
nineteen. Abdel Fatah had expensive habits – he smoked a lot and frequented
the cafés with his friends, buying numerous cups of coffee. After a few weeks
of this he seemed no closer to getting a job than when he'd arrived and an

opportunity came up at the Nashid Brothers for someone to work on the machines. I suggested that he take this work while he carried on looking for something more suitable. He was furious: 'I am a fully qualified engineer,' he shouted. 'Why would I work in a sweet factory? Are you telling me that I've wasted four years studying, that Kamal has wasted his money supporting me?' This problem was experienced by many Palestinians at the time, largely because there were so many of us in Jordan but also because of prejudice. By the end of the summer, Abdel Fatah had realized he was not going to get a decent job in Amman and started to look in the Gulf. He got a job as a preparatory school teacher in Saudi Arabia and left. I missed him when he had gone. He was a sweet-natured man and the idea that someone was looking out for me in this strange world gave me a sense of security.

At the end of his first month in Saudi Arabia, Abdel Fatah received his salary cheque and immediately sent me a large amount of money with a letter urging me to go to Egypt and finish my education. 'You are proving yourself to be a responsible and serious young man,' he wrote. 'I want you to get your higher education certificate and then go to university. I believe in you and know you will achieve your ambitions. I intend to support you throughout your education.'

Although I was later to repay this faith in me by becoming something of a media figure in the Arab world, I was not, in fact, the first among the Atwan brothers to make an appearance on the television. This honour was reserved for Ziad, our younger brother, who started a construction company in the 1970s and won a commission to build a mosque in a poor area of Jeddah, in Saudi Arabia. The mosque was constructed and proudly featured in the Saudi media. Ziad told us that he was to be interviewed on Saudi television in front of his mosque and Atwans all over the Arab world duly tuned in to watch. I was with Abdel Fatah and when we saw it we rolled around laughing because the minaret was leaning at an angle to the rest of the building. We had heard of the leaning tower of Pisa but never dreamed our brother would provide the world with the leaning minaret of Jeddah.

It is a matter of pride to me that my family are so loyal and have always helped each other out. Another brother, Jalal, joined Fatah when he was a teenager and was captured by the Israelis, accused of attacking an armoured vehicle. Aged just seventeen, he was given a prison sentence and was badly tortured; like my father before him, he gave nothing away and was released a year later. The only good thing about his sentence was that he was able to take his higher exams behind bars; these were marked by an Egyptian examiner who made sure prisoners got the best results – not out of sympathy but so that the candidate could subsequently go to university in Egypt, which was a form of indirect exile. Jalal set off for Cairo University in 1976, but the torture had seriously damaged his mind and he was unable to cope on his own in Egypt. He failed all his exams and returned to Gaza where he married a neighbour when he was only nineteen. We brothers solved the problem of how Jalal could earn a living by clubbing together to buy him a taxi and he has been happily self-employed ever since. He gave up all his resistance activities and concentrated on his family – he has four daughters and two sons. Jalal's children grew up to be well-educated, successful individuals, and one of his sons is now the attorney general in Gaza.

Amman was becoming increasingly dangerous for Palestinians and I was fortunate in that I left before matters came to a head; but I was kept informed of events on the ground by my favourite aunt, Halima, and her husband, Abu Jihad, one of Fatah's leaders in Jordan. Although King Hussein, in the heady days following the Battle of Karameh, had declared 'We will all be fedayeen soon', he started to change his mind when he saw how quickly the movement was growing and the extent of the threat the guerrillas could pose to his own regime. By the end of the 1960s there were at least 50,000 trained Palestinian guerrilla fighters in the kingdom, and groups such as Saiqa and the Arab Liberation Front were openly challenging the Jordanian regime, establishing roadblocks and denouncing the King. Nor could King Hussein count on the loyalty of his own army, as thousands of soldiers, including officers, supported the PLO.

The high-profile presence of Palestinian guerrilla groups in Jordan was also creating problems for King Hussein on the international stage where he was trying to build up ties with the US. Matters came to a head in September 1970: on 6 September 1970 the PFLP hijacked four planes which they intended to land in the Jordanian desert on an RAF airstrip formerly known as Dawson's Field but renamed 'Revolution Airport' by the PFLP. Two planes were indeed landed there, a third was blown up at Cairo airport but the fourth, Israeli El Al Flight 219, ended up in London after the hijackers were overcome by sky marshals and passengers. The hijackers of the El Al flight were Leila Khaled and a Nicaraguan, Patrick Argüello – an indication of how the Palestinian cause was becoming part of the global revolutionary movement. Argüello was killed and Leila Khaled arrested at Heathrow airport. (I always remember Leila Khaled's amused comments regarding the way the British authorities dealt with her; her first visitor at Ealing police station was an immigration officer who was so bureaucratic that he asked her why she had tried to enter the country without a visa.)

On 9 September another Palestinian guerrilla group hijacked a BOAC (British Overseas Airline Corporation) plane which they also force-landed at 'Revolution Airport', demanding the release of Leila Khaled and other PFLP prisoners. By now King Hussein had three hijacked planes on his territory and faced an escalating threat to his own national security. The hijackers then blew the planes up, taking 300 passengers hostage, 65 of them British. Despite being a signatory to the 1963 Tokyo Convention which stipulates no negotiation with hijackers, Britain capitulated to the hijackers' demands and King Hussein was left looking weak, ineffectual and embarrassed.

In 2000 the BBC acquired British cabinet documents under the thirty-year disclosure rule which show that King Hussein asked Edward Heath's government for help in ridding Jordan of Palestinian guerrillas for good:[1] he wanted the British, his closest ally in the region, to encourage Israel to bomb Syrian troops poised to back the fedayeen if Hussein attacked them. The documents show that Britain passed the buck to the US and that Washington did indeed contact Golda Meir with a view to the unpalatable scenario of Israel rushing to the aid of the Jordanian king against his fellow Muslims. The Soviet Union now intervened, pressing Syria to withdraw from the north of Jordan, leaving the Palestinians alone to face their fate as the Jordanian army set about their bloody business (nor did the 17,000 Iraqi soldiers stationed in Jordan come to the guerrillas' aid).

The infamous 'Black September' massacres started on 16 September 1970 and lasted until July 1971 by which time more than 3,000 fedayeen and refugees had been killed. By this time, I had already moved on to the next leg of my own personal exile: Egypt.

---

1.   http://news.bbc.co.uk/1/hi/in_depth/uk/2000/uk_confidential/1089694.stm

3

A Cairene Education

In November 1969, I arrived in Egypt to continue my education, more than two years after my departure from Gaza with this aim in mind. Home to the oldest Islamic university in the world, Al-Azhar, which was founded in the tenth century, Egypt had long enjoyed an unrivalled reputation in the Middle East as a centre of learning. I was fortunate in that Nasser's government was providing scholarships for impoverished students from neighbouring countries at this time and I was only one of many Palestinian refugees who benefited from this generosity.

I flew from Amman into Cairo and a different world. At the threshold of the vast continent where civilization first emerged, here you could sense all of Africa stretching southwards and the streets were throbbing with noise, traffic and crowds. Everywhere you looked there were smiling faces, which was a welcome change from Jordan with its grim-faced citizens. In Amman, whoever you met had a litany of woes, from a street sweeper to a millionaire. In Egypt there was an equality of happiness; it seemed to me that people laughed and joked from dawn till dusk, regardless of their circumstances. The people clinging to the sides of overcrowded buses smiled throughout their perilous journey and the scores of train passengers who were obliged to travel on the roof were as happy and relaxed as people enjoying the luxury of a cruise liner. The Egyptians were simple and humble people and I felt at ease among them.

The political and economic system under Nasser was more or less egalitarian and there was a genuine sense of progress. Socialist principles influenced everything, from the food (in November, for example, everyone ate cauliflowers and oranges because this was all that was available in the markets) to culture (theatre tickets and publishing were heavily subsidized). These were optimistic times despite the humiliations of 1967; it was as though the Egyptians were trying to defeat defeat itself.

In Cairo, the past was close to hand but I had no interest in antiquities. I didn't put a tourist hat on and go rushing off to gaze at the pyramids; my own future was my main concern. My plan was to go to Alexandria where I hoped to finish my secondary education with a view to returning to university in Cairo afterwards.

Alexandria

Alexandria was cleaner and less crowded than Cairo; everything, from the wide boulevards to the modern tram system, was orderly and calm. With sizeable Greek and Italian minorities, the city had a cosmopolitan, quite European, atmosphere and I soon learned that its inhabitants do not consider themselves Egyptian; they are 'Alexandrians' and when the tourists have left after the summer season is over, they sigh and say, 'Now we have our beloved Alexandria to ourselves once more.'

This was the most affluent environment I had been in. People were well turned-out and the shops were full. I was staying with my cousin, Jihad, who was studying there, and for the first time in my life, I actually had my own room in a 'normal' flat in a nice residential area.

A beautiful city had stood on this spot for over 2,000 years and centuries of architectural expertise informed the elegant tree-lined streets, the magnificent squares and the colonnades along the main thoroughfares. This was a grand Mediterranean city reminiscent of Greece or Lebanon; the traces of Alexander the Great, after whom the city was named, were palpable. At nineteen years old, I was captivated by it all and drank in every detail of the city, succumbing to romance for the first time in my life.

On the practical front, things were not so easy. I had a lot of trouble finding a school in Alexandria that would take me since a million Egyptians had fled from the Suez area to avoid Israeli bombardments during the War of Attrition that followed the Six-Day War and their children filled the schools. I decided that I could justifiably present myself as a refugee fleeing from a war zone created by the Israelis – in my case Gaza – and on this basis begged the authorities to find me a place. I must have made an impression because I received an affirmative letter within days.

I was to attend al-Orwa al-Wathqa ('the trusted link'), an educational establishment that had been set up by Jamal al-Din al-Afghani, the pious Islamic philosopher and reformer. This school may have borne his name but the connection with moral integrity stopped there. It was by far and away the worst school in Alexandria, peopled for the most by juvenile delinquents and thugs. Al-Orwa al-Wathqa was situated next to a park, and breaks and lunchtimes were passed there. Not that the students wished to enjoy some fresh air – many were more interested in smoking hashish away from the watchful eyes of the headteacher.

Nasser's championing of the Palestinian cause ensured me an elevated social status in Egypt compared with the prejudice I had known in Gaza and Jordan. Here, Palestinians were viewed as revolutionaries and heroes of the resistance and my peers were keen to get to know me. My nationality worked to my advantage with the staff too and I wasn't slow to exploit it: each morning there was a school parade during which the Egyptian flag was hoisted and saluted. I was lazy and hopeless at getting up on time; with no parents to harry me I was invariably late for this ceremony, which resulted in getting publicly whipped across the hands with a cane. I went to see the headteacher and suggested that as a representative of the Palestinian resistance movement (which I wasn't) I should be treated like the teachers and given a special dispensation not to attend the morning parade. From that day on, I arrived just in time for the start of lessons and was saluted at the locked school gates by the guards as they let me in.

Lessons were a nightmare, with more than fifty boys in each class. They were disrespectful to the teachers: ridiculing them, throwing paper darts, cracking jokes and shouting at one another. The only way the all-male staff could survive was to swallow their pride and carry on as if they were oblivious to the anarchy raging around them. I don't know how I managed to learn anything but I eventually passed the secondary-school certificate – *Tawjihi* – with flying colours.

'National Education' was the only subject the pupils were vaguely interested in. These twice-weekly lessons concentrated on Arab heritage, imperialist history and the struggle in Palestine. I would often be called to the front to talk about my experiences and impromptu question and answer sessions would evolve. I remember one such session when a curly-haired boy at the front stood up and said, 'Abdel Bari, what do the Jews look like?' I was surprised by this question. 'Why do you ask me this?' I replied.

'Are they horrible to look at?' he asked.

'No,' I replied. 'What did you think?'

'We thought they must have claws and fangs like monsters,' he said and the other boys agreed. I started to laugh at the absurdity of his idea but then it struck me how sad it was. 'No,' I told him, 'the Jewish people are human beings just like us. They don't have claws and fangs, but America has armed them with guns and missiles while we have none and that is how they have occupied our beloved Palestine.'

I loved walking in the streets in Egypt, just to see what was going on – I still walk everywhere in London for the same reason. One day, when I was walking back from al-Orwa al-Wathqa, a throng of people appeared in the middle of all the cars and lorries, walking alongside a horse-drawn cart bedecked with coloured cloths and streamers; the horses were plumed and blanketed and in the cart were two girls aged around eight years old and dressed in white like miniature brides. 'What is it?' I asked my neighbours in the crowd that had stopped to watch.

'It is a *Khitan* party,' said the man next to me. I had no idea what this was but I could see that the girls looked rather apprehensive despite being the centre of attention. I went on my way and didn't think anymore of it, until some time later when the Egyptian psychiatrist and feminist writer Dr Nawal El-Saadawi started a protest campaign against female circumcision and I read her harrowing accounts of this cruel and barbaric practice. This was the fate that awaited those little girls.

Female circumcision is a legacy of Pharaonic times and involves cutting out the clitoris (and sometimes sewing up the entrance to the vagina). The crude reasoning behind it is that if a female is incapable of experiencing sexual pleasure she will not fall prey to temptation and sin. The operation is generally performed without any anaesthetic, using unsterilized razor blades and needles. Severe haemorrhages and serious infections are commonplace and often fatal. The shock and psychological trauma resulting from the experience can endure for the rest of a woman's life.

Dr El-Saadawi's outspokenness won her many enemies. She received death threats and was even imprisoned by President Sadat in 1981. The protest she started continued unabated but the practice was not banned by law until 1997 and I have heard that it is still carried out in remote villages today. When I first arrived in London, I was often challenged about female circumcision and it became a focal point for much of the Islamophobia I witnessed and experienced. This emotive subject is used to tarnish the image of our faith but in fact it has little to do with Islam.[1] It is a cultural phenomenon originating in the Nile area where it has been practised by Muslims and Christians alike for centuries.

One day the headteacher, Mr Khalil, called me to his office. He was short and bald with thick glasses, his ancient suit was badly tailored and the thick material shone with years of being ironed. The Egyptians love making jokes about the Pharaonic times and the boys used to say this suit looked 'as though it had come from Pharaoh's tomb'. Mr Khalil gestured for me to sit down on the other side of his over-sized desk.

'Atwan,' he said, 'you are the Palestinian resistance representative, yes?'

'Er ... yes?' I replied, wondering where this was leading.

'The mayor came to see me regarding Victory Day,'[2] he said. 'I told him about you and we've arranged for you to address the crowds about the Palestinian cause and the PLO.' I was aghast because I knew next to nothing about Palestinian politics at that time yet had no alternative but to agree.

The day came soon enough and though I had resolved to make copious

---

1. A procedure similar to male circumcision is mentioned in the *hadith* when the Prophet Muhammad says, 'Cut off only the foreskin (outer fold of skin over the clitoris; the prepuce) but do not cut off deeply (i.e. the clitoris itself), for this is brighter for the face (of the girl) and more favourable with the husband.'
2. National celebrations were held to commemorate the withdrawal of British and French troops from Suez in 1956.

notes, I had done nothing at all in the way of preparation. I went to al-Tahrir Square, Alexandria's main public gathering place, and found tens of thousands of people there. From an enormous black stage, distinguished orators addressed the crowd through powerful speakers, their voices echoing over the throng. I was numb with trepidation as I stood in the wings but almost immediately I heard my name being announced and had to make my way onto the stage. The previous speaker had been shorter than me and I had to adjust the microphone stand, grimacing awkwardly as my breathing and fumbling fingers were amplified across the square. Petrified, I looked out at the sea of faces.

'Um ...' I couldn't find my voice. '*Salam alaikum*,' I managed but my voice sounded shaky and weak. 'Thank you for inviting me,' I said, relapsing into silence. I coughed and started to feel angry with myself. Wasn't I a Palestinian? Didn't I have a duty to tell the world about the suffering of my people? Words from the fiery speeches of the first PLO leader, Ahmed Shukairy, bubbled up from my subconscious and I began to speak with genuine passion, interspersing my own thoughts with Shukairy's Arab nationalist slogans. I could hear my own voice as if it was somehow separate from me, becoming more strident and confident by the minute. When I stopped, the crowd erupted into applause, stamping their feet and whooping. A cry went up repeated by thousands of voices, 'Long live Palestine! Revolution until victory!' I was delighted and the others on the platform, including the mayor, came over to shake my hand, congratulating me.

This experience changed me forever and I realized that not all success emanates from the conscious mind – sometimes you have to trust instinct and the knowledge that is stored in more hidden parts of your psyche. I accepted several more speaking dates and started reading up on politics and history, books like *A Return Ticket* by Nasser Nashashibi, *The Arab Awakening* by George Antonius, and articles by Muhammad Haikal.

The Death of Nasser

28 September 1970 was like the day JFK was shot, or when the planes hit the World Trade Center – everyone in the Arab world remembers where they were when they first heard the news that Nasser was dead. I was sitting in

a fleapit cinema in Alexandria watching a triple bill of old films. Suddenly, a man burst through the doors at the back and ran in front of the screen where he started railing against us like a madman, silhouetted against the blown-up face of a movie star. 'You bastards,' he shrieked, shaking his fist. 'You are watching films and entertaining yourselves while our beloved Gamal Abdel Nasser is dead.' The man was seized by four or five security guards and cinema ushers who carried him, screaming and cursing, out of the building and gave him a bloody nose in the process.

The consensus among the audience (who habitually chatter all the way through films in any case) was that the man was either a lunatic or one of the *agents provocateurs* operating in Egypt at the time, spreading rumours and stirring up trouble. Ten minutes later, however, the film was switched off and the lights came up; we realized that it must be true. Nasser was dead. We soon found out that he had died of a heart attack shortly after an exhausting round of talks at the Arab summit meeting convened to discuss the Black September massacres of Palestinians in Jordan.

That evening it seemed as if the whole Alexandrian population was out on the Corniche. People wandered stunned and silent or stood motionless with tears in their eyes. When friends met they would quietly embrace and cry together. Pockets of sound came from cafés, where the radio broadcast details of Nasser's death and paid tribute to our great hero. It is one of the few times in my life that I have heard broadcasters weep live on air. The mosques threw open their doors and you could hear the Qur'an being recited from inside. Nightclubs, shops and cinemas were closed for days and the electricity was cut off as a sign of mourning.

There were incredible scenes of grief throughout the Arab world and Nasser's funeral in Cairo, three days later, was attended by five million people. I watched it on television in a café and we were all moved when the people seized the coffin from the soldiers who were carrying it and bore it themselves; the procession was six miles long and it remains one of the largest funerals in history.

General Nasser had led Egypt since 1954 and was seen by many as the great hope of the Arab world. His ideology inspired me then and still does today. Egypt had become the focal point of an Arab renaissance: the capital of Arab culture and the pan-Arab political movement. One of Nasser's slogans was 'Arab Oil for the Arabs' and he fervently believed that Arab resources should be used for the benefit of the Arab people and not to line the pockets of Western leaders and businesses.

Nasser promoted a new age of Arab defiance and resistance; his implacable opposition to Israel and his socialist domestic agenda appealed to me and millions of others. Nationalizing the Suez Canal, in July 1956, had provoked the Suez Crisis and cemented the growing relationship between Egypt and the Soviet Union. The US and British governments made much of Nasser's 'red' credentials and the writer Peter Mansfield has described how British PM Anthony Eden's hatred of the Egyptian leader 'bordered on the hysterical'. In 1964, President Nikita Khrushchev awarded Nasser the Soviet Gold Star and the Order of Lenin along with the title 'Hero of the Soviet Union' but this was a marriage of convenience where Nasser was concerned. He had little liking for communism, observing in the preface to his book, *Communism As It Really Is*, that the ideology is 'incompatible with religion and individual liberty'.

Nasser's personal honour and bravery engendered a host of legends. Although I was only four at the time I knew every detail of the 1954 assassination attempt: when Nasser was shot at while addressing a crowd of 30,000, he did not duck or run for cover but waited silently for calm before uttering one of his most memorable sentences, 'They want to kill Nasser. Every one of you is Nasser.' The crowd, of course, went mad. And later, when his armies were defeated in the Six-Day War with Israel he offered the people his resignation live on television, announcing his intention to 'return to the masses, performing my duty in their midst like any other citizen'. Millions took to the street to protest his decision, not only in Egypt but all over the Arab world.

The significance of Nasser in my life came full circle when, in 1995, I was invited to speak at the Institut du Monde Arabe in Paris. They were holding a seminar to commemorate Nasser, twenty-five years after his death. Also on the panel were two French former ministers and other distinguished guests who talked about Nasser the great statesman, pan-Arabism and Middle Eastern politics in general. I was the last to speak and decided to take a more personal approach as I rose to my feet in front of a capacity audience: 'The only reason I am here at all is because of Nasser,' I began. I told them how Nasser championed the weak; how I, despite being a dispossessed, impoverished, Palestinian refugee heading nowhere, had received the best education available in the Middle East thanks to the generosity of Nasser's regime; how Nasser's vision had enabled me to turn my life around. I ended with the story of the letter Nasser sent me when I was a little boy in the refugee camp and was touched to see that several members of the audience were moved to tears by this simple testimony.

Cairo

I felt an affinity for Alexandria and could have settled there. The Arab dialect in the city is similar to our Palestinian one, perhaps because we share the Mediterranean Sea. I had been offered a place at Cairo University, to read for an arts degree specializing in journalism, which I started in October 1970. The site of Cairo housed the capital of Egypt since the dawn of civilization although the existing city was established in 641 CE by Amr Ibn-Elass. The optimism and happiness I felt there from the outset are reflected in the name of this extraordinary city – in Arabic *al-Qahirah* means 'triumphant'.

Shortage of accommodation was, and still is, the city's major problem. When I moved to Cairo the population was already five million, although that is nothing compared with the twelve million who struggle to survive there today. Economically, times were hard: war had drained Egypt's coffers and, trying to undermine Nasser, the US had stopped selling Egypt grain on credit. As a result Nasser's social housing programme was slashed and homelessness was commonplace. People took to building their own homes on agricultural land to the north of the existing city, sold by opportunistic landowners, and in the desert to the east. Known as *aashwa'i* (meaning 'random') these makeshift satellite towns mushroomed. There was no question of planning permission and none was sought. Often unable to afford a finished home, families would build one floor or even one room at a time, on their small plot of land, resulting in an unsightly jumble of roofless buildings of up to six or seven storeys.

The first room I rented in Cairo was in one such *aashwa'i* town called Embaba. The streets between buildings were so narrow that if there had been a fire it would have been impossible for the emergency services to come to the aid of the occupants. At ground level there were shops, puddles and piles of rubbish where goats, chickens, cats and stray dogs foraged, not to mention the rats that called them home. Above, line upon line of colourful washing waved from windows all the way up to the sky, which was invariably blue.

Embaba was a no-go area for the police, home to drug dealers and criminals of every hue. There were constant turf wars between rival gangs and stabbings and shootings were commonplace. I quickly found a way to survive on those streets, however: football. There were two main teams in Cairo at the time – Zamalek and al-Ahly and so fierce was the rivalry between their supporters that the 1970–1 cup final was unable to finish due to crowd violence. I, however, supported a real underdog team called Tersana. Thus, when I was asked for the time by a dangerous-looking youth in an alleyway one day, I noted his al-Ahly supporter's scarf and said, 'nearly time for kick-off and I hope those Zamalek bastards get massacred'. He was delighted and shook my hand instead of whatever else he had planned for me. I became quite expert at guessing which team potential attackers supported and could insult the opposition in all sincerity. I only got this wrong once, which ended with a stick-wielding Goliath chasing me all round Embaba.

My football analysis was much sought after in the neighbourhood and the man who earned his living by ironing people's clothes (to have your own iron was an unthinkable luxury) used to come to me on the eve of every match to hear my latest thoughts and predictions. Since he then refused to take my money but ironed everything I gave him, I was among the best-pressed students in the University.

There is no Egyptian word for 'slum' because even in the most apparently impoverished area you will find pockets of well-off people benefiting from the cheap housing. In Embaba there was a lawyer who had already built a five-storey block of flats, one for each of his married siblings, and as each of the remaining three announced their engagement, so he would build them a flat on top of all the others.

The opposite is also true: my next home, for example, was in an upmarket part of Cairo called Dukki. People were highly impressed when they enquired where I lived and I gave this posh address. Little did they know that I was actually occupying a makeshift shack a wealthy merchant had constructed on the roof of his house using planks and tarpaulin. It was fortunate that my possessions were few since I was always moving from one district to another during my four years in Cairo, usually having been evicted for making too much noise or being unable to pay the rent.

University of Dissent

Cairo University, which was established in 1908, is both the oldest and largest secular Arab university in the Middle East (the American university in Beirut was founded in 1866). The building itself is monumental and it was a proud moment for me when I walked up those magnificent stairs and under the columns for the first time. It was October 1970 and I was entering the Faculty of Arts. The first year of my degree would consist of general studies and languages but after that I was to major in journalism and the media for a further three years.

There were students from all over the Arab world. Men and women were educated side by side; you wouldn't have found a veiled woman at this time, and many girls had adopted the Western fashion for miniskirts. Nowadays, the opposite is true and you would be hard-pressed to find a woman not wearing the veil, which has become a potent symbol of anti-Western sentiment for some, and Islamism for others.

Cairo University was a hotbed of revolutionary political activity. These were heady times and the late 1960s were momentous years in terms of global politics: 1967 had seen huge demonstrations and protests in the US against the war in Vietnam, a mass movement which also harnessed the energy of the civil rights struggle in America. Martin Luther King's 1963 'I have a Dream' speech had inspired a whole generation of oppressed people and boosted our belief that change was not only possible but imminent. Of immense significance to us, too, was the 1964 conversion to Islam of World Heavyweight boxing champion, Cassius Clay, who changed his name to Muhammad Ali. Two years later the American-born Ali would famously refuse to fight in Vietnam, saying, 'I got nothing against no Viet Cong. No Vietnamese ever called me a nigger.'

Marxist-Leninist revolutionary activity in Latin America also inspired us. Fidel Castro transformed Cuba into a communist stronghold on America's doorstep, and his left-hand man, Che Guevara, became a roving *agent provocateur*, trying to foment revolution, first in Africa – described by Castro as 'imperialism's weakest link' – and then in Bolivia. His execution on 9 October 1967 at the hands of the CIA (hiding behind the Bolivian Army) inflamed socialists everywhere and assured his enduring status as a revolutionary icon.

Global insurrection continued in Paris with student unrest erupting into full-scale revolution on the streets in May 1968. The students occupied the Sorbonne and turned it into a commune, and ten million workers across France went on strike in solidarity with them. I remember reading about it in Jordan and watched the drama unfold on a television belonging to a wealthy friend, witnessing in admiration the construction of barricades and my peers' running battles with the police.

As a Palestinian, it would have been impossible not to have been involved in politics. At that time it was assumed that if you were Palestinian you were revolutionary and because everyone else was fighting for the Palestinian cause, solidarity with other oppressed peoples was expected in return. Most of our student demonstrations in Cairo had been pro-Palestinian, anti-Israeli and we had a whole raft of complaints against the US as well. As Sadat's[1] policies began to bite we now embarked on more localized, domestic protests, focusing on his economic agenda and the way he was undermining Nasser's legacy. Sadat was swift to comprehend the power of the media and was preparing the Egyptian people for a new political reality via the pages of newspapers. He sacked all the Nasserite editors and promoted pro-Western ones instead, at the same time tightening state control over the media. Under the guise of allowing greater press freedom he encouraged criticism of Nasser and his Soviet allies (who were expelled from the country after the 1973 Yom Kippur War) but would not tolerate any regarding his own government.

I was part of a group of journalism students that produced a weekly newspaper. We were organized in cells under the umbrella of the Students' Union; other parties tried to hijack our group but we steered clear of them. Because we were short of funding – in fact we had none – the paper took the form of a poster with the laboriously copied, handwritten articles laid out side by side. In the course of our studies on the history of journalism we had discovered that this kind of poster-newspaper was popular in Soviet

---

1.   Nasser was succeeded by Field Marshal Anwar Sadat who remained in office until his assassination on 6 October 1981.

Russia just after the revolution and so we adopted the idea. We pasted these up on walls clandestinely, usually at night, one in each department.

Our poster-newspaper was considered so radical that the university authorities called in the police and they would regularly come in and tear it down from the walls. We, in turn, substituted fresh copies in the hope that people would have a chance to read them before they were removed once more. This level of persistence stood me in good stead when I started my own paper against all odds years later.

One day the Palestinian resistance organization, Fatah, sent an envoy to me. They wanted to recruit me for their media branch and delivered their proposal via a young Palestinian woman, who offered me a job on their radio station. She told me there would be an income of more than £40 pounds a month, which was double what my brother, Abdel Fatah, was sending me to live on. They wanted me to conduct interviews live on air which I found tempting, but I said no because I felt their political agenda was at odds with my more left-wing, pan-Arab nationalist inclinations.

Student demonstrations and protests escalated as Sadat distanced himself from the Soviet Union, aligning himself with the much hated US. The cost of living increased and there were full-scale riots and clashes with the police. Journalists now came from all over the world to report on what was happening in Egypt, comparing it to Paris in May 1968. Our university was viewed as the Egyptian equivalent of the Sorbonne as far as this new uprising was concerned. Sometimes they had to close the campus for days at a time because matters got so out of hand.

I remember one particularly dramatic confrontation between the students and the authorities in January 1972. One of the student leaders had been arrested during a sit-in on campus and the place erupted. (It is incredible how spontaneous uprisings find a cohesive form, as if a collective consciousness is at work.) Groups raced around shouting 'Everyone down to Tahrir' (one of the main squares in the centre of Cairo) and before the police could grasp what was happening there were approximately 25,000 students on the march.

Once in the square everyone sat down; in the middle there was an empty stone pedestal, which normally displayed a statue of the leader, surrounded by a small garden. The fact that the pedestal was unfilled held tremendous symbolic value; I can only imagine that the municipal authorities hadn't yet been able to organize a statue of Sadat. People used it as an impromptu podium and jostled with each other to give hair-raising speeches that were enthusiastically applauded.

There was a café in the square which was frequented by left-wing intellectuals and they were delighted by the spectacle unfolding under their noses. They wrote up proclamations and statements, emerging from their comparative comfort every so often in tailored overcoats to deliver them in charged tones. Poets and singers – I recollect Ahmed Fouad Negm and Sheikh Imam being there – also turned up and performed to an appreciative crowd.

Many of my comrades from these heady times have gone on to have successful political careers. Hamdin Sabahi is now an Egyptian MP and Muhammad al-Shabah has become a well-known journalist and activist. These two were the most radical and were often imprisoned for leading demonstrations and protests. I, meanwhile, was trying to keep a lower profile to avoid being expelled from university and deported before I could finish my degree, which would have been a disaster for me and my family. Quite a lot of Palestinians had already fallen foul of the regime in this way and had been thrown out, most of them finding refuge in Iraq.

Our presence in Tahrir Square was not frowned upon by the ordinary citizens of Cairo. Far from it. As night fell, elderly ladies came around with food and blankets for us because it was so cold. After midnight, we all started chanting 'Down with Sadat' and 'Nixon is Satan' which finally goaded the police and security forces into charging the crowd, firing teargas and using water cannons, lashing out at anyone in range with their batons. But people didn't give up and ran down the main shopping streets in smaller groups shouting 'Cairo arise!'

Since my English was fairly good, I agreed to be the spokesperson for the protestors, getting my first taste of dealing with the world's press. Unfortunately, this also drew me to the authorities' attention which would later have serious repercussions.

Brotherly Love

I had arrived at Cairo University almost destitute and had been unable to earn any money as I had to work so hard to catch up on my academic studies. Two pairs of trousers and two shirts saw me through my entire education in Egypt. The jacket I wore was borrowed from a cousin's friend who had become too fat for it. I was progressing, however, and everything was going according to plan, due to Abdel Fatah's continued sponsorship of my studies.

The conditions in the southern part of Saudi Arabia where he was teaching were worse than basic and he told me later that he had been living in what was little more than a hut. There was no electricity and so no possibility of air conditioning to alleviate the extreme heat of the summer months. Not only were the physical conditions near unbearable but there were no amenities to help while away the long hours of holidays and weekends. He must have hated being there, yet he forced himself to stay because of his financial commitments to me and the family back in Gaza. I think it was a combination of the hardships of life there, together with the difficulties he had endured in Palestine, that led to him having a mental breakdown in my second year at university. He was dismissed from his position and dispatched to Jordan, where family members took care of him and secured treatment for his condition. Six months later, he returned to Saudi Arabia and got a job in Jeddah, working for the municipal authority. At least he had the comfort of being able to live with our brother Kamal, who had also moved to Saudi Arabia, but we never saw the old Abdel Fatah again. Though he was popular with the girls, he didn't marry. He used to joke that he couldn't limit himself to just one woman but I think it was because of his mental illness; he didn't want to burden anyone with his problems.

Abdel Fatah was diagnosed with lung cancer at the end of 1989, which should not have surprised anyone since he had chain-smoked since the age of fourteen. At the hospital, the doctor told him, 'I want you to stop smoking and we will put you on chemotherapy.' Abdel Fatah got his cigarette packet out of his pocket, ready to throw it into the waste-bin. 'Okay doctor,' he said. 'If I stop smoking how long will I live?'

'You will probably live between six months and a year.'

'And how long if I carry on smoking?'

'Maybe four or five months.'

Abdel Fatah pocketed his cigarettes again and sighed. 'I want to live,' he told the doctor, between coughs. 'But I want to live with a cigarette in my lips and the hair still on my head. I don't want your chemotherapy. Why should I go through all that suffering just to live a few extra months?' He died in May 1990. I loved him and miss him still. I will never forget him or his incredible kindness and generosity.

Time Out

Cairo's streets were a constant source of entertainment. In the daytime, they were crowded, hot and sticky, the air thick with pollution and the roads always blocked by traffic jams. Drivers took no notice whatsoever of traffic lights and seemed to have their hands glued to their horns. It was common to see people getting out of their cars and starting a fist-fight. The pavements were almost impassable. Meeting friends, people stopped in groups to chat, blocking the path for the rest. There were people selling fruit, tea and snacks every two metres, surrounded by clusters of customers; crowds gathered to watch snake charmers or the many monkey trainers whose charges wore human clothes and performed tricks. I remember one such performance in particular: a little green monkey had on a long nightdress and a sleeping cap and pretended to fall asleep on command, pinning a white sheet firmly under its chin with its paws. This cameo was titled 'the Old Maid'.

Many cultures have a day when the dead are remembered but I wonder if any celebrate death with such fervour as the Egyptians. Cairo's 'Day of the Dead' festivities begin at dawn when the first horse-drawn carts appear bearing entire families from babes in arms to toothless elders. There are drummers and musicians playing pipes and *oud,* and everyone joins in singing and dancing with wide grins and ululations. The horses trot briskly along with the flow of ordinary traffic and head for the graveyards where the day is spent feasting. Instead of mourning departed friends and ancestors, the day is spent in joyous remembrance of them.

The Cairene fondness for the dead led to an unusual solution to the city's homelessness problem – some hardy souls had taken up residence in the cemeteries; their ancestors had constructed dwelling rooms around the graves to house relatives during the forty-day period of mourning and these now provided permanent housing for the living. I visited a vast, seven-kilometre-long cemetery known as the 'City of the Dead' where whole families had set up home among the gravestones which were put to good use as shelves and tables. Washing was strung between them to dry and children played tag, laughing and squealing in the dusty gloom. Makeshift kitchens were created in corners and there were even some old sofas and armchairs. There were birds in cages and domestic animals shared the space with men, women, and children who slept on mattresses and mats on the dirt floors. By the year 2000, more than five million people were living in the graveyards and last time I went there I found the inhabitants bathed in fluorescent light and in possession of fridges and colour television, having procured an electricity supply from the mosque.

Every city loves its river; the Parisians have the Seine, Londoners the Thames, and the people of Cairo are no exception, they adore the Nile – which cuts through the whole city – with a passion. I spent a lot of time walking by the great river, getting to know the parallel world that existed on its banks and on its waters. Fishermen trawled the river right in the heart of the city and lived in their small boats for want of better accommodation; they caught and sold fish from the minute they woke up but couldn't afford to eat it themselves, subsisting instead on broad beans.

On the first day of spring, I found the banks of the Nile taken over by a wonderful festival. This was a day even the poorest people could enjoy and the whole city looked forward to it. The children had painted hard-boiled eggs and were exchanging them as gifts. I wandered down by the river, delighted by the kaleidoscopic scenes of celebration and was invited to eat with different groups of picnickers, despite the fact I was a complete stranger.

'Come with us and try these!' they shouted, showing me oranges, salt-fish, broad beans and bread. There was a cacophony from wind-up record players, the strains of the great Egyptian diva Umm Kulthoum as well as other Arab musicians; from wandering bands, the beat of drums, the wail of pipes and the rhythmic strumming of an *oud*; and from the festive groups themselves a perpetual backdrop of chatter and laughter. As the day ended in a spectacular sunset the crowds dispersed, leaving all their rubbish behind them for my comrades in the Cairene refuse department to clear up.

While I was in Cairo the Nile became the repository for more unusual waste – two cars and a bus! It seems the city's collection of ancient vehicles were prone to brake or steering failure, on several occasions sending driver and occupants careering into the waters.

The best time to go down to the riverbank was at night when the water's inky blackness reflected the moon and stars. It was a regular haunt for lovers who strolled there hand in hand, whispering and laughing and, cloaked in darkness, exchanging forbidden kisses.

Because I was so impoverished, living on less than £20 Egyptian a month (the equivalent of £5 sterling at that time), courtship was out of the question for me. Besides, most of the girls on our course were from the Arab upper classes, educated in foreign schools like the French Lycée and the British School in Cairo. They were undeniably attractive but completely out of bounds for me, except as classmates. I was destined for a few more bachelor years.

A Dedicated Fan

Cairo in those days was the capital of culture. The Nasser regime understood the importance of art in an inclusive society and the government provided substantial subsidies for film making, book publishing and theatre. The Egyptians were producing 300 movies and documentaries a year, and had also spawned the internationally renowned film star, Omar Sharif. Sharif was actually born Michel Demitri Chalhoub, which does not have quite the same ring to it but when he converted to Islam in 1955, in order to marry the Egyptian actress Faten Hamama, he took on the Muslim name which would later become so famous.

My favourite form of entertainment was the theatre and I first saw the plays of Molière and Shakespeare on the big state-funded stages of Cairo. But most astonishing were the private theatres which were a law unto themselves: the actors didn't bother with the script except as a starting point so that a play written to last an hour and a half might go on all night, because the actors ad-libbed, heading off on different tangents, depending upon the mood of the audience. While I was there, the British play *To Sir, with Love* came to Cairo having been translated into Arabic and renamed *A School of Thugs*. I went to see it three times and on each occasion it was different, the producers having replaced various members of the cast until, by the end, only the leading actor remained of the original line-up. These plays would never start at the advertised time but would lurch into action when the audience turned up, or when the actors felt like it. The audience used to bring melon seeds and pistachio nuts with them and the sound of shells being cracked and a constant nibbling formed a backing track to the drama. Sometimes, in their eagerness to make people laugh, the actors would overstep the mark and end up saying something obscene that would be reported by an offended member of the audience. Several plays were halted after the censors had been alerted.

I also loved live music and attended several concerts with a relative, Assad, who had recently joined me in the Egyptian capital. Cairo attracted the best Arabic performers but tickets were prohibitively expensive. One day, I saw posters advertising a concert by Farid al-Atrash. *Atrash* in Arabic means 'deaf', although the singer was by no means afflicted in this way. This is an issue in the Arab world where generations carry a family name which has its genesis in one ancestor's long-forgotten misfortune. Thus perfectly healthy people are called *Arraj* meaning 'lame', or *Awar* meaning 'one-eyed', and so on. Anyway, I was a fan of al-Atrash: not only did he have a mellifluous voice and a repertoire of wonderful romantic songs but he was also a virtuoso *oud* player. We went to the box office as soon as we heard he was playing, but all the cheap tickets had been sold, leaving only the most expensive seats in the house, priced at £5.

'Let's get them,' I urged Assad.

'Five pounds is all I have for food for the whole month,' he replied.

'Five pounds is all I have for *everything*,' I said. 'I'm still going to get one – what about you?'

'No way,' Assad was firm. 'You can tell me about it afterwards.'

Inside the concert hall, Atrash's fans were frenzied with anticipation and hero worship. Long before the concert started, even though the stage was empty, they kept on bursting into applause. A man brought a chair onto the stage for Atrash to sit on when he played the *oud*, provoking an eruption of shouting and screaming. When the movie star Samir Sabri came on to introduce him, there was such an uproar that I didn't hear a word he said. As Atrash himself finally appeared the crowd went crazy, leaping to their feet and crying. He waited for people to calm down and take their seats, and picked up his *oud* to make sure it was in tune: just these notes set them off again. This time I joined in, but I was screaming because I'd spent all my money on this ticket and it didn't look as though they would ever let the man sing. Eventually, Atrash got going but was constantly interrupted by applause, so that a song that would usually last ten minutes took half an hour and of course there were a great many encores. The concert hall was several miles from my flat and as the compelling magic of Atrash's performance came to an end I was faced with the horrible realization that I would have to walk home because I had no money for the bus fare. I almost starved for the rest of the month but it was worth it.

Some time after this experience, I realized that if we went to watch musicians perform in nightclubs rather than concert halls we could get in for free. My reasoning was this: the main acts didn't usually go on until about 2 AM, by which time the people running the venue were drunk. 'Let's go to see Olya,' I suggested to Assad and whispered my plan. Olya was a Tunisian known for singing populist and Libyan folk songs, and she was appearing in a nightclub out by the pyramids. Assad looked dubious but agreed to give it a go. The ruse worked like clockwork. We walked up to the door laughing and chatting, nodded at the doormen who were looking the worse for drink (and were probably stoned on hashish to boot), and sauntered straight in. Never one for moderation, I repeated this exercise three more times during Olya's residency and used this new-found currency of guile to see other artistes too.

With my head still full of the fabulous sound of Atrash's *oud* playing, I decided to take up the instrument myself. I bought what must have been a fifth-hand one and tried to play it, accompanied by howls of complaint from my flatmates. I decided to arrange some lessons at the Institute of Music. My tutor was called Sheikh Mustafa and he had a beard and a well-developed belly. He wore a red *tarbush* and one of two outfits: either a long grey *jalabiya* or an old double-breasted pinstripe suit whose heyday was long since gone. In his deep voice, he would sing old songs, trying to emulate Sayed Darwish, a famous musician from the 1920s.

Sheikh Mustafa was a well-respected teacher and he dedicated much of his time to nurturing new musical talent. Unfortunately, I was to prove a disappointment to him. I was impatient and plagued him with frustrated comments and complaints, as if my lack of ability was somehow his fault. After a month, I was still unable to play more than three consecutive notes and during our lesson would stare in annoyance at the fingers of my left hand which seemed incapable of finding the correct position, resulting in discordant sounds and curses from me.

'There must be something you're not telling me,' I said. 'This is not normal.' Sheikh Mustafa, who had until then been calm and reserved, stamped his foot and leaped to his feet.

'How much did you pay for this instrument?' he asked me, snatching the *oud* from my hands.

'Five pounds,' I said. 'I thought if I got a cheap one now, I'd splash out on a better quality one when I become good at it.'

'You will *never* be good at it,' he snapped. 'You will *never* be a musician of any type, good or bad.' He put the *oud* on the table and took out his wallet. 'Here is five pounds,' he said. 'Please take it and leave this instrument here. I don't want to see you again. Goodbye.' It was not until my children started learning the recorder that I understood what the poor man must have gone through, listening to me struggling to play even one correct note.

Work Experience

As part of the journalism course, I was sent to do a month's work experience at *al-Mousowar*, a weekly magazine. I was greeted by one of the editors, Foumil Labib, who was going to supervise the students' time there. Foumil described the different sections and asked me where I would like to work.

'The show-business pages,' I said without hesitation. He was shocked.

'But ... you are Palestinian!' he reasoned. 'You must want to work in the politics section surely?'

'It's because I'm Palestinian that I don't want to work in the politics section,' I said firmly. 'I know I will spend the rest of my life writing about politics and this will be my last chance to explore the world of entertainment.' He asked me to give him three story ideas. He liked them and my wish was granted.

One of my first assignments was to interview the composer Helmi Bakir. We became friends, and I enjoyed his down-to-earth outlook; I once came across him in a downtown garage in the company of hashish-smoking mechanics. He told me he preferred their company and anecdotes to mixing with the rich and powerful at vacuous cocktail parties.

Another assignment featured an up-and-coming actress called Sophia Amri who had made a big impact on Foumil. He kept on pushing her name into stories and trying to get her featured as much as possible – this was a large circulation, glossy magazine with a lot of influence. Foumil came up with the idea of a feature on 'new faces' that would focus, of course, on hers. I was surprised when he produced a sheaf of professional photos of Sophia Amri which he seemed to keep in the top drawer of his desk. The media played a major role in promoting these young stars and many were exploited by newspaper and magazine editors, although I am certain that Foumil had a genuine belief in Sophia Amri's undeniable talent.

I thought no more of Miss Amri until several years later when I was working as the London bureau chief for *al-Madina* and she had become a star of stage and screen. I was taking a flight from Abu Dhabi to Cairo and there had been a problem with the scheduled plane. A charter plane was being used instead and as it had no first-class seating they were putting all the passengers with first-class tickets in the front four rows instead. At the last minute, Sophia Amri got on the plane burdened down with carrier bags from expensive boutiques and luxurious hand-luggage. At the top of the steps, the air hostess told her all of this would have to go in the hold and an argument ensued which Miss Amri lost. She was still fuming from this confrontation when she was told there was no first-class accommodation.

'Where am I to sit then?' she asked.

'I am sorry, madam, but in the main part of the plane. The front four rows are for first-class passengers,' the air hostess explained.

'Impossible,' came the reply. 'I can't be expected to sit with … ' she scanned her fellow passengers and her glance fell on me '… just anyone!' Finally, persuaded that she would either have to leave the plane or take her seat, she lowered herself down beside me, clicking on her seatbelt in an irritated manner. After about half an hour, she was obviously rather bored and decided to strike up a conversation with me. 'So what do you do?' she asked.

'I'm a mechanic,' I said. 'I repair cars.' I glanced at her casually. 'And what about you?' I asked. 'What do you do? Are you a teacher?'

'Of course not. I am Sophia Amri. Don't you ever go to the cinema or watch television?'

'No,' I said. 'The cinema is immoral. I have never heard of Sophia Amri.' She looked so hurt by my feigned ignorance that I started to feel sorry for her, but it was too late for a confession and I soon fell asleep.

I met Miss Amri again in 2001. I was at the BBC Arabic service and the director told me she was in the studio doing another programme. He asked me to stay and have some tea with her. I agreed and scrutinized her with interest when we sat down. She had aged well and seemed calmer and more dignified. She took a good look at me and said, 'I know I've seen you on the television, but I am sure I've met you somewhere before too.'

'Do you remember on a flight from Abu Dhabi to Cairo when you were sitting next to a mechanic and there was no first class and you were grumpy?' I asked, laughing. 'Well, that mechanic was me!'

'I remember!' she said. 'Why did you do that?'

'I wanted to tease you,' I confessed. By the end of our tea we had overcome our differences and she invited me to watch her play in the West End. I visited her backstage afterwards to offer my congratulations on her performance, which I jokingly told her was better than the one I had witnessed on the plane. Sophia Amri has since become an ambassador to UNESCO and her new role becomes her very well.

Away Day

In my summer holiday, in 1973, I had an unusual assignment to undertake. My second brother, Kamal, who lived in Saudi Arabia, had decided to get married. His bride-to-be was a Palestinian girl of eighteen called Camilla who was living in Rafah refugee camp. My mother had been active in locating the perfect bride for Kamal and had taken charge of most of the arrangements. There was to be a wedding party in Gaza and I would then escort Camilla from Gaza to Jordan where she would get a plane to Saudi Arabia.

It was a flying visit and rather a depressing one. I stayed with my mother, sleeping on the floor of her nine-foot-square room, and it saddened me to see that her circumstances had not improved at all, nor had anything about Rafah; in fact it had deteriorated. The Israeli occupiers hadn't repaired the roads – not even the main one which was built under the British Mandate – or maintained the hospitals, parks or any public amenities whatsoever. I tried, however, to be cheerful for my mother's sake. There was nothing to be gained by bemoaning the plight that she would endure for the rest of her life since she refused to leave Gaza, always clinging to the dream that one day she would return to Isdud. I noticed a change in our relationship now; before I had talked to her as a boy and been treated as one, but now I was a mature man.

The wedding party was a dour affair, symbolic, somehow, of the Palestinian tragedy. There was the bride, in her white dress, caked in make-up applied with an inexperienced hand, sitting in a refugee camp in Gaza with nothing but a framed photograph of the groom beside her since he was holed up in Saudi Arabia. Personally I am not opposed to arranged marriages if both parties wish to find a partner in this way. Forced marriages, of course, are completely unacceptable. Arranged marriages can have as much chance of success as those we choose for ourselves; when we are young we are prone to making mistakes which our elders, who know us well, can avoid on our behalf. Camilla seemed happy and excited about meeting her husband for the first time as we talked on our way to Jordan. Their marriage has had its fair share of ups and downs but they have eight children and are still together.

Having seen Camilla off in Jordan, I decided to extend my trip and travel to northern Lebanon where my favourite aunt, Halima, was living in the Nahr al-Bared refugee camp where she and her husband, one of Fatah's leaders, Abu Jihad, had fled after being expelled from Jordan during the Black September massacres in 1970. Although I had kept in touch with Halima over the years, my clearest memories of her are still in Deir al-Balah where she used to help my mother look after us children and more than once got rid of the head lice that plagued us. My father's youngest sister, she was tall, slim and always wore traditional Palestinian dress. She hadn't been to school and was illiterate, but understood everything and had the heart of a lion.

Nahr al-Bared is the second largest refugee camp in Lebanon, sited near Tripoli. Not far from the beach, it was like a cement jungle when I went there and I doubt it is any better now. People had built their own houses between the shelters provided by UNRWA, creating a shanty town intersected by narrow alleyways and blighted by open sewers. It seems absurd now but in my mind I was comparing this camp with Rafah and finding reasons why it was better. I imagine refugees still make these comparisons which are akin to weighing up one hell against another.

Abu Jihad's house was full of bombs, grenades, and guns which Halima used to tidy away from chairs and table tops, making little 'tsk's of irritation as if they had been newspapers or packets of cigarettes. They had anti-aircraft batteries on the roof to combat the Israeli planes that used to periodically bomb the refugees. Abu Jihad took me to visit some of the other camps, including Sabra and Shatila in southern Beirut which would be the scene of one of the world's worst massacres in September 1982, when 3,500 refugees were slaughtered by Lebanese Phalangist militia at the instigation of Ariel Sharon, then Israeli Minister of Defence.

I was only able to stay with them for five days because I had to get back to Cairo for the start of the new academic year, and left them with promises to return, but that was never to be. It seems that fate had directed me to go to Nahr al-Bared: One week later, I received a telephone call in Cairo telling me that the Israelis had bombed their house and Auntie Halima had died of a heart attack. She was only in her late twenties.

In the summer of 2007, Nahr al-Bared was in the news again because it had become the base for *Fatah al-Islam*, an al-Qa'ida offshoot, which engaged in some fierce fighting with the Lebanese Army. Hearing that the camp was under heavy bombardment, I phoned an acquaintance to find out how Abu Jihad was faring. He called me back himself a few hours later and I learned that he had remarried and was still living in the camp with his children, who now numbered sixteen! He missed Halima very much, he told me, but was carrying on with his life and the fight, just as she would have wished him to.

No Forwarding Address

I had intended to do an MA at Cairo University, mainly because I didn't know what to do next or where to go. It didn't occur to me that this would be a problem but when I went to renew my student visa I was told to come back in two hours by a grim-faced receptionist. Upon my return I found a police officer waiting for me.

'What do you want?' he asked, without even suggesting we sit down, looking at me down his nose as if I was something unpleasant.

'I want to extend my visa,' I explained.

'Why?'

'I am thinking of doing a Master's – '

'Don't imagine we don't know all about you,' he said in an aggressive manner. 'We've been keeping an eye on you and have a file on you this big.' He held his hands a metre apart. 'We know about your past, your involvement in illegal demonstrations, the speeches you have made and your writings criticizing President Sadat and other regimes in the Middle East. You will not be getting any kind of permission to stay beyond the date of your current permit. If you are still here after that, we will arrest you and throw you in jail.' Anyone who has ever seen the inside of a Cairo jail will understand just how much of a deterrent that was. I had no choice but to start packing up.

At the end of term, there was a party for the graduates of our course in the Journalists' Union club. This should have been a happy occasion; I had a degree and all likelihood of a good career ahead of me, yet I felt downcast and anxious. Towards the end of the evening people started exchanging addresses, promising to keep in touch with each other. Since I had no forwarding address, I tried to keep out of the way, busying myself with pouring another soft drink or getting a bite to eat from the laden table. My tutor, Mofeed Shehab, who later became a prominent member of the Egyptian government, and with whom I had got on well, came over to me.

'I'd like to get your contact details,' he said.

'I don't have any,' I replied, trying not to sound bitter.

'Well, I'd like to keep in touch,' he smiled kindly. 'I want to keep an eye on my star pupil,' he joked.

'To tell you the truth I have no idea where I am going to be living,' I confessed. 'I have to leave Egypt. My own country is under Israeli occupation and I – ' to my horror my voice started to crack, betraying my emotion. Mofeed put his hand on my arm. 'My dear Abdel Bari,' he sighed. 'Forgive me, I didn't think. How difficult to be a Palestinian refugee. How difficult not to have a fixed address and not to know where you are going.' I realized that if I didn't leave, my own gloomy situation would bring everyone else down, so I said my farewells and walked out into the night.

Though I left Egypt in a rather miserable way, my time there changed me forever and taught me much that has informed the rest of my life. The Egyptians are an inspiration: they face the most terrible privations and difficulties with jokes, which is probably why their comedians are the best in the Arab world. In my experience, they are patient, generally peaceful – unless provoked – and exceptionally generous. In spirit, the Egyptians are essentially egalitarian and socialist. One custom that I became familiar with in Egypt was a form of communal saving called *Jama'ia*: a group get together and regularly contribute a small amount until quite a large pot exists; this is then used to finance expensive things like weddings or hospital treatment for individual members when the need arises. We operate such a system at *al-Quds al-Arabi* and have been able to offer substantial help to colleagues in this way.

4

Career Moves

At one time I might have become the Arab answer to Gordon Banks. I love football and in my time was an accomplished goalkeeper. I briefly considered becoming a professional footballer instead of a journalist and two of my childhood gang, Abdel Rahim Falah and Abu Jamus, did in fact go on to become semi-professional footballers in Jordan. We had enough practice, despite the fact that there was only one worn-out and bumpy football pitch for the whole population of each camp. We used to play for hours anywhere we could find enough space, on the dusty wasteland or scorching sand, and always barefoot – I don't think any of us had ever even seen a real football boot. The fact that none of us possessed a football was no impediment either. We used to improvise with old socks, a balloon, and string. The inflated balloon was stuffed inside the socks then bound with string; another layer of socks was pulled over this and so on until we had a fairly hefty approximation of a football.

Only one boy in Deir al-Balah possessed a genuine football. His name was Kamal and he came from one of the few well-off Palestinian families living next to the camp. Kamal was far from generous with this football, cannily rationing our use of it so that we would do virtually anything just for an hour's game. He was quick to exploit our desperation, especially as he was hopeless at football himself and would never normally have been invited to join in. Seeing us gathering on the wasteland or the beach, marking 'goals' with rags and stones, he would appear nonchalantly carrying his football as if he were on his way elsewhere.

'*Salam alaikum*, Kamal,' we used to call.

'*Wa alaikum as salam*,' he'd reply, making as if to carry on past us.

'Come and play football with us?'

'I've got to go to my cousin's house,' he'd say (or his aunt's or his teacher's but always a feeble excuse).

'You can be captain of one of the teams.' This would stop him in his tracks.

'Yes?'

'Yes.'

'And I get to choose my team?'

'Yes!' It was worth the sacrifice of having a bumbling captain if it meant playing with a real football. Everyone hoped he wouldn't pick them for his team because this meant being careful not to step on his toes, literally or metaphorically.

As goalkeeper, I was key to our unspoken strategy. Kamal would never pick me for his team so that I was defending the goal he took aim at. On the rare occasion that it managed to find its way into the goal I, of course, would fail to save it and Kamal would enjoy the congratulations of his team mates. Sometimes things would go wrong and I would accidentally impede the ball while trying to avoid it or one of his own team, unable to restrain himself, would intercept his slow progress down the dusty pitch and kick the ball away to a more energetic team mate. Such misdemeanours would result in the ball being withheld for several days. These petty concerns were put into perspective, however, when the Israelis invaded Gaza and all our games ended.

I took up football again when I was at university. I had managed to put on a bit of weight in Jordan, and was now stronger and fitter than I had ever been in the camps. I was asked to join both the university and the foreign students' team and, miraculously, was provided with my first pair of football boots as well as goalkeeping gloves. One day, the foreign students played against a celebrity team, in front of a capacity crowd at the home stadium of Cairo's top team, Zamalek. I remember there were various musicians, the comedian Sayed Mellah, and actors such as Mahmoud

Yassin and Nour El-Sharif; some of them were good but others so unfit that they were out of breath and exhausted after running the length of the pitch just once, and didn't get anywhere near the ball. The celebrity team was beefed up by a substitutes' bench occupied by star players from the Zamalek team.

If I do say so myself, my goalkeeping was courageous: my reflexes were sharp and I hurled myself through the air and onto the ground with little care for my personal safety. After the game, in which we trounced the celebrities, one of Zamalek's scouts asked me if I would like to train with their reserves. I agreed and started attending sessions twice a week. After a while they offered me a contract to join the team as a reserve. This was an exciting offer and I was tempted, but it was my third year at university and I had to get down to some hard work. Besides, professional football was not well-paid in the Arab world then, and such a career is short-lived, and dependent on age and fitness.

My son Khalid, born and raised in London, inherited the football bug from me and was obsessed with the idea of being the next David Beckham. He had great confidence in his prowess as a footballer and this made him rather idle where schoolwork was concerned. Khalid was good at the game, but I knew from my own experience that in all likelihood he wasn't good enough to be a premier division player and even if he were I would still have my reservations about such a precarious choice of career. This was a tricky moment of parenting since, of course, nobody wishes to demoralize their children or damage their self-esteem. Salvation came in the form of a 1995 television series about Chelsea Football Club's training academy. The programme showed how thousands of young hopefuls applied to get in but just three made it, and of these, only Jody Morris was signed to Chelsea. Even then, after months of training and rough treatment at the hands of the coaches, he played in the team just once in his first year. I had watched the opening programme and my wife, Basima, and I decided that the best way to get Khalid to relinquish his footballing dreams was to let him watch this series. It worked. He accepted that he was going to have to do something else and so started studying hard. Khalid, however, did play in both his school and university teams and this was a source of pride and happiness to us all. Incidentally one of his friends, Brett Johnson, is now a professional footballer playing for first division Northampton Town.

There have been a few Arab players in British teams over the years. Palestinian Walid Badir, a skilled midfield player, built like a tank, was bought by Wimbledon in 1999, for a million pounds, and he scored a goal against Manchester United. I interviewed him shortly after his arrival in London and felt that he was out of his depth. He was being paid £10,000 a week, an unthinkable amount of money for a poor Palestinian boy from the remote village of Kafr Qassem. It soon became obvious that Walid was spending a significant amount of his salary on junk food and he put on too much weight to play at his former standard; after just one season he was sold back to Maccabi Haifa, an Israeli team. I was glad to see that he had regained some of his earlier form when he played against England in the 2007 European Cup qualifiers.

Rachid Harkouk was one Arabic player who did do well in Britain. Half-Algerian, half-British, he was signed by Terry Venables for Crystal Palace in 1976. He moved to Queens Park Rangers in 1978 and Notts County in 1980. Rachid could kick the ball with explosive vigour and got the nickname 'Rash the Smash'. Unfortunately, this nickname could also have applied to his other on-pitch activities, like losing his temper and assaulting opposing players. He collected red cards like some people collect stamps and was usually kept on the substitute bench until right at the end of a game, when the manager would release him like a pent-up bull onto the pitch, often to score the winning goal. When I interviewed him, I asked why he couldn't control himself better. 'I am Algerian – North Africa is hot and boiling and so is my blood,' came the reply. He played in the Mexico World Cup in 1986 and then disappeared. I met his father in 2001 who told me that Rachid was driving a van for a living and was twice divorced.

Football can be a lethal pursuit. Just watching it can be hazardous. I narrowly missed being among the forty-seven people who were trampled to death in Cairo Stadium, in 1974, when the police let in too many people. I was in the stadium, a few metres from where the barrier eventually gave way, but left minutes before the tragedy; having been jostled and pushed by the crowds struggling to get to their places I sensed that there was going to be a problem and forced my way out against the flow.

I had another brush with death due to sport, whilst studying in Alexandria, where I used to play basketball at the Christian youth club. After one particularly vigorous game, I went to have a hot bath in my cousin's flat. It was cold outside so I closed all the windows and the next thing I knew my face was being slapped and pinched by our neighbour. The gas boiler was faulty and I'd been almost asphyxiated by carbon monoxide. My cousin told me later that he'd called an ambulance, but in Egypt this is little more than a token gesture. If you are lucky enough to have access to a telephone that actually works it is a miracle if anyone at the other end, in the 'emergency services', bothers to answer your call. Should they, you will face such a lengthy barrage of idiotic, bureaucratic questions, first about yourself and then about the patient, that the latter will be long dead by the time they decide to get an ambulance on the road. So I was lucky that our neighbour was a medical student and one look at my blue face had convinced him that if I wasn't brought around I'd be dead.

A Dangerous Occupation

I was obsessed with newspapers from an early age. In the refugee camps few people could afford brand new ones, but old papers were sold cheaply by enterprising individuals who would spread them out on the dusty earth along with ancient magazines. I did a deal with the man who owned the only actual newspaper kiosk in our part of the camp. In return for a few Egyptian pence, he'd let me read that day's papers and then put them back, on the condition that I didn't make any marks or creases on the pages. My older brother, Abdel Fatah, had convinced me of the importance of reading the newspapers; always with an eye on his appearance he pointed out that you could advertise the type of person you were by the title of the newspaper you carried tucked under your arm.

At the beginning of the 1970s, the only relatively free press in the Arab world was based in Lebanon. Some of the newspapers were privately owned, as opposed to state-controlled, and there were several journalists whose work I admired, for example Ghassan Twaini who wrote for the Lebanese paper *al-Nahar* and Mohammad Hassanein Heikal who used to be the editor of *al-Ahram* in Egypt. I respected them because they had the courage to express their own opinions even when these were in marked contrast to the official line and liable to get them into trouble. Heikal, for example, was jailed for three months because of his forthright criticism of the late President Sadat.

Sometimes Arab journalists paid for their outspokenness with their lives, as in the case of Selim al-Lauzi, whom I very much admired and who published and edited a Lebanese weekly magazine called *al-Hawadess*. He had fled Lebanon, like much of the Beirut-based media, when the civil war erupted in 1975. The media reported his death a year or so later without going into any details but his widow, Omaya, told me what had really happened: al-Lauzi had decided to risk a flying visit to Beirut for his mother's funeral. His body was found on wasteland shortly after his return to Lebanon. He had been tortured to death, his fingers cut off and his limbs mutilated by acid. This was a political assassination and there were several suspects; he had been critical of many dangerous men and organizations, from Colonel Gaddafi to the Ba'athist regime in Syria as well as certain radical Palestinian groups. The identity and motives of his assassins remain a mystery but his death represented a strong message to all journalists who dared to criticize the powers that be. Much as I would have liked to, I couldn't write the truth about al-Lauzi's death at the time because the newspaper I was working for was unwilling to antagonize the governments and groups implicated in his murder. It was not until 1996, when al-Jazeera invited me to take part in a programme about censorship in the Arab media, that I finally had a platform from which to speak the truth. Minutes after the programme was broadcast, Omaya called me in tears to say how much it meant to her the truth had finally been revealed.

The international NGO, Reporters sans Frontières (RSF), issues an annual analysis of press freedom around the world. The 2006 report shows that little has changed in the Middle Eastern region since my own time there as a journalist. They found that in Libya, Iran, Syria, Tunisia and Saudi Arabia the state exercises total control over the media. Of all the countries listed, North Korea was the least free in the world, at number 168, but Iran was ranked 162nd and Saudi Arabia 161st with Syria, Egypt, Algeria, Libya, Sudan, and the Palestinian Authority close behind. By 'least free' they are not referring only to censorship, but to a widespread infringement of civil liberties, not to mention torture, kidnapping, imprisonment and, sometimes, assassination of journalists. In the Middle East, journalism remains a dangerous profession if you wish to report the truth.

I thank God that I have escaped arrest or imprisonment in the course of my career but that is not to say that I have escaped all repercussions for speaking out. Several Arab countries including Saudi Arabia, Egypt, Syria, Kuwait and Iraq have banned me from entering their territory. I have even received death threats from Arab governments displeased with my reporting. In 2004, I wrote several articles in my paper, *al-Quds al-Arabi,* criticizing the Jordanians for their human rights violations; a short while later our Amman correspondent, Bassam Badareen was called to the Intelligence Service offices where he was given the following message to deliver to me: 'Tell your boss that our arms are very long and can reach him in London.' I had a similar experience with the Syrian authorities in 1998 after I published accounts by torture victims of their horrific experiences in Syrian jails.Where threats of physical harm fail to work, assaults on a journalist's reputation and integrity often follow. In the summer of 2002, during the build-up to the US invasion of Iraq, seven Saudi Arabian daily newspapers launched a vicious smear campaign against me that lasted several weeks. I have long been a fierce critic of the Saudi royal family's corruption and they had obviously decided to try to discredit me, with a view to silencing me. Short of ammunition they accused me, among other ludicrous things, of being an Israeli spy, announced that my newspaper, *al-Quds al-Arabi*, was financed by Mossad, and that I was a CIA puppet programmed to tarnish the image of certain Arab regimes. Ironically, the Israelis were running their own smear campaign at the same time, maintaining that my paper was financed by Saddam Hussein.

All of these could have been laughed off but the Saudi campaign soon became personal and stories were printed suggesting that I had not left Saudi Arabia voluntarily but had been expelled for immoral activities. I decided to sue. The Saudi Embassy refused to give my solicitor in Saudi Arabia, Saleh Hijelan, power of attorney to act on my behalf so I instigated legal proceedings in Britain. In an astonishing move, even by Saudi standards, the government changed the law regarding cases brought against Saudi newspapers so that there was now no legal forum for my case to be heard in Saudi Arabia. Furthermore Saleh Hijelan became the target of a hate-campaign himself. He had successfully defended British nurses Deborah Parry and Lucille McLaughlin in their 1996 trial for the murder of Australian colleague Yvonne Gilford and was later awarded an OBE as a result. In

Saudi Arabia, however, he was vilified as a defender of the morally corrupt, including me! The irony is that I was subsequently sued three times by Saudi princes in this country because they thought stories published in my paper reflected badly on them. Unable to afford the fees to instruct a top libel lawyer we were obliged to settle out of court on each occasion.

Later, Saudi newspapers would employ Stalinist methods to pretend I simply didn't exist. Once, for example, I was a member of a four-person Palestinian delegation that met Tony Blair in Downing Street, but when a photograph of the occasion was reproduced in the Saudi press it had been doctored so that I was no longer to be seen and my name was left out of the report.

No wonder then that my family were, in general, opposed to my choice of career. I remember my mother, in tears, pleading with me to train as a doctor instead. I wanted to be a journalist because I was full of anger after a childhood spent in the refugee camps and all the injustices I had witnessed there. My anger needed expression; I could have joined the resistance but decided that words, rather than bullets, would be my ammunition. I had social reasons for my choice of career too: success in journalism can break through class barriers, providing a swift route for an impoverished refugee to escape from the bottom of the pile and move to the top.

Through the Desert

I have to admit that where my career is concerned I have often been blessed with good fortune. A case in point is the story of how I published my first freelance article. In the summer of 1974, the Egyptian authorities refused to renew my visa. I had to leave Egypt by the end of the month or face imprisonment but I had no idea where to go. On the penultimate day, I bumped into an old friend and told him about my dilemma. 'Can you drive?' he asked. When I assured him that I had a full licence and experience he told me a curious tale: a wealthy businessman had hired a chauffeur to drive his car from the Libyan capital, Tripoli, to Cairo and back again. Unfortunately, the chauffeur had inconvenienced his employer by dying of a heart attack, leaving both the businessman and taxi stranded in the Egyptian capital. A new driver was now required. 'I'll do it', I said, without hesitation. I had few personal possessions which was just as well because the car and boot were stuffed with luggage belonging to the businessman and his former driver. With just one bag and no money at all, I set off across the desert towards Libya and an uncertain future.

My employer, Hafiz, was short, fat, and bald. Although he was wearing a flowery shirt that implied freshness, he himself was soaked with sweat. He chain-smoked cigars, puffing in my face as he sat next to me, and I didn't dare complain. Hafiz was in a big hurry and utterly egocentric: 'There won't be any time to rest,' he said. 'You will have to drive non-stop until we get there.'

The journey from Cairo to Tripoli is 2,000 kilometres, most of it across the desert. We set off at dawn and I drove as fast as the run-down vehicle would allow. The road would often disappear under the sands that billowed across it when the wind picked up and at night there were neither lights nor markings. We were surprised several times by desert foxes scampering across the road and once saw a small herd of gazelle. Snakes slithered across the sands but the most dangerous beasts in the desert were our fellow drivers. The sands bordering the road were littered with crashed or abandoned cars.

At the Libyan border, we were interrogated by the guards and I discovered that I wouldn't be permitted entry unless Hafiz stood as my guarantor. This gave him an unwelcome amount of power over me since one word from him could result in my expulsion from the country, but there was nothing I could do about it. I had an inkling that it might also make him stingy when it came to paying me; foolishly, I hadn't agreed a fee with him in advance.

Twenty kilometres inside Libya, I heard the sound of snoring. Hafiz was asleep and I, too, was exhausted. I pulled over by the side of the road and, trying not to wake that slave driver, slid down in my seat for a welcome nap. We woke up at about midday in a sauna bath that used to be the car. The fierce sun had been beating down on us for hours and we jumped out, opening all the doors in the hope of alleviating the situation. It was just as hot outside with no breeze and no shelter in sight. 'Let's go,' said Hafiz. 'We'll have all the windows open as we go along to let the air circulate.' As we closed the car doors he looked at me with a frown and asked, 'Why did you stop anyway?'

'I didn't want to wake you up,' I said. 'The road was bumpy ...'

'Hmmm.' He didn't sound convinced but lit up another cigar and cracked open a bottle of vivid orange pop. Just before draining it he reluctantly handed me the last salivary dregs with an air of pious resignation. 'Thanks,' I said.

When we arrived in Tripoli, I parked the car outside Hafiz's offices. He didn't invite me in after all the trials and tribulations we had been through together but unceremoniously took the keys from the ignition. I got my bag from the back and he locked the car. 'Well, goodbye then Abdel Bari,' he said, extending his sticky paw.

'Goodbye.' I shook hands and smiled at him expectantly. Irritated, the skinflint extracted a wallet from the back pocket of his trousers and fished out a £10 note. 'Here,' he said. 'It's more than you deserve – I said non-stop but caught you sleeping on the job.' I was disappointed, penniless as I was, and opened my mouth to object. Then I remembered the business at the border and decided to hold my peace and trust to fate.

'*Mashallah*, God has willed it,' I said, not without irony, and slinging my bag over my shoulder set off into the unknown.

Gift from Gaddafi

Experiencing an oil boom at the time, Libya was full of foreign workers and accommodation was scarce. I managed to find somewhere cheap to stay but the bargain rate I negotiated in a backstreet hotel was arrived at by the most unusual sleeping arrangement I had yet encountered. There were eight mattresses in a row with only a few centimetres separating each. The idea was that twenty-four men could share these by agreeing to sleep for no more than 7 hours and 57 minutes at a time. Three minutes changeover time saw occupant number one rising and going out to work, study or tramp the streets while occupant number two lay down on the still warm mattress to slumber through the next slot. Occupant number three would arrive 7 hours and 57 minutes later and so on. 'You only need the bed when you're sleeping,' Tibra, the small and chubby wife of the hotelier, reasoned as she took the first week's rent up front. 'So why pay over the odds for it?' I couldn't fault her logic.

Tripoli boasted just two newspapers: *al-Balagh* and *al-Fajr al-Jadid*. Both were part of the same organization, financed and controlled by the government and its flamboyant leader, Colonel Muammar Abu Minyar Gaddafi. The revolutionary leaders were revered and the Colonel's portrait could be found everywhere. Gaddafi's revolution had been inspired by Nasser's Egypt but the countries had little in common. The majority of the small (5.7 million) population was nomadic, moving with their flocks and living in tents or primitive mud houses, but there were also sizeable urban centres along the northern coast including Tripoli and Benghazi.

I tried to find a full-time editorial position in Tripoli but neither of the papers would have me. The only ray of hope was an invitation from *al-Balagh* to submit articles on a freelance basis. Meanwhile, unable even to afford Tibra's 'hot-bedding' hotel, I had temporarily moved in with my cousin, Salah, who was now living just outside Tripoli, sharing a small villa with three teachers.

At the time, in the mid-1970s, the US were worried by the rising power and influence of the Shi'i clergy in Iran and were propping up the Shah's regime which would eventually fall in 1978. I decided to write an article on the subject and considered it a good omen when I noticed a copy of *The Times* on a newsstand with a special supplement about Iran, stuffed with all the facts and figures I would need to back up my arguments. Unfortunately, *The Times* cost 2 dinars, precisely the sum I had left in my pocket. I decided to forgo eating and make this investment in my future instead. I researched, wrote and rewrote the story by hand, as a typewriter in those days was a luxury. Even today, I still prefer to write my articles and editorials by hand.

When the piece was finished to my satisfaction I went to the editor's office and handed it to him in person. He took one look at the title and shook his head. 'We couldn't possibly publish such a story,' he said. 'Our editorial policy does not allow for criticism of Middle Eastern leaders, no matter who they are or what they have done.' And to my horror he took my handwritten pages and placed them on the spike.

I returned to the villa and sank into a depression, I had rarely felt this hopeless and was so demoralized that I could hardly be bothered to get out of bed in the morning. I was slumbering a few days later, when my cousin came running into my room, closely followed by two of his colleagues, shouting and laughing with excitement. 'Wake up, wake up, you bastard!' Saleh shouted, brandishing a copy of *al-Balagh* 'Your story is on the front page.' I thought I was dreaming but dragged myself out of bed and stared at the tabloid paper he was holding right under my nose. I couldn't believe my eyes when I read 'Why the Americans need the Shah to police the Gulf by Senior Writer, Abdel Bari Atwan.' 'Senior Writer?' And just a few days ago I had been spiked. At lunchtime, the radio news broadcast the story in its entirety and in the afternoon the television included it in their round-up of the day's press.

I went into Tripoli to find out what had happened. When he heard I was in reception, *al-Balagh*'s editor came down to greet me: 'We've been looking everywhere for you,' he beamed, kissing me three times with great warmth and explained what had happened. Shortly after my story had been spiked, a media officer from Gaddafi's Ministry of Information had turned up in the editor's office. Gaddafi, it seems, had fallen out with the Shah of Iran. 'We want some anti-Shah stories,' the officer said. 'What have you got?' The editor unimpaled my story from the spike and handed it to him: the official took the article for Gaddafi to have a look at and he, it seems, was thrilled with the story. It was at his insistence that it was front-page news and its author promoted to 'Senior Writer'.

I was offered four jobs on the strength of that article, including one at *al-Balagh*. I decided to stay with them out of loyalty, even though they had initially spiked my story and the salary they offered was the least competitive.

After I had been in Libya about a year, I began to feel frustrated by the lack of professionalism in the state-run press. I had been working hard but wasn't learning enough from my seniors who were not, for the most part, journalists by profession but who had won their positions through allegiance to the party. The Libyan press was infiltrated by government agents and newspaper editors were directly appointed by the Ministry of Information or even Gaddafi himself. Muhammad al-Zwai (who became ambassador to London when diplomatic relations were restored with the UK in 2001) was a frequent visitor to our offices and had his nose in everything we did. Our editor-in-chief, Salem Wali, was part of the ruling Free Officers Movement and a close friend of Gaddafi who visited the newspaper in person several times while I was there, driving his ancient blue Volkswagen Beetle. On one occasion, we were asked to send the whole front page over to Gaddafi's tented headquarters where it was changed beyond recognition and returned to us for publication. Nobody commented.

When it was time to renew my contract, I wasn't surprised to be told this would entail a visit to the secret services central office. Two uniformed officers grilled me about my allegiance to the revolution and informed me that in order to 'protect' it and promote Arab nationalism I should be 'very flexible'. 'Keep in touch with us,' one of them elaborated. 'Tell us if you notice anything unusual, any criticisms of the state, anyone speaking in a non-revolutionary manner ... '

'It sounds as though you are asking me to inform on my colleagues,' I objected and decided I would rather leave. I later discovered that this was a widespread practice throughout the Middle East and a fellow journalist told me that, when he worked for an Egyptian daily in the 1960s and 1970s, the editor used to ask reporters to bring him 'special' stories about what was happening on the streets which were not for publication but to be kept on file and copied to Gamal Abdel Nasser and his government.

Because government interference is so widespread in the Middle Eastern media, people sometimes assume that any story published in an Arabic newspaper has originated from, or at the very least been approved by, the authorities. Due to this assumption, I once unwittingly created havoc on the international stock markets. In 1977, the Organization of the Petroleum Exporting Countries (OPEC) was split into two opposing sides, one headed by radical members like Algeria and Libya who wanted to increase prices by 10 percent, and the other led by Saudi Arabia who wanted to cap the rises at 5 percent under US pressure. The Venezuelan president, Carlos Andrés Pérez Rodríguez, acting as mediator, came to Riyadh as part of his goodwill tour. I wrote an editorial in the Saudi paper, *al-Madina*, urging unity and stating that there should be an agreement on pricing levels. All the news agencies leapt on this story thinking it was an official Saudi government response to the Venezuelan mission, agreeing to the 10 percent rise. The markets globally went into a frenzy. Had I been a speculator, I could have become a millionaire overnight but I realized what had happened far too late and, anyway, journalism and millionaires rarely appear side by side in a sentence.

Saudi Arabia

In late 1975, I decided to leave Libya and move to Jeddah in Saudi Arabia where my brother Kamal and his family were living. Kamal worried about me being a journalist and had been busy looking for alternative employment for me. He organized a job interview with a friend of his who was working as a translator at a Mercedes Benz dealership, translating their brochures and other documents for them. Thank God, this friend was not impressed with my appearance and told me, rather rudely, to get myself smartened up and have a haircut. It was the era of long hair and I was young. I took it personally and walked out, never to return.

I was briefly employed as a private tutor to a young Saudi princess, which gave me a fascinating glimpse of the ostentatious luxury inside the palace with its acres of glistening white marble as well as an insight into the strange, claustrophobic lifestyle imposed on these ostensibly privileged young women.

I was soon able to resume my journalistic career when I was offered a job at *al-Madina* newspaper. The editor at the time was Muhammad Hafiz who later became one of the founders of *al-Sharq al-Awsat*. His family owned *al-Madina*, which had been established by his father and uncle in Madina, later moving to Jeddah. He was a professional journalist and we got on well but he was not prepared to offer me a writer's job immediately. Since I spoke some English, he said that he would test me out as a possible translator and sent me to work with a Sudanese sub-editor called Soba'i Osman, who gave me a sheaf of Reuters' printouts in English and told me to make some stories from them. I did well and was soon hired as a junior reporter. Some time later, I brought a Reuter's wire to Soba'i to show him something: 'What does it say?' he asked.

'I thought you spoke fluent English?' I laughed.

'I can't speak a word of English. In fact my Chinese is better than my English,' he confessed. I was astonished and a little outraged. 'But you were meant to be testing my English when I first came here. I was going to be a translator. How could you possibly judge me?'

'Well, your Arabic is very good,' Soba'i replied. 'You got the job because of your Arabic, not because of your English.' Soba'i Osman later became managing editor of *al-Madina* and a good friend. He was unusual for a newspaperman in that he was sensitive and artistic; he wrote several success-ful novels and was fond of literature. He encouraged me to write creatively and later took charge of the literary supplement of *al-Madina* where he published several of my short stories. When I gave up fiction some years later because of an increasingly busy schedule, Soba'i wrote in his column that it was a great loss that I had been taken from literature to politics. I was flattered but not convinced. Sadly we lost Soba'i in his early fifties.

As a Palestinian, I greatly admired Yasser Arafat, the PLO (Palestine Liberation Organization) leader. When I heard that he was in Jeddah in 1976 I determined to meet the great man myself, hoping for my first 'scoop'. Arafat and his entourage had come to Saudi Arabia to perform the minor pilgrimage known as *Umrah*. I found out where they were staying and contacted them through an intermediary to arrange a meeting. My official purpose was to be briefed on the Lebanese civil war, which was at its peak, and the implications it would have for the Palestinians but I was hoping for a one-to-one interview with Arafat. I felt nervous, clutching the notebook in which I had written out all my questions. What would Arafat, the figurehead, the father of the Palestinians, think of me, a humble junior reporter? What would I say? Would I even be able to speak? When I arrived at the villa his bodyguards told me that Arafat had gone to per-form *ihraam*, the ablutions necessary before the pilgrimage itself, and that I would have to wait.

This made my nerves worse and my hand was trembling as I sipped the glass of tea someone had thoughtfully provided. Then the door opened and Arafat came in wearing nothing more than a white towel around his waist. I nearly dropped my glass in shock – here was no camouflage-wearing, gun-toting guerrilla leader but a short, bald, middle-aged man with a spreading waistline. I started to feel more at ease and we sat together chatting and joking for awhile. To my disappointment, Arafat declined my request for an interview and suggested that the PLO press spokesman could provide the information I required. My expression must have given me away because he started laughing and asked if I would accept his Foreign Minister, Farouk Kaddoumi, as a substitute. At the time, Kaddoumi was third-in-command of the PLO and my spirits and pride were revived.

As the interview progressed, I noticed that Arafat was listening to my questions intently. After half an hour, he went off and came back in his usual uniform brandishing a Polaroid instant camera. He took pictures of me talking with Kaddoumi and when we had finished, gave them to me and said, 'There, you see, I was your photographer today. What more could you ask for? The leader of the PLO takes pictures for the talented young journalist Abdel Bari Atwan.' I asked to have my photo taken with him and this time Kaddoumi did the honours. When I wrote my article I included all these details and it was a resounding success. There was no tradition of adding this kind of 'colour' to stories in Arabic newspapers and doing so was to become my trademark. I was to encounter Arafat many times after this and have devoted an entire chapter of this memoir to him.

Life in Saudi Arabia offered few distractions for a young, single man. The most exciting thing that happened in our offices at *al-Madina* was an unexpected visit by a jean-wearing Texan lady, 'Ms' Mary Randolph, whose husband was posted in Jeddah. She had lost her pet Yorkshire terrier, Jiminee, and wanted to advertise a reward for his safe return. Not only was Ms Randolph the first woman ever to set foot in those male-only offices but her fondness for Jiminee was completely incomprehensible to my Gulf colleagues. I felt some sympathy, having had a pet dog as a child, but here the canine species was seen as a health hazard rather than a companion, Saudi dogs spending most of their time scavenging on the rubbish heaps, fighting and, quite possibly, carrying rabies. Worse, they are considered profane by strictly observant Muslims who will wash their hands in mud or sand seven times after having touched a dog.

Being the designated English speaker it fell to me to explain the paper's reluctance to publish the notice, which I packaged as 'cultural differences', with the entire staff of the paper gathered round us in reception. Ms Randolph countered that she couldn't sleep without Jiminee beside her, oblivious to the gasps and sniggers her fondness for the canine provoked among my colleagues. I promised to do what I could but the advertising department was adamant; our receptionist fielded angry calls from Ms Randolph for several days before she took matters into her own hands and pasted hand-made posters appealing for Jiminee's return all over Jeddah. I hope she found him but I doubt it – the packs of wild dogs in Jeddah are notoriously tough.

Meanwhile *al-Madina* acquired a new, enthusiastic, and professional editor called Ahmed Mahmoud. He was hard working, arriving at the office at 7 AM and rarely getting home before midnight. Mahmoud improved the paper and circulation increased fivefold in the initial two years of his editorship. With no social life to speak of, I found myself working similar hours to my boss and my commitment and enthusiasm soon led to promotion and better pay. Eventually I was rewarded with my own column ... and a picture by-line which was every Arab journalist's ambition at the time. My writing became popular due to my idiosyncratic, critical and outspoken style, which was a rarity in the conservative Saudi press, and I later learned that it had been the bane of Saudi Minister of Information, Dr Mohammad Abdu Yamani's, life. 'I was torn,' he told me when we met in London. 'I really enjoyed your column and it was the first thing I turned to when the papers arrived in the morning, but I was anxious the whole time, wondering when I'd get the call from the royal family ordering me to deport you!' I always had a soft spot for *al-Madina*, which had provided me with valuable experience and opportunities at a crucial time in my career, and was deeply saddened when I discovered that my old paper had joined the smear campaign against me in 2002 which I mentioned earlier.

Although I was happy with my job and doing well, I found Saudi Arabia stifling. When I was headhunted by *al-Sharq al-Awsat*, a pan-Arab paper with big ambitions, and offered the chance to go to London I was tempted. The plan was to launch the paper in London in 1978 and print it simultaneously on four continents in twelve cities. I already admired the paper's editor, Jihad al-Khazen, who was behind some of the most interesting publishing ventures in the Arab world at the time including *Arab News*, the first English-language daily in the Middle East. When he heard that I had some reservations he asked me to come and see him. 'Abdel Bari,' he said, 'until your circumstances change, I would suggest that it is infinitely preferable to be a refugee in London than in Jeddah.'

Still not convinced, I went to see the veteran Palestinian journalist, Yusuf Salah. Yusuf had grown up under the British Mandate and dressed like an English aristocrat in a three-piece suit with polished brogues, his dyed hair smoothed back from a fine-boned face. I told him about my job offer and he chuckled and said, 'Abdel Bari, that is just too good to be true.' He put it in a political context, pointing out that most Arab countries had banned Egyptian papers which had become a mouthpiece for President Sadat's new friends, the US and Israel. 'They need another voice of Arab "moderation"', he said. 'There's a gap in the market and in the information war.' I must have looked crestfallen because Yusuf patted my hand and said, 'And so what? It's good money and it's a chance to go to London. You could do a Masters degree there too. My advice is go and give it a chance.'

Back and Forth

The social and cultural aspects of my move to London are considered in a subsequent chapter; career-wise it was somewhat turbulent. I was well paid at *al-Sharq al-Awsat* and initially enjoyed the working environment. Journalists and editors had been exposed to greater press freedom and professionalism in London and this had a dramatic effect on the Arab media in general. I was producing good stories which were often on the front page but gradually I noticed a change in editorial policy and an increase in censorship. A lot of the editorial team had worked together before in Lebanon and I started to feel sidelined. As the paper's political line emerged it became clear that it was diametrically opposite to mine. Whereas I was Palestinian, anti-Zionist and socialist, *al-Sharq al-Awsat* was pro-America, pro-Camp David,[1] pro-Saddam (because of the imminent Iranian Revolution), and supported most of the Gulf regimes.

I began to feel the strain and my physical condition deteriorated as a result of the almost daily conflict at work. My weight dropped and I developed shooting pains in my stomach. My doctor diagnosed a duodenal ulcer and a few days later it burst. I was rushed to hospital by ambulance, semi-conscious and suffering from internal bleeding; I realized that my professional situation was untenable.

Once more, I was in the right place at the right time. My old paper, *al-Madina*, had decided to open a London bureau and they asked me to

---

1. The Camp David Accords were the result of secret talks regarding a solution to the Palestinian problem between Egyptian President Anwar Sadat and Israeli Prime Minister Menachem Begin in September 1978. There were two agreements which were signed at the White House, and witnessed by United States President Jimmy Carter. However, since they excluded the Palestinians they were unacceptable to the majority of Arabs.

head it. Within weeks I was my own boss and the bearer of the grand title, 'London bureau chief'. I found an office on the fifth floor of the International Press Centre, a modern office block in Shoe Lane, just off Fleet Street, and bought telephones, a fax machine, and an electric typewriter that I never once used. In the *Guardian*, I placed an advertisement for a personal assistant, stating that I would offer some journalistic training, and was surprised to receive over 3,000 replies, the majority from graduates with good degrees.

The International Press Centre was home to a number of prestigious organizations: on the floor below us was the London bureau of *The New York Times*, presided over by Heather Bradley, a power-dressing American woman in her early forties. The lift used to open right into her suite of offices and I remember once a group of Afghan *mujaheddin* wearing flowing robes, turbans and beards came to be interviewed by me but accidentally got out at *The New York Times* on the fourth floor. One of these, Sibghatullah Mujaddidi, laughingly recounted how the initial puzzlement of both sides had given way to humour, the offer of coffee and an escort to lead them to their correct destination. Mujaddidi later became the interim president of Afghanistan.

My new position meant that I could choose my own stories and I began to travel widely, attending all the most significant political events in the Arab world, sometimes witnessing history in the making. At the Arab League summit in Tunis in November 1979, for example, I had my first encounter with the man who would become such a thorn in the Americans' side: Saddam Hussein. I was standing with other journalists outside the Hilton hotel where the conference was being held when Saddam got out of a black limousine. He had only recently become president after the resignation of Bakr in July but he marched imperiously up the steps surrounded by bodyguards and a retinue of lackeys; he completely ignored us whereas most leaders (especially newly appointed ones) would have made some effort to charm the media. In fact, the majority of those who had already passed had had the courtesy to come and shake hands and exchange pleasantries with us. Out of curiosity I followed his considerable entourage into the conference centre.

I think I was the only journalist who witnessed what happened next: as he entered the hotel lobby, the son of Tunisian President Habib Bourguiba, also called Habib, came forward to greet President Saddam, a broad smile on his face. This eloquent diplomatic gesture was misinterpreted by Saddam's bodyguards who, not recognizing the president's son and taking him for a potential assassin, attacked the unfortunate Habib en masse, pinning his arms behind his back and propelling him forcibly against a wall. Tunisian officials intervened and put an end to the undignified brawl. Having established the true identity of their victim, Saddam's bodyguards allowed the shaken and annoyed Habib Jr to return to their master's side. But if he was hoping for an apology he was mistaken. Saddam looked him up and down as if he himself had been inconvenienced by having to wait and continued on his way. It is a testament to Habib's diplomacy that nothing more was made of this incident. Further, it demonstrates the fact that Saddam was already capable of generating fear in other leaders.

I used to get a number of interesting insights into Saddam in those early days from Yasser Arafat. In private meetings, and before he had officially become the Iraqi president, Saddam was already making threats. He openly accused Arafat and the PLO of nurturing potential opposition to the Ba'athist regime and was enraged by PLO hospitality to Iraqi dissidents. By the late 1970s Saddam had formed strong links with groups opposed to the PLO, such as the Abu Nidal Organization (ANO), which had a base in Baghdad at the time. Arafat suspected, and I think he was right, that Saddam's intelligence services had some involvement with the 1978 assassinations of PLO representatives in London, Brussels, Paris, Rome and Madrid perpetrated by the ANO. Arafat had good reason then to be careful around Saddam Hussein, and this could explain his support for Iraq when the war with Iran broke out in 1980.

Like most correspondents, I joined the Foreign Press Association which is housed in a very fine building just off the Mall and has more than 700 members. I used to go there from time to time and enjoyed sharing tips with other journalists from all over the world. In the early days I was frustrated by my lack of success in gaining any interviews with top-ranking government ministers and was complaining about this one day over lunch to the London bureau chief for the Italian paper La Repubblica. 'You'll get one when they need you for something,' he said, in between mouthfuls. 'You mark my words.' In 1980 the count was proved right when ITV broadcast a television drama called Death of a Princess.

The film was a dramatized account of a real situation that had occurred in Saudi Arabia when a young princess and her lover were publicly executed for adultery. The journalist who made it, Anthony Thomas, had conducted interviews with Saudi nationals who gave vent to their frustration with the conservative and repressive regime they were living under. The Saudi regime was furious and threatened to impose a trade embargo on Britain, blaming Margaret Thatcher's government for allowing the film to be shown on television. As London bureau chief for a major Saudi newspaper I was seen as an important pawn in the diplomatic game of chess that ensued and was offered an exclusive interview with Douglas Hurd, then foreign secretary in Mrs Thatcher's government.

Politely ignoring my questions about British foreign policy in the Middle East, and Palestine in particular, Douglas Hurd talked at length about his respect for the Saudis and how much he regretted this recent souring of relations. He urged the Saudi people to understand the cultural and political differences between the two countries and insisted that, since the media is not under state control in Britain, the government has no say over what is broadcast. I reported all of this and it was read by the right people. In my small way, I limited the fall-out of an incident which was considered of such historical significance in retrospect that it was even referred to in the comedy series *Yes Minister* when Sir Humphrey speaks of 'the worst diplomatic crisis since *Death of a Princess*'.

Two years later I was invited to interview Margaret Thatcher along with two other Arab journalists. Again there were diplomatic reasons for this apparent favour: she was about to broker the infamous al-Yamamah arms deal between BAE Systems (and its predecessor, British Aerospace) and Saudi Arabia worth £45 billion. Naturally I was curious to see inside 10 Downing Street and to meet the famous 'iron lady'. There were no barriers at Downing Street at the time, and you could drive to Number 10 without encountering any security other than a single policeman standing in front of the door. A secretary answered and ushered me into the entrance hall, which was not an impressive room for anyone who has been in a Saudi palace. A few seconds later we were in Mrs Thatcher's office. She was there waiting for us and shook each of our hands in turn. Taller than I expected, she had bright blue eyes and a sharp, penetrating look, together with a general air of moral and psychological strength. If I am honest, I was a little scared of her.

I was opposed to Margaret Thatcher's politics and expected to feel some antagonism but she put us at ease, giving us a guided tour of Number 10. The whole event was carefully stage-managed so there was a disappointing absence of amusing incidents. I was hoping to meet Dennis Thatcher, the prime minister's husband who was always portrayed in the media as being rather hapless, but he didn't appear and I hardly dared enquire where he was.

During the interview, we took it in turns to ask questions which had all been vetted in advance and which were answered in a serious and earnest tone. Afterwards we had tea and biscuits and the official Tory photographer came to take some pictures. As we were posing I discreetly passed on some unusual information: 'King Fahd of Saudi Arabia has written a poem about you,' I told Mrs Thatcher. 'Have you heard about it?' She shook her head, looking at the camera. 'He considers you the perfect woman,' I said. She was so surprised that she gave me an amused smile. The photographer snapped away enthusiastically but she waved her hand at him sternly to show that these would not be for publication and despite my entreaties I wasn't allowed a copy. The only unexpected thing I had managed to extract from Mrs Thatcher was that smile, and that I was not allowed to keep.

My dream job as London bureau chief came to an unexpected end less than two years later when Ahmed Mahmoud, the editor-in-chief on *al-Madina* and by now a good friend of mine, got himself into hot water with an article about the Syrian President, Hafez Assad. In 1984, one of his journalists wrote an article claiming that there had been a *coup d'état* while Assad was in hospital following what appeared to be a fatal heart attack. Unfortunately for the journalist and Ahmed Mahmoud, Assad recovered and complained to his connections in the Saudi royal family about the article and the perceived lack of integrity of its editor. Both men were dismissed and a new editor-in-chief, Hamza Abu al-Farajj, was appointed in Ahmed Mahmoud's place. Abu al-Farajj and I did not get on.

I returned to the *al-Sharq al-Awsat* stable as managing editor first of their new magazine *al-Majallah* and then of the paper itself but the same political problems recurred. Things came to a head on 14 May 1988 when the First Intifada, which claimed nearly 1,200 Palestinian lives, was at its peak. There had been many deaths that particular day and we had some horrific pictures of Israeli atrocities that I wanted on the front page. It so happened that Wimbledon had won the FA cup that day and to my dismay

Deir al Balah Refugee camp (UNRWA Archive)

The Atwan siblings, Deir al Balah refugee camp, 1965
Back row, left to right: the author, Abdel Fatah, Ziad, Jalal.
Front row, left to right: Fatima, Bashir, Amal

Reunited in Rafah refugee camp, 1995
From left to right: Bashir, Kamal, Zarifa, the author

My mother brings Bashir
to visit, 1968, Jordan

With my cousin Jihad
in front of the flats
we were living in,
1969, Alexandria

With friends at Cairo University, 1972

In Alexandria, 1974

Journalists' football team where I played as goalkeeper, Libya, 1975

Marching for Palestine, 1979

One of my first interviews, 1975, Libya

With Yasser Arafat, 1989, Tunis

With Osama Bin Laden, 1996

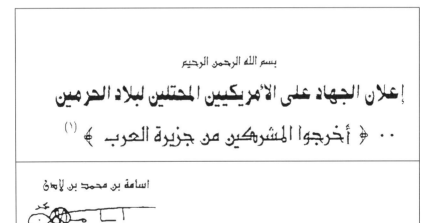

بسم الله الرحمن الرحيم

إعلان الجهاد على الأمريكيين المحتلين لبلاد الحرمين

.. ﴿ أخرجوا المشركين من جزيرة العرب ﴾ (١)

اسامة بن محمد بن لادن

The famous fax, 1996
'A declaration of Jihad against Americans occupying the
Land of the Two Holy Sanctuaries', with Osama Bin Laden's signature

At the launch of *The Secret History of al-Qaʻida*,
2006, London

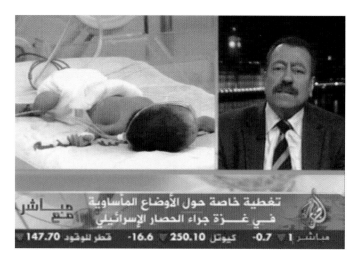

تغطية خاصة حول الأوضاع المأساوية
فــي غــزة جراء الحصار الإسرائيلي
مباشر 1 ▼ 0.7-   كيوتل 250.10 ▼ 16.6-   قطر للوقود 147.70 ▼

Describing the hardships endured by the people of Gaza,
January 2008, on al-Jazeera television

the editor-in-chief, Osman al-Omeir, decided to run with this story instead. 'It gives us all hope,' he said. 'They beat Liverpool – like David and Goliath'. The irony that we had our own David and Goliath story going on in the 'intifada of stones', as it was known, because stones were all the Palestinians had to fight the might of the Israeli armies, was lost on al-Omeir who was, and remains, a close personal friend. In my heart I resigned then and there. I left the paper for good on 14 September 1988.

5

The Arab Independent

When I handed in my resignation at *al-Sharq al-Awsat* I was a married man with two small children and a hefty mortgage, but I decided not to rush into my next job. I had been approached with an attractive offer by Jamil Mroeh, the editor-in-chief of *al-Hayat* newspaper which had recently moved to London, but wanted to work independently and was considering establishing a *Spectator*-type Arab-language weekly. My main aim now was to create something new that would really make an impact on the world of Arab publishing.

In October 1988, I travelled to Algiers to attend the annual Palestine National Council (PNC) meeting. During one of the breaks, Walid Abu Zalaf, the eldest son of the family who had set up the first and oldest Palestinian paper, *al-Quds*, asked if he could have a word with me. Walid told me that the family wanted to publish an international version of their paper and went into detail regarding their plans for a pan-Arab, independent daily. 'Good news!' I told him. 'It will happen soon, *inshallah*.' Patting him on the shoulder I was about to move on.

'Abdel Bari,' Walid stopped me. 'We want the paper to be based in London.'

'You'd certainly have more editorial freedom outside the Middle East,' I commented. 'But London is very expensive – '

' – and we want *you* to be editor-in-chief!' He interrupted, sounding quite exasperated by my failure to see where all this had been leading.

Although I took my time making a final decision, I knew from the outset that this was an opportunity I couldn't turn down. The idea of a free voice in the Arab media was something brave, new and long overdue. Despite the fact that the budget available for this unprecedented venture – to be called *al-Quds al-Arabi* – was miniscule, the ambition, optimism and belief were there in abundance. There was a chance of success, but I fully realized that there was a greater likelihood of failure.

There were already three well-established major offshore pan-Arabic newspapers operating out of London (Beirut having become untenable as a media centre). Two had been there since 1977: my former employer, *al-Sharq al-Awsat* which is owned by Prince Faisal bin Salman, son of the governor of Riyadh, and *al-Arab,* owned by the former Libyan Minister of Information, Ahmad al-Houni. These had been joined in 1988 by *al-Hayat*, which had ceased publication in Beirut in 1976 due to the civil war and is owned by Prince Khalid bin Sultan, Chief of Staff and son of the Saudi defence minister.

These papers dominated the Arab media in London. Generously funded, their offices were housed in grand buildings and they could afford the best writers and production teams. Compared with these giants, *al-Quds al-Arabi* came into the world like a sickly premature baby. Most of the Arab media thought it would cease to exist after a few brave months of struggle. The doubters reasoned, quite rightly as it turned out, that no top writers would leave well-paid positions to join such a precarious venture. Not only that, it would be politically risky for any journalist to join a publication so critical of many Arab regimes. Such people risked never working again.

My plan, however, did not require expensive, experienced or well-known writers. I wanted the paper to have its own independent character and style and decided the best way to generate this was to work with young, ambitious people who could be trained on the job by a core group of more seasoned journalists. In this way we would, organically and collectively, develop a house voice and ethos, whilst honing the new writers' individual skills.

I found a home for *al-Quds al-Arabi* in the shabby suite of offices in Hammersmith where we are still based. *Al-Hayat* was the first Arab paper, and probably one of the first papers in the world, to use computers for layout and design. I saw that this was not only faster and more efficient but much less expensive than traditional typesetting methods and we adopted this technology from the outset, scraping together a collection of computers of varying stages of antiquity; many are still in use today and we suffer endless 'compatibility problems' due to the haphazard mixture of Apple Macs and PCs in our offices.

Initially, the entire team, from editors to receptionist, consisted of eighteen people and even today we are just twenty-five. From the outset staff members were headhunted – mostly unsuccessfully – by other newspapers offering much higher salaries. In 1991, the Kuwaiti government-in-exile set up a newspaper in London called *Sawt al Kuwait*'and managed to poach three of our four designers. These young men were pioneers of computer-based layout and design and not easily replaced. We had to struggle on with just one designer who endeavoured to train up two others while overseeing everything himself. The Kuwaiti publication collapsed after seven months and our deserters came back full of apologies. 'It was the money,' said one, with forthright honesty. 'Damn that temporary Kuwaiti oil well!' said another. I took them back and suddenly we had a surfeit of designers.

For me, the most important qualities in business and friendship are loyalty, respect and forgiveness. On some Arab papers it is common to cut employees' salaries or suspend them by way of discipline, but if we have a problem I deal with it in a discreet way, face to face with the people involved in the privacy of my office. I politely explain what is wrong and usually my point of view is accepted and any mistakes rectified.

From the moment of conception our newspaper's gestation was fraught with difficulties. We were ready to go into production just three months after I had agreed to head the project but faced new problems on the printing and distribution front. *Al-Sharq al-Awsat* cancelled their deal with us at the eleventh hour, saying they did not believe we would have the means to pay them. They were right! We were rescued by a former colleague, Tom Johnson, who had great faith in us; he had just set up Newsfax and was already printing the *International Herald Tribune*. On the distribution side, Ibrahim Swaidani of Quick-Marsh was also prepared to take a risk and offered us financial credit.

We produced three 'zero' issues as a rehearsal and were disappointed with nearly everything about them but, young and enthusiastic as we were, decided to go ahead anyway. The first edition, on 26 April 1989, appeared in the afternoon instead of the morning and was full of mistakes but we were happy that the baby was finally delivered. Early issues of the paper were poor in every way and went largely unnoticed, except among those who willed our downfall.

Circulation Problems

When Saddam Hussein invaded Kuwait, *al-Quds al-Arabi* was one of the few newspapers in the Middle East to take an editorial position critical of the US, deploring the presence of half a million foreign troops on Saudi soil. We exposed America's hidden agenda to expand its hegemony in the region and linked these ambitions to oil. As a result, we were banned in most of the Gulf States and Egypt; our circulation fell dramatically, even though we were doing well in Europe. We faced continual financial problems. Yasser Arafat had bailed us out a few times but he himself was now all but bankrupt having been blacklisted by those same Arab states, which accused him of siding with Saddam Hussein. Advertising revenue is the lifeblood of any newspaper and can be used as a covert form of censorship; the majority of expensive advertisements in *al-Quds al-Arabi* were placed by Gulf companies who now withdrew them.

One day, a short, squat man wearing an overcoat appeared in our offices accompanied by a taller one in his shirt sleeves who never spoke but stared around impassively. 'Overcoat' informed me that he was a bailiff and had come to value our assets. These amounted to several old computers and a collection of cracked coffee cups; 'shirt sleeves' looked distinctly unimpressed. This pair became a regular fixture, sent by the courts to obtain payment of various bills from the rent to stationery.

I received delegations from both the Kuwaiti and Saudi governments offering to help us to the tune of millions of pounds, if I would change the political allegiance of the paper. Of course I refused. On another occasion, a British PR company representing the Kuwaiti government-in-exile invited me to lunch with the governor of the Central Bank of Kuwait 'to discuss a matter of mutual interest'. I declined but kept their letter as a souvenir.

Meanwhile, we were at crisis point. The freight company had refused to ship the paper because we were so late with our payments and for a few weeks we were distributed in London alone. I called a meeting of the staff and put the situation before them, hiding nothing and asking for ideas to bail us out. After half an hour's discussion someone, I don't remember who, said, 'Listen, do we want to keep this paper going?'

'Yes,' came the unanimous response.

'There is only one way,' this brave soul continued. 'We all have to take a cut in salary. Mr Atwan, how much of a cut would keep us from going under?' I consulted with our accountant, Pat Sandram. 'Are we talking about everyone?' she asked.

'Is there anyone who would not be willing to take a pay cut?' I asked. Nobody said anything. 'Everyone.' I told Pat. She fed some figures into a calculator and shook her head. 'It would have to be 50 percent,' she announced.

'Half pay,' I said. 'How many of you would be prepared to work even harder and produce an even better paper for half of what you earn today?' To my amazement every single hand in the room shot up and people shouted out their approval for the plan. It was an emotional moment and I noticed that Pat, too, had tears in her eyes.

Gradually, we managed to steady the ship. Circulation in the countries where we weren't banned continued to increase, and many of our creditors were patient and supportive, remaining so through to this day. Newsfax even wrote off some of our debts for which I am ever grateful. Nevertheless, it was almost seven months before the staff were back on full pay and I am sure many unspoken personal sacrifices were made during this period. Nobody knew it at the time but my colleagues Sanaa al-Oul and Amjad Nasser, as well as Pat Sandram and myself, went without any salary at all for four months, but we managed to survive.

Arab Media Revolution

Al-Quds al-Arabi became a good, independent newspaper by any standards. In terms of the Arab media it was an earthquake, undermining and shaking up an entrenched conservative, state-controlled and complacent system that had been in place for decades. We were as revolutionary in terms of the print media as al-Jazeera would be to broadcasting some years later.

The staff had emerged from the financial crisis more enthusiastic and determined than ever and our reputation for outspoken and fearless reporting grew. We were not afraid to criticize certain regimes for their corruption, woeful human-rights record, and lack of democracy. Admittedly, we made some mistakes in those early days: we were on occasion overly aggressive and at times the editorial was so radical that it could be accused of being unbalanced and unprofessional. We didn't check stories as closely as we should have and because we weren't able to pay top commentators we sometimes had to compromise our editorial line and accept over-zealous outpourings for publication.

I found myself on the wrong side of the libel laws on more than one occasion due to inexperience, since this form of legal protection does not exist in the Middle East. Today it has become commonplace for wealthy people from the region to litigate in the British courts. During the first Gulf War I received a letter from the well-known libel lawyer Peter Carter-Ruck, suing me for £50,000 in damages after a journalist on my paper had confused a Kuwaiti prince with his cousin. Another time, I quoted the *Sunday Times* which had alleged that the late Sheikh Muhammad bin Rashid al-Maktoum, the ruler of Dubai, was one of the people behind the collapse of a famous international bank. Almost immediately I received a writ from Allen & Overy, one of the biggest law firms in the world. Libel lawyers are expensive and there was no way we could afford a defence. I wrote an apology and put it on the front page and the Sheikh was generous enough not to pursue this any further. He knew he could ruin *al-Quds al-Arabi*.

The most extraordinary libel writ we ever received came at the end of 2001. I had published a story, following up on an article that originally appeared in the *Sunday Telegraph,* which alleged that Saddam Hussein's intelligence services had employed the services of several Iraqi entertainers in London to poison exiled members of opposition groups. Our article was a humorous take on this and featured a fictitious Iraqi belly dancer in an invented club on the Edgware Road. The next day, we had an irate phone call from a young woman who informed my incredulous receptionist that her name was 'Malyeen', which means 'millions'. She was put through to me.

'Abdel Bari Atwan?' a smoky voice enquired. Assured that it was me she continued in angry tones: 'Why are you libelling me?'

'What do you mean?' I asked (the very word libel by now sent shivers up my spine).

'Listen, I like your paper and read it everyday but you had no right to say I am poisoning Iraqi exiles.'

'We didn't – ' I began but was silenced before I could finish my sentence.

'You said an Iraqi belly dancer on the Edgware Road. Well, everyone knows that's me,' Malyeen insisted. I was amazed at this unfortunate coincidence of fact and fiction and, once again, we were obliged to pay several thousand pounds compensation.

Privileged Access

My work as editor-in-chief of *al-Quds al-Arabi* has sometimes been rewarded with unusual invitations from unexpected quarters. President Saleh of Yemen, for example, asked me to visit him several times in the late 1990s. On one occasion he took me to one of the modest town houses he owns in the capital, Sanaa. He has several such houses apart from the presidential palace, four of them set aside as homes for his four wives. After our preliminary enquiries regarding each other's health and families, he suggested that we chew *qat* together. *Qat* is the popular name for the shrub *Cata Edulis*, common in the Horn of Africa and the Arabian Peninsula area and which contains cathinone, a mildly euphoric stimulant. I had never taken it, or any other 'recreational drugs', before but I knew that in Yemen, chewing *qat* has much the same social significance as having a cup of coffee and did not want to offend the President of Yemen by refusing this hospitable gesture. I have since learned that the usual method of imbibing *qat* is to form a half-chewed ball of it which is then tucked into the cheek and 'milked' of its juice. Unaware of this, I chomped on leaves and twigs like a goat, chewing and swallowing it instead. My unorthodox approach resulted in terrible stomach cramps and diarrhoea; not only that, I was unable to sleep all night. I haven't repeated the experience and President Saleh clearly changed his mind on the subject too, issuing a statement in

1999 which urged the Yemeni nation to stop taking *qat*, pointing out that it is time-consuming, and suggesting that they spend their leisure hours playing sport or reading instead.

In 2000, I was invited to Sanaa again, this time to interview Saleh in the presidential palace. Built in the ancient Yemeni manner, which is similar to Moorish architecture, you enter the extensive grounds through iron gates guarded by soldiers. There are surprises and contradictions everywhere in the compound: in the middle of the carefully tended gardens the president has erected a huge army tent; the floors are covered with valuable traditional carpets but the furniture consists of cheap plastic tables and chairs. Inside the palace walls are two swimming pools, a gym and a bowling alley.

When our interview was over he invited me to stay for lunch. We went into another room and some servants rolled out a plastic tablecloth on the floor, placing cushions in a circle around it. Steaming bowls piled high with food, rice, meat and vegetables were brought in for us to share. We were about fifteen people, the guards and cabinet ministers all ready to dig in together, using their hands as is the custom in that part of the world.

It is usual for Yemeni people to change their trousers before eating to relieve the pressure of a tight waistband. Saleh was no exception and, in an egalitarian manner, dropped his trousers in order to put on a *wasra* – a cotton garment in the style of a Scottish kilt. As he did so a small handgun fell out of his trouser pocket. I picked it up and looked at it. It was a Colt with a custom-made pearl handle.

'That's a beautiful gun,' I said, forgetting that in Yemen, as in many Arab countries, it is considered polite to give the visitor any item he or she might admire whilst in your home. We sat down to eat and I tried to pass the gun back to Saleh.

'Please, Abdel Bari, accept it as my gift!' Saleh said with a smile, waving his hand as if to say 'put it away and let's have our lunch'. I was horrified. How could I get out of this without appearing ungrateful or discourteous? Visions of my arrest and imprisonment as a hijacker or terrorist flashed before me.

'Thank you' I said, 'but I couldn't possibly take it!'

'Why not?' The president looked at me with a frown. His bodyguards shifted a little beside him.

'First, because I don't know how to use it,' I explained, but the president looked unimpressed. 'Secondly, because I live in London, not the mountains of Yemen where warring tribes need to be armed, and thirdly because if I board a plane with it I will be arrested!'

'Take it with you,' Saleh said, patting my hand encouragingly. 'And don't worry. You are travelling with Yemen Airways. I will send instructions that they are to let you carry it.'

'Well, that's kind,' I said, 'but what about Heathrow? You aren't allowed to carry a gun in England. It will be a scandal and I'll be locked up for years.'

'Don't worry,' he said. 'I will send it through the diplomatic bags and you can pick it up from the Yemeni embassy on Cromwell Road.' I was panicking now, racking my brains for something that would get me out of this scrape. I loosened my collar and mopped my brow. Then I heard the sound of muffled laughter and saw that the president and his bodyguards all had their hands over their mouths. Laughing out aloud, Saleh took the gun from me. 'I accept your refusal, Abdel Bari,' he said, wiping the tears from his eyes. 'And now, let us eat.'

Later, Saleh showed me around the rest of the palace. He had a room devoted to housing the presents he had received from world leaders. There were two enormous glass jars that he had been given by a Chinese delegation, filled with white liquid and lizards and snakes at the bottom of each. He had a gold sword from PFLP leader George Habash; a gold incense burner on a metre-high stand from King Fahd; the Emir of Abu Dhabi, Sheikh Zayed, had presented him with an ornamental boat, also made of gold; and Colonel Gaddafi had contributed a top-of-the-range Rolex watch. One wall was covered with shelves for gifts from Yasser Arafat – about twenty models of the Dome of the Rock in various sizes. After Saddam's invasion of Kuwait, Yemen was one of few countries to welcome Arafat and he visited often, evidently forgetting each time that he had already given Saleh a model of the Dome of the Rock a few months before. There were also some presents from African leaders consisting mostly of carvings, daggers and decorative spears. It was an impressive exhibition unique in the Arab world.

As we strolled in the grounds, Saleh mentioned that he was directing an opera. I laughed and said, 'But you are a military man!'

'Come with me and see for yourself,' he said and drove me to a remote area outside the capital where a large group of men were waiting to rehearse a traditional Yemeni opera for the tenth anniversary of Yemen unification. It was a surreal sight to see the president, in his military uniform, standing in the courtyard of an ancient building, waving his arms about, directing a group of men in traditional Yemeni costume as they sang and danced. Saleh told me afterwards that these men were all soldiers who had been ordered to take part in the performance.

In 1992 I was invited to visit Colonel Gadaffi, the Libyan leader, after he had heard me on BBC Arabic radio. I flew to Tripoli via Amsterdam and the Libyan Airlines flight arrived four hours late, after midnight. There was no one there to meet me, which was a surprise, since I had expected a formal reception as his guest. The airport was empty; all the other arrivals had been met and the workers had clocked off. I had no idea what to do or where to go, so I took a taxi to the only hotel I knew of, the Grand.

'I'd like a room for the night, please,' I told the receptionist who looked me up and down.

'Are you a Native American?' he asked.

'Why do you ask?' I was baffled.

'Because Colonel Gaddafi has given his annual award to the Native Americans because of their persecution by the US. All the rooms are taken by a delegation from Death Valley.'

'I am a native Palestinian,' I ventured but he didn't like the joke.

'Sorry, we can't help,' he said and turned away. Another hotel worker appeared and recognized me from my television appearances. He started a hushed conversation with the stubborn receptionist and he eventually came up with a room not much bigger than a broom cupboard, which was filthy and had no lock on the door.

In the morning, I phoned the Ministry of Information who were apologetic and said they were sending a car to pick me up. I then phoned my wife who was worried about me since she had heard of people disappearing in Libya. Nobody came to the hotel and I was so tired and frustrated that I fell asleep again. When I next opened my eyes I found two men standing over the bed staring at me. They were to be my hosts.

'What's the programme?' I asked them once I had got dressed and managed to squeeze a coffee out of the reluctant hotel staff.

'We've booked a flight for you to go to Sirit tomorrow. This is the birthplace of Gaddafi and you will be attending a meeting of the General People's Congress which will enable you to understand the workings of Libyan democracy.'

'Okay,' I said. 'That sounds fine. How long will it last?'

'Three weeks.'

'Three weeks! But I have a newspaper to run. When do I meet Gadaffi?'

'When you have seen how our democracy works it may be possible. We'll consider your request.' They told me that a car would come for me the next evening at 7 PM and ordered the receptionist to find me a decent room, which he did. Having spent the rest of the day wandering around Tripoli I had an early night and rose at 6 AM, took a taxi to the airport and bought a ticket out of there on the first available Swiss Airlines flight to Zurich.

It wasn't until 1999 that I actually met the Colonel in person. This time I was met at the airport and driven straight to the Aziziyah Barracks, Gaddafi's military base in Tripoli. There were three identical khaki tents in the garden, carpeted and colourful inside with comfortable cushions and chairs to sit on. Gaddafi likes to receive his visitors in a tent to remind them of his Bedouin roots. It was August and boiling hot with just the slightest breeze from a series of garden sprinklers irrigating the grass. I was asked to wait in one of the tents and sat, looking around me, noting a collection of books about globalization, political theory and the fall of empires. Despite his terrible reputation among journalists for poor time-keeping, Gaddafi came into the tent after ten minutes and straight away apologized that we hadn't met during my previous visit to his country. He was wearing military clothing but didn't stop coughing and sneezing into his handkerchief. Before getting down to business he served me chilled fruit juices and made sure I had everything I needed.

As soon as he sat down, he placed a tape recorder on the table and pressed the record button. Then he brought out a sheet of paper which he smoothed on the table beside it. Even upside down I could make out that this contained closely typed lines of information about me and my background. Gaddafi was well prepared, and remains the only person I have ever interviewed who did not succumb to my pre-interview chatting techniques and who turned the tables on me by recording every word of our interview from the outset.

When King Abdullah of Jordan was crowned following the death of his father, King Hussein, in 1999, he was extremely wary of the media but having seen me several times on the television, told his advisers that he would speak to me because I seemed 'approachable'. It would not be an exaggeration to say the Abdullah had become king by accident and felt quite unprepared for the role. Just before he died, King Hussein declared that his brother, Crown Prince Hassan, was not to succeed him. After thirty years in waiting this was a devastating blow. Hassan had been running the country while the king was in the Mayo Clinic being treated for cancer, but his conduct had obviously displeased his older brother. King Hussein wrote him a long letter, dated 25 January, which was published in the *Jordan Times* and also posted on the king's website. A diplomat to the end, by making his decision public and in the most eloquent and well-reasoned way, King Hussein made his choice incontestable.

The rumour doing the rounds at court, when I got there, was that Hassan's wife, Princess Sarvath, had damaged relations with the dying king by busily redesigning the royal apartments and styling herself as future queen. The Hashemite court is a multinational affair: the unfortunate Princess Sarvath, for example, is from Pakistan; King Hussein's last wife, Queen Noor, was born Lisa Halaby in the US, and his second (of four) wives, Queen Muna, was an English woman, née Antoinette Gardiner.

The matter of accession was all anybody talked about the whole time I was there and it really was the stuff of soap operas. In his letter, the king had made no secret of his affection for his son, Prince Hamza, Queen Noor's eldest boy, whom he touchingly describes in his letter as being constantly by his bedside in the Mayo Clinic, only leaving when the king ordered him 'as his ruler' to return to his training at Sandhurst. It was probably the fact that Hamza was only eighteen when his father died that prevented his accession. Right at the end of the letter, which must have been an agonizing read for Hassan, the king named Abdullah, his eldest son from his marriage to Queen Muna, as his successor.

Some courtiers expressed doubts about King Abdullah's ability to reign because he was half-English and had been brought up in the West. King

Hussein had married Antoinette Gardiner on 25 May 1961 and Abdullah was born 30 January 1962. Greater mathematicians than I have suggested this is less than the normal gestation period in human beings. In any case, Abdullah's advisers were keen that he should get used to dealing with the media and prove his Arab credentials at the same time.

Reflecting on how different my role in Jordanian society had become since my dustcart days, I watched the beautiful mountain scenery from the window of a Mercedes Benz as I was driven to King Abdullah's residence in the mountains outside Amman by Mr Abdel Karim Kabariti, chief of the royal court. King Abdullah greeted me in his private office, looking fit and muscular; he had clearly been working hard on his appearance. I soon realized that his Arabic was poor but, to his credit, he insisted on speaking it the whole hour that I spent with him. I asked him questions in English because I didn't want him to struggle but he would still answer in Arabic. He was completely unpretentious and confessed that it had never occurred to him that he would be king and had therefore devoted himself to a military career in both the British and Jordanian armies. In the former, he became colonel-in-chief of the Light Dragoons and in the latter, major-general.

I felt a lot of sympathy for this likeable young man and understood how difficult it was going to be for him to fill his father's shoes. I asked King Abdullah if his father had offered him any words of advice when they met just prior to his death. The king looked thoughtful and appeared moved. 'Yes,' he answered, 'he said, "Abdullah, you must follow your heart. You have the guts for the job but you must always follow your heart."' Unfortunately, in his broken Arabic the way the king pronounced this made it sound like, 'You must always follow your dog' and it was difficult for me to keep a straight face, especially as he said it twice. He spotted my reaction and realized that he had made an error and hastily corrected himself in English, 'I mean follow your heart, of course,' he said with a smile. He was humble enough to listen, make mistakes and learn and I have to say that after three years his Arabic was perfect. Once I joked with him about his wife, Rania, who like my wife, Basima, is Palestinian, but was brought up in Kuwait. I pointed out the similarity and added, 'My wife is giving me a hard time. I hope yours isn't?' King Abdullah laughed and said, 'No, not at all. In fact she is in Bosnia at the moment trying to help the victims of war.' He talked very fondly about Queen Rania and was in general happy to converse freely. I believe this discussion brought us closer and whenever I met him thereafter he preferred to talk to me off the record – which was difficult professionally because he told me many a good story which I couldn't then print.

At the end of 2002, I went to see King Abdullah when he had just returned from a meeting in Washington with George W. Bush. We sat down for some coffee and I asked him how it went. 'Appalling,' he said, wiping his palm with a handkerchief. 'It was the worst possible meeting.' He went on to tell me how he had warned the president against a war in Iraq, assuring him that Saddam had no weapons of mass destruction. President Bush, however, had ignored him and intimated that he fully intended to invade Iraq and depose Saddam with or without the Jordanian monarch's approval. King Abdullah's more self-interested concerns regarding a possible relocation of Palestinians from the West Bank to Jordan in the event of such manoeuvres were curtly met with a promise to safeguard Jordanian national security. It seems that what had upset King Abdullah most of all was the president's attitude towards him, which he considered discourteous, and his refusal to meet his eye during the whole exchange. Nevertheless, King Abdullah admitted that he had agreed to go along with the American military agenda though it clearly stuck in the craw to do so.

My most unlikely 'fan' as a result of my television appearances was Saddam Hussein, the President of Iraq: I heard from Azzam al-Ahmad, the PLO ambassador to Iraq, who was well connected with the Ba'athist regime in the early 1990s, that Saddam was watching CNN with his Foreign Minister, Tariq Aziz when I was interviewed in the aftermath of the April 1993 assassination attempt on George Bush Sr, during his triumphal visit to 'liberated' Kuwait after he had left the White House. The US had retaliated by bombing Baghdad, killing the prominent Iraqi artist Saoud al-Attar among many others when they destroyed the Rachid Hotel. I questioned the rationale behind this heavy-handed response and whether Saddam could be held accountable at all since he was under sanctions at that time. I then suggested that the whole assassination attempt could have been a set-up to give the US an excuse for military action against Iraq. Saddam turned to Tariq Aziz and asked, 'Is he Iraqi?' Tariq Aziz informed him I was not.

'What is he?'

'Palestinian.'

'Has he ever visited us?'

'No, he hasn't.'

'Is he one of those Palestinians who support the Ba'ath party?'

'No, he is independent. He is an editor of a newspaper.'

'Are we financing his newspaper?'

'No, we are not.'

'Well if an independent analyst like this is on our side then we know that we are winning.' Saddam concluded. 'Call Arafat and tell him that we are delighted that a Palestinian with such good English can argue so well for our side on American television.'

Tariq Aziz called the Palestinian embassy in Baghdad who, in turn, conveyed the message to Arafat. Of course, Arafat couldn't resist taking the credit for my opinions himself and telephoned Tariq Aziz immediately. 'Atwan spoke well,' he acknowledged, 'but I had thoroughly briefed him in advance.'

Saddam subsequently sent me three invitations to visit him in Baghdad through envoys and Iraqi ambassadors in London but I refused. As a journalist I was curious, and had heard many stories about the incredible security arrangements that were made around such visits because of the constant danger of assassination by the CIA, or any number of other enemies Saddam had managed to accumulate. Abdullah Hourani, from the PLO executive committee, told me that when he visited Saddam during the sanctions era he was put in a blacked-out car and driven for ten hours to a small house in a remote part of Iraq to meet him. I'd heard of people having to wash their hands in a special chemical solution before meeting him in case they intended to poison him with a handshake; or being strip-searched in case they were concealing weapons or electronic homing devices.

Three months before the US invaded Iraq in 2003, Saddam again sent an envoy, Abu Ahmad, to speak to me. I was in Qatar, making regular appearances on al-Jazeera television, commenting on the imminent disaster. 'Listen, Saddam likes you,' Abu Ahmad said. 'And he wants you to be on his side. Come to Baghdad to hear what he has to say. Other British nationals like Tony Benn and George Galloway have been so there is no reason to be afraid.' I agreed to go out of courtesy, even though I had no intention of doing so; rumours had already been put in circulation by the Iraqi opposition that I was paid or funded by Saddam Hussein, and I was not about to become his mouthpiece. The only grain of truth in these rumours is that I once met the Iraqi ambassador, Mozafar Amin, at a mutual friend's dinner party in London and he surprised me by offering to help *al-Quds al-Arabi* financially. During the sanctions era I had also been offered oil coupons, which could be traded illegally for large sums of money, by other Iraqi intermediaries. None of these offers were accepted.

Although I certainly didn't approve of his regime, the televised execution of Saddam Hussein on 30 December 2006 sickened me and made a martyr of the man for some by broadcasting his bravery on the gallows round the world. The American reliance on television to mould public opinion at home and abroad is often misguided and sometimes dishonest. Many will remember the humiliating footage of Saddam's capture, for example, but I was told by his lawyer, Khalil Dulaimi, that this was all staged for the cameras. He had actually been apprehended several days earlier, having been betrayed by one of his men who pretended he was going out to buy bread but went instead to the nearest US post and told them where Saddam was hiding. According to Dulaimi, Saddam was subsequently drugged and filmed in the dugout being 'arrested' by jubilant US soldiers who inspected his head for lice and the condition of his teeth as a petty act of humiliation.

Some Iraqis will now remember Saddam as a hero who fought the occupiers; his own blood-thirsty deeds have been somewhat dwarfed by the horrors and lies of this latest war. His domestic legacy may yet be that of a modernizer who equipped Iraq with a booming scientific and technological base, abolished illiteracy, nationalized the oil industry for the benefit of the masses and made his country a feared power in the Middle East. Throughout the Arab world his reputation is posthumously assured as the man who fired forty rockets at Tel Aviv, championed the Palestinian resistance, compensated the families of martyrs and defended Damascus against invading Israeli tanks in the Ramadan War of 1973.

Leading the Way

Al-Quds al-Arabi became known not only for its political stance but also for its unorthodox coverage of the arts and literature in a cultural section edited by the well-known poet, Amjad Nasser. Amjad is a Jordanian who spent many years with the Popular Front for the Liberation of Palestine (PFLP). He wanted to break away from the traditional Arab forms of classical poetry and was controversial in his own attitudes and method. He had created an informal school for up-and-coming poets and novelists and turned our newspaper into a platform for them, as well as artists working in other forms. The result was that work which would never see the light of day in the conservative press now filled our cultural pages, and raised the paper's profile and popularity with the young.

We have also done our bit for equality of opportunity. It is difficult for women to get ahead in much of the Arab media and I hope the success story of my deputy, Sanaa al-Oul, might encourage others in her field. Sanaa came to our offices when the paper had been running about a year and insisted on seeing the editor-in-chief (me). She sat in reception for half an hour and eventually, intrigued by her persistence, I invited her into my office. Sanaa got straight to the point: 'Now listen, Abdel Bari Atwan, I have long admired your writing. I want to learn from you and I want to work here.' I was taken aback. 'Well, I don't have any vacancies on the staff,' I said.

'I am doing a Master's in journalism at City University,' she replied. 'You don't have to pay me. It will be my work experience. What do you say?'

'Do I have a choice?'

'No.'

'Okay.' I laughed. I admit I was impressed; I like determination. Sanaa started the next day and was so enthusiastic, reliable and hard working that she soon became indispensable. Sanaa grew into an excellent political journalist and I promoted her through the editorial ranks until she became my deputy. I sometimes think of her as a shock-absorber because she is so good at dealing with criticism, conflict and problems; far better than a lot of men who would fly off the handle. When I went to interview bin Laden, she was the only person I confided in. I didn't even tell my wife and family where I was going. As far as I know, we remain the only Arabic paper to have a woman deputy. I have one other female journalist on the staff, Maha Bourbar, who is in charge of Palestinian affairs. Sanaa and Maha both married men from our rival newspaper, *al-Hayat*.

People have compared our newspaper to the Arab League because the staff come from all over Arab world. We have become a close-knit group. During Ramadan, we take it in turns to organize or prepare a meal for the whole staff and we break the fast together when the sun goes down.

11 September 2001

As a result of my November 1996 trip to Afghanistan where I spent three days with Osama bin Laden and his men in their hideout in Tora Bora (a full account of this can be found in Chapter 8 of this book), I was regarded as something of an expert on al-Qa'ida and my comments and analysis were regularly sought by global news organizations. Nothing, however, could have prepared me for the events of 11 September 2001.

I was in my office when I received a phone call from a friend. 'Turn on the television,' he said. I couldn't believe my eyes when I saw smoke billowing out of one of the Twin Towers, those beacons of capitalism and Western civilization. At first I, and most of the world's media, believed it was an accident but when the second plane hit and news came through that the Pentagon had also been targeted I was certain that this was the work of al-Qa'ida. The symbolism as well as the scale and audacity of the attacks bore all their hallmarks and the method used to destroy the Twin Towers reminded me of the 1998 truck bombings in Dar es Salaam and Nairobi, where one vehicle was used for a first strike, swiftly followed by a second to administer the fatal blow. Of course, this was far bigger than any terrorist attack in history, and I was surprised that al-Qa'ida had the resources to do it, but Osama bin Laden had vowed to 'deal a blow to America that will shake it to its very foundations' and he has never yet failed to fulfil his threats, one way or another. My office filled up with members of staff and we all watched as the devastation unfolded.

Along with most people in Britain, I felt shocked and horrified, especially when the victims started throwing themselves from the burning building. The world had never seen anything like this except in movies. I still believe that, if the Americans had harnessed the sympathy the world felt with them then, history could have turned out differently. Instead, President Bush and Tony Blair presented 9/11 as 'an attack on Western civilization', constructing a new enemy out of the entire Muslim world, as if they were repackaging the cold war, launched a major bombardment of Afghanistan, and, two years later, invaded Iraq.

My phone started ringing as I sat glued to the television in my office. It was Alistair Lyon of Reuter's. We knew each other well and he didn't bother with any formalities. 'Bari, what do you think?' he asked. I replied, 'This is the work of al-Qa'ida.' We have eight telephone lines at *al-Quds al-Arabi* and they didn't stop ringing for the next two months. Everyone in the world's media wanted to speak with me because I had interviewed the world's most wanted man, Osama bin Laden. On 11 and 12 September, there were thirty or so news crews camped outside the offices on King Street, Hammersmith. I had to leave by the back entrance to avoid a scrum and started to feel sorry for celebrities who have to endure this invasion of privacy on a daily basis.

In the aftermath of 9/11 and my commentaries on this tragic event, I was approached by four major television networks (CNN, ABC, CBS and NBC) to be a specialist consultant on al-Qa'ida. Of these I chose CNN, which had, in my opinion, done the best job covering the Gulf War and was well regarded in the Arab world.

Under Pressure

A steadily growing circulation as well as letters and feedback from readers attested to our growing popularity despite *al-Quds al-Arabi* being banned at various times in most Arab countries. Not everyone was pleased by our success, however, and there were frequent attempts to sabotage our operations. Our offices were broken into a number of times by various groups intent on finding links between me or my employees and a range of bogeymen from Saddam Hussein (it was alleged that he was funding the paper) to Osama bin Laden. In the aftermath of 9/11, I found myself the target of hate emails from right-wing groups, who thought I was supporting al-Qa'ida rather than reporting on them. One read, 'Foreign scum. We know where you live and we are going to kill you.'

I received other death threats and each had its own peculiar perspective and logic. There were several from Islamic fundamentalists who did not believe al-Qa'ida was capable of such an attack and thought I was tarnishing their image. They recalled the Oklahoma bombings that were blamed on a variety of fundamentalist organizations including Hizbullah, only for it to turn out that the culprit was an American national, Timothy McVeigh. According to them, I was part of a CIA smear campaign against al-Qa'ida and so they wanted me dead. I remained at the centre of this particular conspiracy theory for a further three years: it was not until October 2004 that Osama bin Laden officially acknowledged responsibility for 9/11.

Then there was the London branch of the Klu Klux Klan (KKK). Nobody seemed to know they had a London branch until I arrived on the scene. One morning at home, I heard the letterbox clank and went downstairs. I found a computer-generated calligraphic letter, bearing their symbol, which read, 'You are defending those Muslim terrorists and we are going to come back and get you.' On this occasion, I called the police who took the threat seriously because the KKK knew my address. I was offered a twenty-four-hour armed police guard at my home, but I refused. Their presence would only cause anxiety to my family and I took the risk that if the KKK had been going to do anything, they probably would have done so when they had the element of surprise on their side, instead of delivering a letter. Until I wrote this book, my family knew nothing of that letter or my dilemma.

Other attempts at sabotage were more discreet. One method I have become very familiar with is the phoney viewers' complaints campaign. During the first Gulf War I was a frequent contributor to the BBC Arabic service which was deluged with letters claiming that I was biased and pro-Saddam Hussein. An alert secretary noticed that all these letters were sent from two or three postal districts and voiced her suspicion that they were not genuine. The BBC World Service reviewed my output over the months and concluded that my approach was well balanced. As a result, I was asked to broadcast my opinions and analysis on a more regular basis.

Post-9/11, I was a regular guest on a programme called *Dateline London* on BBC News 24 and their office started to receive an endless stream of vitriolic emails from a professor at Haifa University. The professor complained that I was condoning terrorism and suicide bombing and begged them to take me off the air. A BBC researcher decided to look into the professor's identity and discovered that no such person existed. More recently I have been the target of a cyber-smear campaign. My entry on Wikipedia was hijacked and several incorrect or doctored entries posted on it, one provided by the MEMRI project which is headed by ex-members of the Israeli secret services.

New Labour and the BBC

In the aftermath of the attacks on New York and Washington we London-based Arab journalists found ourselves being courted by the Foreign Office once again. As the number one ally of the US, the British government had decided it needed to win the hearts and minds of Muslims and that our influence was now required. I was offered interviews with Tony Blair and Jack Straw, and even an article penned by the latter, but I declined. I was not convinced by the sincerity of these overtures, especially since both men were members of the powerful lobby group, the Labour Friends of Israel.

A few weeks later, I was invited to appear on *Newsnight*. I had stopped answering most requests for interviews because I was becoming exhausted. But I made an exception for *Newsnight* because I respected the programme. Putting everything else on hold, I got straight into the car the BBC had sent, arriving at the studios dead on 10.15 PM, and ready for the programme's 10.30 PM start. I was surprised, and not a little annoyed, when a smiling assistant producer came down to reception and said, 'Good evening, Mr Atwan. I am afraid we are not going to use you tonight.' I turned on my heel and walked out. Two nights later, exactly the same thing happened again. I arrived and the same producer appeared, this time looking sheepish. 'I'm sorry – ' she began.

'Why?' I blurted out.

'Because we have changed the format', she said, which remains as meaningless today as it seemed then. 'BBC1 wants you,' she added, by way of consolation.

'I know – everybody wants me,' I replied, trying to keep a smile on my face despite my fury. After all, it wasn't her fault. I got back into the car and headed back to Hammersmith. I vowed that I would never appear on

Newsnight again unless I had a full apology and, above all, an explanation. It was not until six months later that I discovered the real reason behind this chain of events. One day, a veteran correspondent from the *Newsnight* team came to see me in my office. Asking that I didn't reveal that it was he who told me, he first of all apologized for the way I had been treated. He then explained that my appearance had been cancelled at the last minute the first time around because the Israeli Prime Minister Ehud Barak had been invited to participate in the same debate. On the second occasion, it was because Benjamin Netanyahu would have been sitting next to me. 'The Israelis don't like you,' my contact said, 'because you speak so frankly and passionately and always make their man look inadequate. The Israeli embassy has an informal policy never to let anyone appear on a show with you.'

The reader might wonder why the BBC would have an Israeli – albeit a prime minister – discussing al-Qa'ida rather than someone who has not only met bin Laden, but has many years expertise on the subject. The reason, I believe, is the close relationship between the BBC and the British government, and the even closer one between the British government and Israel, which results in a pro-Israel, anti-Arab bias. At the end of 2005, I was invited to make a submission to the BBC 'Impartiality Commission' investigating this issue and was glad of the opportunity to contribute the observations I had made over the years. I pointed out that the BBC habitually offers Israelis a platform to express their opinions and analysis of Arab affairs, Iraq, the so-called 'war on terror', and related strategic issues while the opinions of Arab commentators are sought less frequently. As a result, Israeli commentators are presented as unchallengeable authorities on Middle Eastern politics.

Over a period of time, this has a distorting effect and contemporary history is rewritten as it happens. For much of the BBC's audience, the corporation is their main source of information and education and they trust it implicitly. It is therefore imperative that not only the news but the historical and political context of current affairs are presented clearly and objectively. With regard to the Palestinian–Israeli conflict this is neglected.

I have been told by BBC staff that the Israeli embassy in London regularly sends ideas for stories to producers of the *Today* radio programme (an influential BBC Radio 4 daily news and analysis broadcast) and that these are often picked up. Staff in Jerusalem then work on them, which in some cases results in reporters adopting a passive role rather than the proactive investigative approach that is the backbone of good journalism.

The Israelis concentrate on inputting to high-profile, peak-time programmes like *Today* for obvious reasons. On the rare occasion that a programme examining the Palestinian perspective is aired it is usually off-peak. Even world-renowned Palestinian intellectuals like the late Edward Said get sidelined. I remember in 2003, the BBC had an excellent profile of Said but chose to show it on the small-audience channel, BBC4, and late in the evening. On the other hand, a documentary like *The Last Stand,* shown on Thursday 10 November 2005 and dealing with the Israeli settlers' withdrawal from Gaza, was at 9 PM on BBC2, a prime slot. This was an emotive and one-sided account of this historic event and I am sure viewers' approach to the settlers – who were portrayed as victims and heroes – would have been different had they been in possession of the full historical, legal and political facts.

The most obvious historical comparison is with Apartheid South Africa. Here we had an undemocratic regime overseen by the minority and committed to oppressing, humiliating, exploiting and degrading the indigenous population. We know about this because of excellent media coverage of the abhorrent situation under the Apartheid regime, and the BBC was no exception. When an atrocity was committed against the black people of South Africa we did not witness a rush to provide 'balance' in the form of an Afrikaner carefully explaining his agenda. The BBC was rightly appalled and did not shy away from broadcasting the truth in terms that invited condemnation.

Consideration of the language employed in BBC coverage of the current conflict is revealing. At the beginning of the Second Intifada the Occupied Territories became 'disputed' territories, illegal settlements became 'neighbourhoods' and Palestinian deaths were related in numbers while the humanity of dead Israelis was often marked by giving their names.

Greg Philo's report, *Bad News from Israel: Media Coverage of the Israeli/ Palestinian Conflict* (which the Right Honourable Clare Short described to me as 'saying it all, really'), has recorded numerous instances of how the choice of words distorts the viewer's interpretation of events. For example, 'dozens of Palestinians and Israelis have been killed in a relentless round of suicide bombings and Israeli counter-attacks'. The implication is that the beleaguered Israelis only employ violence when necessary for self-defence.

In BBC programmes and items about the history of terrorism in the Middle East the Zionist terror gangs are hardly ever mentioned. Yet these terrorist groups carried out many atrocities against the British during the Mandate: the Irgun gang blew up the King David Hotel in Jerusalem in 1946, for example, while it was being used as a base for the British secretariat, killing ninety-one and prompting the British government to put up a reward of £50,000 for information leading to the arrest of its fugitive leader. That leader was Menachem Begin who would become Israeli Prime Minister from 1977 to 1982. Nor was Begin the only leader who emerged from a background in terror: Yitsak Shamir (Prime Minister in 1983 and 1984 and again in 1986–92) headed the Stern Gang; Yitsak Rabin (1974–6) and Ariel Sharon (2001–6) were both part of the shady paramilitary group, Haganah. All the Israeli terror groups mentioned perpetrated massacres of unarmed Palestinian villagers which I have discussed in the earlier part of this book.

I, and many others, believe that the 'Zionist lobby' exerts considerable influence on the BBC's editorial policy and programming via the government which, in turn, funds the BBC. The Labour Friends of Israel (LFI) is probably the most influential of several such organizations. This was the first group Tony Blair joined when he entered parliament in 1983 and membership is considered essential as a stepping stone to a ministerial position. The LFI seeks to ensure that Labour policy will remain pro-Israeli and members are regularly consulted on matters relating to the Middle East. Their financial contribution to the party cannot be ignored. According to the BBC, on 7 September 2007, Lord Sainsbury had already given more than £16m and a £2m loan. Michael Levy, duly ennobled by a grateful Tony Blair and retained as 'special envoy to the Middle East', was so successful in his role as Labour Party fundraiser that he was known as 'Lord Cashpoint' until he was arrested and questioned by police in the 2007 'cash for honours' scandal. Given that he has businesses and a home in Israel and that his son Daniel used to work for the former Justice Minister of Israel, Yossi Beilin, it seems unlikely that he could have a wholly impartial perspective on the Palestinian question.

Al-Jazeera

For several years, *al-Quds al-Arabi* stood more or less alone as the vanguard of an independent Arab media; al-Jazeera television, which was to change the landscape of Arabic broadcasting, did not appear until 1996 and its genesis has all the elements of a soap opera: opportunism, wealth, heroic dedication to a cause (in this case truth) and an antagonist bent on its destruction.

In 1994, the BBC announced the launch of an Arabic-language television channel as part of the World Service. Naturally this generated excitement in the Arab world: American channels such as CNN already transmitted to the region but only a minority of Arabs speak English. The fledgling BBC Arabic channel advertised for staff in London and I was concerned that some of my staff might be tempted to leave our impoverished paper for the glamorous world of broadcasting. One day, I received a visit from two smartly dressed women, who looked out of place in our rundown offices, with the paper peeling off the walls and watermarks all over the carpets underneath the leaking roof. They introduced themselves as Portia and Victoria. Victoria did most of the talking. 'Have you heard of the BBC Arabic channel?' she asked.

'Yes,' I said. 'It's great idea. The BBC is highly respected in the Arab world.'

'Why don't you apply for the job of editor-in-chief?' Victoria asked abruptly. I was flummoxed. 'Er, no thank you,' I mumbled.

'Is it the salary?' Victoria persisted. 'We have been told we can negotiate upwards.'

'Exactly who are you?' I asked, still confused.

'Consultants,' said Portia.

'We've heard your paper is in financial trouble,' said Victoria. 'Now might be a wise time for that strategic move.'

'No.' I was resolute. 'It is true our ship is sinking but I am the captain; I either sink with the ship or survive with it. I am honoured to have been asked, however, so please thank your employers.'

Thank God neither I nor any of my staff were tempted to join this venture, because it was over within two years. The project had been set up in conjunction with Rome-based Orbit, a subsidiary of Saudi conglomerate

Mawarid. The channel was broadcast across the Middle East and North Africa, viewed with approval by its Saudi sponsors at first, but soon with increasing alarm. The Saudi media industry has no concept of editorial freedom and when well-known London-based Saudi dissidents such as Dr Muhammad al-Massari and Dr Saad al-Faghi began to appear on their screens openly criticizing the Saudi royal family, it was too much to bear. Charging their BBC production partners with 'cultural insensitivity', Orbit tried to influence production, personnel and editorial decisions. When a *Panorama* programme about the parlous state of the Saudi 'judicial' system and its liberal application of the death penalty was dubbed into Arabic and broadcast throughout the region, Orbit decided to end the venture and pulled the plug on the infant station in April 1996.

Now the staff that the BBC had trained at great expense and to a high standard in 1994 were made redundant and there were few job opportunities for them in Arabic-speaking broadcasting. Enter the canny Emir of Qatar, Sheikh Hamad bin Khalifa al-Thani, who scooped them up to people his dream – al-Jazeera television, based in Doha. The new station was (and is) funded by the emir; he invested $150 million setting it up and continues to pay an annual grant on an *ad hoc* basis to cover any shortfalls in advertising and subscription revenues.

At the time of writing al-Jazeera boasts some 50 million viewers worldwide, having steadily gained popularity with its fearless take on global news and Middle Eastern politics. For the first time truthful debate became possible, as both sides of any issue were voiced, in Arabic and at home. Allowing the Israeli point of view airtime was a bold new step and initially the Arab masses were outraged and the station was criticized by some Arab newspapers, but the necessity for full and fair debate was generally understood and this is now the norm. Only the Saudis remained unconvinced and they banned al-Jazeera from opening an office in the kingdom and from covering the *Hajj* (pilgrimage). Ironically, when the Saudis launched their own satellite TV channel, al-Arabiya, they broadcast in-depth interviews with Israeli leaders and journalists.

Al-Jazeera dealt with all the subjects that had been taboo for decades: human rights, torture, repression, the ill treatment of foreign workers in the Gulf, the squandering of billions by the rulers while their people starved, gender issues and the call for democracy and reform. The quality of broadcasting was highly professional and everyone took notice, including the Americans.

At first, the US favoured and commended al-Jazeera, imagining that a free Arab voice would speak in favour of the American way of life, its global policies and ambitions. Hardly a week went by without an article in an American publication about the new Arab media sensation. In 1999, the *New York Times* columnist Thomas Friedman described al-Jazeera as 'the freest, most widely watched TV network in the Arab world'. Another US journalist, John F. Burns, described it as 'hard-hitting' and praised its audacity. The tide turned during the Second Intifada which broke out on 28 September 2000, after the then Israeli opposition leader, Ariel Sharon, walked into the compound of al-Aqsa mosque in East Jerusalem – the third holiest site in Islam – accompanied by a small army of police and declared 'Jewish sovereignty' over it. Al-Jazeera's coverage sympathized with the unarmed Palestinians who fought Israeli tanks and guns with stones and, in the case of suicide missions, their own lives. This was at odds with the mainstream media in the US which sought, as always, to portray the Israelis as defending themselves against 'terrorists'.

The station further annoyed the Americans when it broadcast a statement by Osama bin Laden on 7 October 2001, shortly after the US attacks on Tora Bora in retaliation for 9/11. Other tapes by bin Laden and Sulaiman Abu Ghaith (his spokesman) followed, justifying the 9/11 attacks on New York and Washington which al-Jazeera duly broadcast. Now the US branded al-Jazeera a mouthpiece for al-Qa'ida propaganda – unlike big US networks like CNN and ABC which also broadcast excerpts of the video tapes, which they had bought or otherwise procured from al-Jazeera. In fact, bin Laden chose the channel for its independence, just as he had chosen my paper for his written communiqués before, and when al-Jazeera started to edit bin Laden's speeches (perhaps under pressure from the US), al-Qa'ida switched to the internet where they had already built up a significant presence.

With the invasion of Iraq in 2003, al-Jazeera broadcast a number of overt criticisms of US policy in the region. I myself was interviewed on the channel, just before the invasion, and stated that it was going to be a catastrophe which would destabilize the entire region for years to come. I predicted that the US would win the superficial 'war' easily because the insurgents would hold back and wait to wage a war of attrition long after the American victory shouts had died down. All of this has come true yet the channel was branded 'anti-American'.

Al-Jazeera broadcasts the reality of war, including the civilian deaths and the humanitarian nightmares it produces. When it screened images of civilian casualties in Fallujah in April 2004, Donald Rumsfeld described their reporting as, 'vicious, inaccurate and inexcusable'. Al-Jazeera's response was simple: 'the pictures do not lie'. The US do not like journalists to be too graphic where death is concerned. I remember watching Peter Arnett (a journalist whom I admire) on CNN, in 1991, the Baghdad sky behind him ablaze, reporting that the bombardment was like the firework display on 'the 4 July in Washington'.

Increasingly affronted by the channel the US and its allies started targeting al-Jazeera personnel directly, presumably intending to issue warnings to their editorial decision-makers. In December 2001, al-Jazeera cameraman Sami al-Hajj was detained in Pakistan, arrested as an 'enemy combatant' and dispatched to Guantanamo where he is still incarcerated without a single charge having been brought against him. Despite al-Jazeera having given the US military the coordinates of its Kabul office to avoid being inadvertently attacked, the building was destroyed by an American bomb in November 2001. Its Baghdad office was also hit as the invasion began in March 2003, killing correspondent Tariq Ayoub outright. Another high-profile reporter, Taysir Allouni, somehow escaped the bombing of the Baghdad office and, suffering from a heart condition, returned to rest at his home in Granada. In September 2003, he found himself under arrest and in 2005 received a seven-year prison sentence from the Spanish Supreme Court for 'aiding al-Qa'ida'.

David Blunkett, the UK's former Home Secretary, told Channel 4's *Dispatches* in October 2006 that during the 2003 invasion of Iraq he suggested to Tony Blair that UK pilots should bomb al-Jazeera's television transmitter in Baghdad, lending weight to the implications that the bombings were not an accident. In November 2005, the *Daily Mirror* published a leaked document from 10 Downing Street that purported to minute a discussion between Tony Blair and George W. Bush in which the latter proposed bombing al-Jazeera headquarters in Doha when the battle for Fallujah was at its height in April 2004. Presumably, Prime Minister Blair managed to talk his ally around, reminding him that Qatar is a friend in the region.

In February 2004, the US administration decided to counter al-Jazeera with its own Washington-based Arabic-language channel, at a cost of $62 million per year. Named *al-Hurra* (the Free One) – apparently without a hint of irony – the radio and television stations produced such bare-faced pro-American propaganda that they swiftly lost any credibility they might have enjoyed in the Arab world. In an attempt to redress the balance the channel allegedly paid what the *Financial Times* described as 'unusually large'[1] fees to certain Arab journalists, left-wing intellectuals and nationalists to contribute to its schedule. The *al-Hurra* project had further unintentional ramifications when the level of Arab mistrust generated by this expensive PR exercise spread indiscriminately to include all American media outlets.

Al-Jazeera launched an ambitious new English-language station in November 2006, broadcast from London, Washington, New York and Qatar. The project was immediately targeted by the American right, whose machinations against the channel resulted in the term 'Jazeeragate'. Joanne Levine, executive producer of programming in the US operation, reported that Arab personnel were subject to racism and discrimination, that the company was unable to get liability insurance, and that one of the big five US accounting firms, as well as a major international bank, refused their business in Washington even though they work for them in Doha. The conservative United American Committee posted a letter on its website for 'concerned citizens' to copy and send to the local cable networks, urging them not to carry al-Jazeera. Among the reasons cited were that the channel would broadcast 'Islamist propaganda' and be a 'hi-tech *madrassa*'. It remains to be seen how the fledgling channel will fare in the face of such determined opposition.

Al-Jazeera has turned the world of Arab broadcasting upside down, as Hosni Mubarak ruefully observed when visiting its headquarters in Doha. He noted how small the prefabricated premises were compared with those occupied by Egyptian National Broadcasting. According to Wadah Khanfar,

---

1.   Guy Dynmore, 'Troubled TV Network Draws Fire', *Financial Times* (6 Nov. 2005).

who became head of al-Jazeera in 2006, he added, 'Here you have a little matchbox but what enormous fires it has ignited around the world.'

A Well-Known Face

It is largely due to my frequent appearances on al-Jazeera (the Arab version) that I have become a well-known face in the Arab world. My appearances, and my reputation for speaking my mind, are popular with the majority of the station's 50 million viewers but not always, it seems, with the US and its allies. In 2003, I was invited to Doha as a studio guest to comment on the invasion of Iraq. I had been there five days, more or less constantly on screen, and had agreed to stay a little longer even though I had a paper to run back in London. The US was monitoring the station's output and started accusing them of an anti-American bias in their coverage. In an endeavour to be even-handed, al-Jazeera decided to broadcast an interview with the then Secretary of State, Colin Powell, who came up with a lively performance designed to win Arab hearts and minds. He promised that the war was not against Arabs or Muslims but only to oust Saddam, and that a just solution to the Arab–Israeli conflict would be top of the US agenda once the war was over. Following the interview, I was asked to comment and I expressed my scepticism, reminding viewers that we had heard this particular American line before – from George Bush's father, the last time the US attacked Saddam Hussein – and that the Palestinians were still as far from peace and justice as ever. The phone rang in the controller's office as I was on my way out and I heard an American voice complaining that 'Atwan sabotaged Powell's goodwill effort'. Some significant threats were made, it seems, because twenty minutes later a production assistant came into the canteen where I was having a coffee and asked me when I would be leaving for London. Al-Jazeera didn't contact me for several months after this and I heard from an insider that they received hundreds of phone calls and emails from disgruntled viewers asking why I wasn't on any more and accusing them of silencing me. Sensing that they were creating something of a crisis by my absence, they decided it was better to let me speak and things went back to normal.

The Palestinian author Said Aburish often relates the story of how we were walking down a street in Nice together when I was spotted by two North African workers who were labouring at the bottom of a cavernous hole. Much to Aburish's delight, the two clambered to the top and jumped out just to hug me and shake my hand. Public exposure has its downside too; after the attacks of 7 July 2005 in London, I was interviewed on Sky News, BBC and ITV, and pointed out that Tony Blair had made Britain a target for al-Qa'ida by supporting George Bush in the invasion of Iraq. Walking home afterwards, I was recognized by a group of teenagers who crossed the road and surrounded me in an intimidating manner. Fortunately, they only spat in my face before leaving me alone, shaken but unharmed.

6

Culture Shock

I have already written about my move to London from a professional point of view; it also affected me deeply on a personal level. When I arrived in March 1978, I had never been to a European country before and my expectations of Western culture were based largely on the handful of US television dramas I had watched in the Saudi desert and letters I had received from Bakir Oweda. Bakir was a Palestinian friend from my days at al-Balah in Tripoli; like me, he was born in Gaza but now resided in the British capital. 'London is fantastic,' he wrote. 'This is freedom! You have to come.' After Saudi Arabia the notion of 'freedom' was at once compelling and daunting.

I had culture shock the minute I walked through the arrivals gate at Heathrow with my suitcases piled precariously on a trolley. An explosion of colour after the monochrome monotony of Saudi Arabia, scores of different languages as passengers were greeted by people from all over the world, tannoy announcements in English, illuminated shops and cafés and bars ... my eyes travelled along the row of cards held up by taxi drivers and chauffeurs and, finding my name, looked at the bearer. The uncovered face of a pretty young blonde woman! Unthinkable in the culture I had left just hours before. Somewhat flustered, I introduced myself and discovered that my driver's name was Tanya. 'Can I help you with your luggage, Sir?'

she asked. I didn't trust anyone but me to keep the wobbly pile of cases in place and put a protective hand on top of it. 'I can take it to Barking,' I said. There is no 'P' in Arabic and I continued to replace every P in the English language with B for years to come, often to the great amusement of my English friends. To her credit Tanya didn't flinch but smiled courteously. 'We need level 3,' she said.

I walked sheepishly behind Tanya to the car park, pushing my trolley and trying – unsuccessfully – to avoid taking too much notice of her shapely figure encased in a short (by my standards) skirt and jacket. Wrestling with overwhelming shyness I found myself unable to speak to this exotic native as I sat in the back of the gleaming *al-Sharq al-Awsat* limousine that Tanya effortlessly piloted. And to think that in Saudi Arabia women are not permitted to drive at all!

Though I could get by on a basic level, and indeed had been considered quite an expert on the subject among my peers in Egypt and Saudi Arabia, my English was not really up to a proper conversation. I had learned what little I knew by reading and from my UNWRA teacher in Deir al-Balah refugee camp. A Palestinian refugee himself, Mr Azzat had managed to beat all his own mistakes into us and to this day I hold him responsible for the ones I make in my adopted language. Instead of 'clothes' I still say 'clothe-is', for 'comfortable', 'comfotbul' and so on. Nearly thirty years on, I know full well that I am mispronouncing these words but am still afraid to say them correctly, expecting Mr Azzat to jump out of my subconscious with his stick if I dare to vary his version of the English language.

No Sex Please, We're British

Tanya deposited me outside the apartment block in Marble Arch that was to be my home for the next few months. The flat was provided by the paper and I had two room-mates, Ahmed and Saad. Ahmed was a senior on the paper in his forties. He was constantly grooming himself in the mirror, either slicking back his hair or trimming his moustache. With his expensive suits and aftershave, he seemed desperate to make the most of his last few weeks of freedom before his wife arrived. Saad was a short, Lebanese Muslim who spent most of his spare time reading the Qur'an and praying.

In his mid-twenties, he was shy and blushed to the roots of his hair if he had to speak to a woman. He fretted about those 'Western angels', convinced they were all trying to corrupt him. The truth is that, like all of us, he was sexually frustrated. Indeed, all we had in common was an obsession with those 'loose' Western women we had heard so much about but who were disappointingly thin on the ground in reality. In addition to our ludicrous preconceptions, we were astonishingly naive, which actually made us prime targets for a cynical *femme fatale* as Ahmed was to discover one afternoon when he brought home a stranger he had just met in the street. 'This is my girlfriend,' he told us in Arabic. 'Please, my friends, could you leave for a few hours so we can be alone?'

Saad and I were forced to walk the chilly grey London streets with our hands dug deep in our overcoat pockets. We wandered aimlessly around Hyde Park, staring at the ducks bobbing among sludgy bubbles, empty crisp packets and sweet wrappers on the Serpentine. I had been working on an article and was annoyed at Ahmed's selfishness, I was also irked that, married as he was, he had managed to find a girlfriend while I was an eligible bachelor and had hardly talked to a woman since my arrival in the country. Saad passed the time by reciting Qur'anic verses between chattering teeth.

Two hours later we returned to find Ahmed sitting dejected and alone on the sofa. 'It didn't work out,' he said.

'Why not?' I asked. 'What do you mean?'

'I don't think she liked me,' said Ahmed. 'She only stayed a few minutes.' Saad didn't enter the conversation but stood by the electric fire warming up and pretending not to be listening. 'I think I moved too fast,' Ahmed continued. 'I tried to kiss her and she jumped up and left.'

'Well, how long have you known her?' I asked.

'I only just met her,' Ahmed replied. 'I went out to buy the papers and she started talking to me. She invited herself in for a coffee – ' A look of understanding suddenly flashed across his face. He picked up his jacket and felt for his wallet. 'Damn it,' he said. 'It's not here. She must have been a thief!'

'No, my friend!' Saad couldn't restrain himself. 'She was a prostitute!' he trumpeted unable to conceal his sense of moral triumph.

Ahmed leapt to his feet and stormed off to his room, slamming the door behind him. Immature as we were, Saad and I spent the next half hour whispering and sniggering, possessed by *schadenfreude* and only stopping when Saad remembered it was time for evening prayer.

Bakir Oweda, recently divorced, had made me promise that I would call him as soon as I had a day off. He wanted to show me 'his' London and we were soon reunited; he arrived in his Mazda one Saturday and took me on a sightseeing tour which culminated in a visit to the heart of British government in Whitehall. As we drove slowly past the Ministry of Defence and the Foreign Office I reflected on the inordinate power this small collection of buildings housed and on all the problems in the world that had had their genesis here. Not least those of my own country.

Later we walked in Trafalgar Square where I was intrigued by the sheer number of pigeons and how well they were treated by the people there, who fed them for no apparent reason other than to have their photograph taken with them. In Gaza my mother had fattened them up for food and just one bird would be a feast; this multitude could have fed the entire starving Palestinian refugee population for weeks. Our choice of restaurant, Pizza on the Park, was determined by nostalgia for our shared past – Libya having been occupied by the Italian fascists from 1934 to 1947, Tripoli boasts some excellent pizza restaurants, most of which Bakir and I had visited together. We both agreed that the 'Gaddafi' (topped with olives and fiery chillies) was infinitely superior to anything on the menu here.

Bakir suggested we visit a club, my first taste of Western nightlife. We slouched against the wall, observing how our Western counterparts sauntered up to girls and asked them to dance and how they invariably said 'yes'. 'You have a go, Abdel Bari,' Bakir urged. I later discovered that he wanted to use me like miners use canaries: if I failed to survive the unknown, he would not venture there himself. Most of the girls there terrified me, to be honest, and I already had my doubts about the much-hyped Western female's availability. Worried that if I asked for a dance, I would be refused and my confidence and pride would be irretrievably damaged, I resisted Bakir's promptings for more than an hour. Then I spotted a girl who seemed rather lonely and watched her discreetly for a while. Nobody asked her to dance and all her friends had deserted her; she was a little plump and seemed relatively approachable. I took a deep breath and walked over. She looked me up and down and before I had even opened my mouth, shook her head firmly and looked the other way. Mortifying.

In those early days I struggled with my, admittedly stereotyped, impression of Western women who conducted themselves, and dressed, so differently from the women I had encountered in the Middle East. Later I would come to appreciate the opportunity to work and socialize with the opposite sex on an equal footing and have long counted several women among my closest, and most trustworthy, friends and colleagues.

It seemed to me that the British were obsessed with sex and this was a big part of the culture shock I was experiencing. Everywhere I went, advertisements, music, television shows and banter among workers were of a sexual nature. I was therefore surprised by the title of a popular West End play at that time, *No Sex Please, We're British* and by the subsequent discovery that the British were innately quite prudish, and found sex at once shocking and funny, hence the popularity of the *double-entendre* among their comedians – I am thinking of Les Dawson, Frankie Howerd and the 'Carry On' films.

In the Marble Arch area, phone booths were plastered with homemade advertisements for 'encounters by telephone'; though I am sure these were designed to create encounters of a more sordid kind, I was not unfamiliar with the concept. The Saudis were pioneers in a peculiar form of telephone courtship whereby a man dials a random number and, if he's lucky, a female voice answers the phone. Provided there is no interruption from a father or brother the conversation can progress (one thing they won't be talking about is the weather because it is always the same in Saudi Arabia, boiling hot). They'll chat about songs, pop stars and so on until one of them plucks up the courage to be a little more personal. The conversation can sometimes become risqué since the chances of being discovered are small and both parties are strangers. Sometimes a romance develops, possibly an engagement. A cousin of mine who lives in Saudi Arabia fell in love with a gorgeous voice and proposed to the girl over the phone. They married and are still together, despite the objections of his family who discovered, when they met her on his behalf, that she was a great deal older than him (which they considered a disadvantage). Most people in Saudi Arabia have a tale to tell about this phenomenon.

The more I discovered about Britain, the greater the gap I perceived between the values of our Arab society and Western norms. I found it incredible, for example, that couples lived together and had children without being married or that they would accept such a precarious situation and call it freedom. I felt backward in some ways but morally outraged in others; this confusion and imbalance sometimes made my new life difficult and characterized my experience in London for several years.

Stereotypes

I used to enjoy travelling by bus, especially sitting at the front on the top of a double-decker from where I had a bird's eye view. In the Arab world when you get on a bus it is customary to greet your fellow passengers but when I said, 'Good morning' to the occupants of the number 11 the first time I got on board I met only steely stares and silence.

In the late 1970s, Londoners had firm ideas about all foreigners and if you were a Palestinian you were considered likely to be a guerrilla or a plane-hijacker. Even among my fellow journalists, my entry to a press conference or reception was often met with worried looks (an uncomfortable experience that I was to endure again in the aftermath of 9/11 and the London bombs in July 2005). After a few months of this I was so irritated that, at a Foreign Office press briefing one morning, I prefaced my question to the Minister thus: 'Abdel Bari Atwan, Palestinian and unarmed', which was greeted with laughter by my colleagues and civil servants alike and broke the ice at least.

Racism was rife in the capital and with my Afro hair and dark skin I was a frequent target. My first such experience was on a bus when the conductor threw me off for not having the correct money, even though a fellow passenger offered to change my five-pound note. Initially embarrassed because all eyes were on me, I was subsequently overwhelmed by anger. I wrestled with the instinct to resist and realized that by giving way to aggression I might jeopardize my future in the country; I quietly got up and left with as much dignity as I could muster.

I had a relative who was making a lot of money in Saudi Arabia; he had bought himself a flat in one of London's most expensive residential areas – St John's Wood – and a brand new Daimler that he offered to lend me while he was away working. I started driving the car around town, but was frequently pulled over by the police. Sometimes I was only asked for ID but on two occasions I was required to empty my pockets and be searched. This was the time of the infamous stop-and-search law, which permitted the police to do just that, and even arrest anyone they chose to, purely on the basis of suspicion that they might commit a crime. Clearly I was a prime target for a racist policeman who would assume I was a thief, so I put the Daimler back in the garage and bought myself a battered Ford Fiesta instead. I didn't get stopped again.

The SUS laws were frequently used against young black men in inner-city ghettos, contributing to a climate of resentment and anger that resulted in palpable tension between the black population and the police. I wasn't surprised when riots broke out all over the country in cities with black ghettos – Bristol's St Paul's was the first to erupt on 2 April 1980 Brixton, London, and Toxteth, Liverpool followed in 1981. The British media and the tabloids in particular perpetuated, even provoked, a climate of xeno-phobia which made life difficult for all minorities, including Arabs, living in London.

Chelsea Makeover

Another Palestinian friend, Adel Bishtawi, had a smart flat in Old Church Street, Chelsea – an exciting, fashionable area which was a magnet for all things strange and unusual in London in the late 1970s. At the time, Adel was married to Kathy Evans, a *Guardian* journalist, and had been in London for many years; he was very 'Westernized' and urbane and I often sought his advice on the unwritten codes that underpinned British society. I stayed with Adel temporarily when I moved on from the Marble Arch apartment and was looking for a place of my own. One day I was complaining about how I had been refused entry into the Hilton hotel on Park Lane where I wanted to observe the well-heeled at play. Adel started laughing and led me by the elbow to the ornate gilded mirror above his fireplace: 'Just look at yourself, Abdel Bari,' he said, chidingly. 'You are wearing third-world clothes in a first-world country. Look at those trousers,' I peered down at the shiny, ill-fitting fabric that encased my skinny legs, stopping short of my shoes by several centimetres. 'And why do you insist on wearing that appalling leather jacket which makes you look like a thug?' he asked. I was hurt but tried to be objective.

Adel continued his inspection and now he patted the thick frizz of hair that shot out in all directions around my head. 'And as for this – ' he began. This was too much.

'It's an Afro!' I objected with passion. 'It's fashionable'

'It might have been ten years ago,' he replied. 'But even so, it's more umbrella than Afro.' I capitulated, since Adel himself seemed to be perfectly acceptable to the British public.

He took me to his own hairdresser, alarmingly described outside as a 'unisex' salon. As we entered, I noticed that all the hairdressers were female. This troubled me as the only woman who had ever touched my head, let alone washed my hair, was my mother. I allowed myself to be led to a washbasin and obeyed the instruction to put my head backwards over it before being abandoned for some minutes in this vulnerable position. Soon a good-looking woman wearing a low-cut top came over and began rinsing my hair with warm water and massaging my head. I found all this novel and enjoyable. 'Do you want conditioner?' the hairdresser asked. In the Middle East we used normal soap to wash our hair and olive oil to tame it but I nodded my consent. Several minutes more massage and pleasant scents followed and then I was placed in front of a mirror, and the hairdresser pulled lengths of springy frizz out this way and that as we discussed the style. She started snipping away and we chatted. 'Where do you come from?' she asked me. My English was still rudimentary and I misunderstood her question, replying, 'Saudi Arabia'. She talked about the situation in the Middle East and I was surprised by her knowledge of that complex political map (it was March 1978 and the Israelis had just invaded southern Lebanon, killing Palestinian refugees as they attempted to oust the PLO from their stronghold there). 'That bastard Menachem Begin is a terrorist,' I began, and carried on in a similar vein for several minutes, not paying much attention to what was going on around my head. When I did check the progress of my haircut in the mirror I looked like a badly shorn sheep and was dumbstruck. 'There we are, sir,' said the hairdresser, flicking at my neck and shoulders with a brush to get rid of stray hairs. As she moved around in front of me I noticed that she was wearing a gold Star of David on a chain around her neck. 'My family live in Israel,' she told me, removing the nylon cape that had been protecting my clothes. 'But I suppose we're all entitled to our point of view.'

Never again did I discuss politics with a hairdresser or visit a unisex salon. When my hair grew back I visited a traditional barber and have been with him ever since. He's a Greek Cypriot who talks a lot. I rarely open my mouth while he chatters on, telling me what bastards the Turks are. On each visit, I hear the same stories but I made a decision long ago to say as little as possible in defence of my Muslim brothers for fear of another politically motivated shearing.

To complete my makeover, Adel took me shopping on Oxford Street. He more or less told me what to buy and I took home a suit, black shoes, a blazer, smart trousers, white shirts and ties. As I considered my new appearance in the mirror at home I remembered, with a pang, my child-hood self: my bare feet, the ill-fitting cast-off clothes I was given to wear, my tangled hair and sunburned skin. I decided to try out my new look on the doorman at the Park Lane Hilton, and approached the entrance in that brisk manner I have noticed English men adopt when they expect no truck from any underlings, assertively tightening the knot on my tie. He didn't give me a second glance as he opened the door and welcomed me in. 'Good evening, sir.'

I had been spending quite a lot of time down the Kings Road and was particularly fascinated by the punks who congregated there. Since they had established their own sub-culture, I felt less out of place among the mohican hair-dos and safety pins than I did in many mainstream London venues and the punks hardly gave an alienated Palestinian a second glance. Shortly after my makeover, Adel and I went into a smoky punk pub I'd often been to before, to have a soft drink, chat and people watch.

After a while we noticed that the barmaid, who was called Fairy Snow, and three male customers were discussing us and looking our way. Fairy Snow lifted up the hatch in the bar and came over to us smoking a roll-up, wearing laddered stockings, safety pins through her nose, and a bracelet made of barbed wire which had cut her arm. Nowadays, they'd have closed the pub down for health and safety reasons but at that time no one had even thought of such matters. Though I'd been in the pub several times and had even had a conversation with Fairy Snow she obviously didn't recognize me and asked us if we were looking for something. We assured her that, no, we were not, and that we were just out for a drink. Then she asked us, 'Aren't you cops?'

'Of course not,' we laughed.

'Then why are you here?' Fairy Snow persisted. 'Do you want to score?'

'What do you mean, score?' I asked. Fairy Snow looked at me as if I were an idiot. 'Score – you know, a joint, some blues,' she said. This was an unknown language as far as I was concerned. 'Oh, no, definitely not,' Adel said, mouthing the Arabic word for 'drugs' to me behind his hand. 'Thank you,' he added, politely.

'Listen,' said Fairy Snow, 'if you're not the police and you don't want to score, why the hell are you here? Please get out and leave us alone. At least undercover detectives give us a bit of a laugh but you're just bad for business with your square clothes and ties.' Adel's makeover had made me fit for the Hilton but an object of suspicion in Chelsea's World's End where I once used to mingle unnoticed.

Connections

In 1979 I moved into a rented flat in Holland Park, living on my own for the first time in my life. It was a novelty to do exactly as I pleased in the domestic environment and for the first few weeks I revelled in throwing my newspapers and clothes on the floor and letting the washing up form precarious stacks in the sink. But big cities can be lonely places and I soon missed having a friendly face around when I got home from work. I was puzzled by the lack of communication between neighbours. In Arab countries you are constantly besieged by your neighbours: they observe your comings and goings and are always 'popping in', often bearing a plate of something delicious they've just cooked. The benefits of this informal social support network are many: the old and sick need never be alone and offers of help abound.

As time went on, I had the strangest feeling that my opposite neighbour was watching me through a spy-hole in the door whenever I came home from work. After many months of this my curiosity got the better of me and I went up to the spy-hole. 'Good evening,' I said, 'I am your neighbour and I would like to meet you. Can I invite you in for a cup of coffee?' After an embarrassed silence, during which I didn't budge but kept smiling encouragingly, a young woman opened the door. Once we both got over our initial awkwardness and shyness, Carol – who worked at the Bank of England – and I became quite good friends. I even harboured some romantic hopes about our relationship and was disappointed when she moved out; especially as her successor was a Welsh lay nun who displayed none of Carol's reserve and would knock on my door at any time of the day or night to tell me about the latest goings-on her church, always staying longer than was comfortable. Nevertheless I resolutely continued my campaign of neighbourliness, greeting my fellow residents cheerfully whenever I met them, regardless of their indifference, and gradually a new culture evolved in our block.

I am still not entirely used to the physical reserve between the British, who greet even an old friend with a handshake. It has changed a little now but is still different from the way Arabs meet with bear hugs and several kisses. It used to be two kisses but then Yasser Arafat started a brand new culture, kissing everybody at least three times. This was acceptable with other Arabs but foreign leaders found it alarming. I several times witnessed the amusing spectacle of a European or American dignitary extending a hand to Arafat only to be swept into a rib-cracking embrace accompanied by smacking kisses on both cheeks which they tried, in vain, to evade.

If I had few opportunities to meet British people socially I had even fewer at work. *Al-Sharq al-Awsat*'s offices were in Gough Square, just off Fleet Street. On the surface, the organization was Westernized, in that we had all the latest technology at our disposal and observed the same kind of daily schedule as any other big newspaper on Fleet Street, but underneath it remained an Arab operation characterized by editorial interference from the owners, slavishness to social hierarchies, backstabbing and nepotism.

It was also a segregated working environment. There were two blocks, one for the editorial departments which were exclusively Arab and male, and the other for the administration which was almost entirely British and female. I invented a rich variety of pretexts to go to the administration side and meet the women there, who were young and good fun. The accountant was called Stephanie and she was outspoken and witty, given to making snide observations about our fellow workers. She wore metal glasses perched on the end of her nose, was quite open about her desire to find a mate and told me about the 'singles' holidays she went on.

One day, I was surprised when Stephanie paid me a compliment. I was signing for my pay cheque and she said, 'You have really beautiful fingers.' I kept this to myself until I could consult Adel who diagnosed 'romantic intentions'. I found this hard to believe but over the next two months Stephanie and I had many pleasant conversations and I decided that I would ask her to come out for dinner with me. It took me another couple of weeks to pluck up the courage but when I went to find her, she was sitting holding hands with a young Englishman who worked in the photo library. She had solved her 'lonely heart' problem and I felt inexplicably relieved.

I made some good friends among the editorial staff. Like most young Arab men, I considered it normal to work and socialize in an exclusively male environment. My companions fell into several categories but could be summarized thus: the intellectuals and the 'bachelors'. Dr Nabil Ayyad was chief among the intellectuals, with a missionary zeal for converting me to high-brow pursuits. He decided to take me to the opera where I spent the first part of the performance shielding my ears against the deafening volume and asking him to explain what was going on which put him in an embarrassing situation with his fellow opera aficionados who glared at me, saying 'Shhh!' In the interval I made my excuses, urging him to stay if he was really enjoying it which he claimed was the case, though I had my doubts.

The 'bachelors', consisting of Eyad abu-Shakra, Hafiz al-Khabbani, Osman al-Omir and myself, had committed ourselves to celibacy and followed a relaxed agenda which consisted largely of picnics in Hyde Park and small, male-only parties in each other's flats where we would dance and sing along to our favourite Arab records and imagine we were back in the Middle East while London's double-decker buses and black cabs glided past outside the window.

One day, Eyad Abu-Shakra came into the office brandishing the *Evening Standard* whose headline concerned a newly established nudist beach in Brighton. This was a cause of controversy both in Brighton and nationally and I decided to write an article about it. Coming from our culture where modesty is so important we found it hard to believe that people would mix on a beach wearing no clothes. The next weekend 'the bachelors' set off to investigate.

When we found the nudist beach we realized it was full of gay men which, I have to confess, was something of a disappointment. We parked ourselves down on the stones, loosening our ties because it was a hot day but remaining fully clothed, even down to our shoes and socks. We started to get some hostile looks and understood that if we didn't take our clothes off too we weren't welcome, a dilemma we hadn't anticipated. Unseen hands threw pebbles in our direction and we scrambled to our feet, heading for the dolphinarium instead.

Bridging the Gaps

In Saudi Arabia, the majority of stories in the print and broadcast media concerned either the 'good deeds' of the royal family or religion. When I first came to London I was overwhelmed by the variety and openness of the British press and applied myself to reading as much as was humanly possible, increasingly conscious of the gaps in my own knowledge, experience and skills.

But while I had a lot to learn, I hoped, too, to make a difference to the way British journalists covered the Middle East. It seemed to me that there was a general (though not exclusively) pro-Zionist bias in their coverage of the Arab–Israeli conflict, for example. With some notable exceptions including Peter Mansfield, David Hirst and Jonathan Dimbleby, all of whom produced incisive and authoritative writing on the subject, the majority of British journalists I met in the late 1970s and early 1980s weren't interested in properly researching Middle Eastern politics and got most of their foreign stories from agencies. I aimed to change this situation by engaging my British colleagues in debate and telling them about my experiences and point of view.

I sensed a general antipathy towards Arabs in the British establishment at this time. I felt side-lined, even shunned, at most professional and social events I attended. I was once invited to a party thrown by a *Daily Telegraph* journalist where I was the sole non-European guest; the only person interested in talking to me was the down-and-out accordion player brought in to entertain the guests from the street outside where he had been busking. Admittedly he was excellent company and told me many hair-raising tales about his experiences of homelessness.

My social alienation was greatly alleviated when I encountered an organization called CAABU (Council for the Advancement of Arab-British Understanding). CAABU had been established in July 1967 after the Six-Day War to promote better relations between Britain and the Arab world, and in particular 'to address the ignorance and prejudice that have all-too-often characterised relations' to quote their mission statement. Now, for the first time, I met British people, including several politicians and members of the judiciary, who were interested in our culture and sympathetic to our causes.

CAABU was based in Earls Court and I often attended their talks and discussions. Once more, I had much to learn, this time about the art of debate. In Arab countries disagreeing with someone's point of view usually ends in recrimination ('Zionist!'), insult ('Idiot!') or a fist fight. Here, for the first time, I learned that a polite exchange of ideas and views is possible and enjoyed listening to both sides of many questions.

Two Great Palestinians

Emblematic of the diaspora, whilst I was living in Europe I met two men whom I would count among the greatest twentieth-century Palestinians. The first was Edward Said whom I first encountered at CAABU in 1981. I was already aware of his outspoken, radical and brilliantly crafted writing through the pages of the *International Herald Tribune* and when he came to Earls Court to give a lecture I was in the front row, listening intently and greatly impressed by his confidence and style. He didn't use notes and peppered even the most serious observations with wit and humour. Afterwards I introduced myself and we immediately got on well. He was strikingly good-looking, charismatic, formidably intelligent but entertaining and very charming company.

When I became managing editor of *al-Majallah* magazine one of the first calls I made was to Edward Said asking him to write a column for us. 'With pleasure,' he replied. 'My rate is a dollar a word.' I was astonished, the Arab media had never encountered such a demand, however justified. 'What if the word is "the" or "a"?' I asked him.

'Big or small, my words are a dollar each,' he insisted. I recently read in *Private Eye* that Julie Burchill, the former Marxist music journalist, demanded £250 per word to pen a column for the *Sun* newspaper, while Tony Blair received £240,000 for a short speech in southern China where an observer (even in that remote region) commented that he had said 'nothing new'. We managed to afford a fortnightly column limited to a thousand words, each of them original, wise and well worth a dollar, and this was a great hit with our readers. Although he was completely bilingual, Edward Said wrote in English and insisted on personally approving the Arabic translations of his work.

In 1992 I went out for dinner with Edward Said after he had given a lecture at the School of Oriental and African Studies (SOAS) in London. He told me how delighted he was with *al-Quds al-Arabi* which was still in its infancy. 'We can't afford you!' I joked ruefully. Some time later I was surprised and touched when we received the first of several articles by him, offered free of charge in support of the newspaper.

Later that year a wealthy businessman who disliked me for political reasons sponsored a conference in London aimed at gathering together the most influential Palestinian media professionals to formulate a strategy for raising awareness of the Palestinian cause in the British press. Edward Said was asked to choose the speakers and I was very hurt and indignant when I was not invited. To add insult to injury, one of his assistants phoned me and asked me to cover the conference in the paper. So vulnerable to insults himself (he could be ridiculously petty) he seemed oblivious of the wound he inflicted on my pride and to my regret I avoided his company for some years. Fortunately we resumed our friendship before his untimely death on 25 September 2003, aged sixty-six. I was greatly saddened by Edward Said's passing and wrote a front page obituary for him, lamenting our differences and the loss of such a genius.

Around the same time as I first met Edward Said, I went to Paris to interview the poet, Mahmoud Darwish, for an *al-Majallah* cover story. Ever since his 1964 poem, *The Identity Card,* which is an angry affirmation that the Israeli occupiers would never stamp out our Palestinian identity, Darwish had voiced what all of us felt. His style was modern, lyrical and,

above all, passionate and he soon became the unofficial poet-laureate of
the Palestinians. Loved throughout the Arab world, he can fill a stadium
when he gives a reading.

I asked him why he had left his beloved homeland – at that time he
had been criticized by some, perhaps jealous of his talent and success, for
his voluntary exile in 1970 when he left first for Moscow and then Cairo.
He describes how his outspoken work and his political activism coupled
with his high profile and popularity made him a frequent target for Israeli
harassment; years of repeated arrests and imprisonment had worn him down
to such an extent that it became untenable for him to remain in his own
country. When I first met him, Darwish was a member of the PLO executive and he told me that he had written many of Yasser Arafat's speeches,
including his famous address to the United Nations on 13 November 1974
which ended with the often-repeated lines, 'Today I have come bearing an
olive branch and a freedom fighter's gun. Do not let the olive branch fall
from my hand.'

There was an immediate bond between us and I started travelling to Paris
to have dinner with him once a month. He is a very private man who does
not readily open himself to others yet we became close friends, speaking
to each other every day on the telephone, sharing jokes and gossip as well
as political thoughts and analysis. He inspired me in those early days and
his encouragement and critique of my writing informed the development
of my style. His conversation was never predictable and once he surprised
me by recalling the dilemma he found himself in, back in the 1960s, when
he started to fall in love with the female Israeli censor who checked the
contents of the papers he was editing, *al-Itihad* and *al-Jadid*!

Like me, Darwish refused to accept the Oslo Accords[1] which came
during the time when he was writing what is, in my opinion, his best
work, including *11 Planets* which appeared in 1992. In 1993 he wrote *A
Non-Lingustic Dispute with Imru al-Qays* which is a damning allegorical
critique of Oslo and resigned from his position on the PLO executive. The
loss of his PLO salary was an additional cause of stress in an already highly
stressful life. In 1997 I received a call to say that he had been hospitalized

---

1. For the full text of the Oslo Accords whereby the Israelis withdrew in exchange for
   cessation of hostilities and the Palestinian Authority was established see http://
   www.yale.edu/lawweb/avalon/mideast/isrplo.htm

with heart problems and was to undergo major surgery. I flew to Paris and was moved to tears to see this great man looking so frail and weak, on a life-support machine, with little drops of blood spattered on his hospital gown. When he came round he was delirious and begged me to take him away from the hospital, oblivious of the tubes that were stuck into his body; he was convinced that someone was trying to kill him. Strangely enough, he was in the same military hospital where Yasser Arafat would later die of a 'mystery illness' which I am certain was poisoning. Thank God, Darwish made a miraculous recovery and is now living in Ramallah, back in his beloved Palestine. Sadly, I rarely meet him nowadays but his poetry always takes me back to the place we are both from, geographically and spiritually.

I remember when Derek Walcott won the Nobel prize for literature in 1992, Darwish called me and asked me to bring his collected works and everything I could find that had been written about him when I next went to Paris. Within weeks he seemed to have absorbed the character and work of his peer. Perhaps he also wanted to know the secret of becoming a Nobel Laureate and it would delight the Arab world if he were made one.

Edward Said and Mahmoud Darwish, like myself, were independent members of the Palestinian parliament in exile, the PNC and we all sat together. Our lunches and conversations on those occasions more than made up for the frustrations of the meetings.

Money Matters

Back in the early days, I was far from well connected and one of the first useful contacts I made in London was not an MP, a lawyer or a journalist but my bank manager. When I was setting up on my own for the first time in Holland Park I didn't have enough of a financial history to get any credit. I mentioned this to an Australian journalist friend called Nigel Harvey who, like many of his countrymen, didn't beat around the bush but said what needed to be said with disarming (sometimes alarming) frankness. 'Invite the bank manager out for lunch,' he said. 'Just let him talk about whatever he wants to, listen to every word, nod encouragingly and put him at ease. He'll like that and then he'll be disposed towards helping you.' And so it was that two days later I accompanied Mr Wright from the Fleet Street branch of a well-known bank to El Vino's, the haunt of hacks and lawyers. Mr Wright was fond of wine and I encouraged him to drink up, ordering a whole bottle for his enjoyment while I drank mineral water. After a few glasses, Mr Wright started talking about his wife, 'She's a nice-looking woman and well meaning enough,' he confided. 'But awfully bossy. She's always bossing me about, acting like she's the man of the house.' With Nigel's advice firmly in mind I said nothing to impede the flow of his complaints as he detailed how his wife wanted to write all the cheques, drive the car and discipline the children. 'Mr Wright,' I said when his internal storm had run its full course. 'Join the club.' I was not married at the time but I felt confident that I could speak hypothetically on the subject. 'You are an important man. You are a bank manager. Why should an important man and a bank manager be troubling himself with domestic utility bills? Shouldn't a great man be driven about rather than having to drive himself? In my opinion, it's perfectly suitable that your wife gets on with these chores leaving you free to concentrate on matters of greater significance, on strategic decisions.' Mr Wright's troubled face brightened. 'Mr Atwan, you are right!' he beamed. By the end of the meal he was so pleased with our reappraisal of his domestic situation that he offered me a £10,000 overdraft facility and a gold MasterCard. Since then, I have never had any problems at the bank, bouncing cheques are a thing of the past and I remain eternally grateful to Mrs Wright's 'bossiness'.

The Loony Left

The few demonstrations I had been on in Jordan and Egypt had met with violent policing. I was unused, then, to the freedom to protest I now encountered in Britain and participated eagerly in the capital's frequent anti-racism and pro-Palestinian marches. In the course of these I got to know several of the group referred to in the red-top newspapers as 'the loony left', including Paul Foot, Ken Livingstone, Tony Benn and the Redgrave siblings.

Some of this group were very sociable and I was invited to their parties and gatherings, enjoying vigorous debates and discussions with all sorts of socialists from Marxists to Trotskyites to Stalinists. They were well informed on global politics, whereas I had concentrated solely on the Middle East until now, and I learned a lot about the situation in Latin America and the nature of US interference there. I was also fascinated by the intricate romantic networks which had evolved between some of them, free from 'bourgeois' moral constraints, which would be completely impossible in the Arab world.

Within the 'loony left' were several subgroups including the Socialist Workers' Party (SWP), Socialist Action and the Workers' Revolutionary Party (WRP). Each subgroup worked hard to recruit new members and had various methods for hijacking causes: the SWP, for example, produced (and still produce) the majority of banners people carried on demonstrations.

The actress Vanessa Redgrave, whom I met several times on marches, was a leading light in the WRP and she intrigued me. The newspapers and maga-zines were full of stories about film stars, their capricious behaviour, divorces and scandals, yet here was one of the most talented actors of her generation who eschewed such folly and strolled through the streets, unprotected by bodyguards, with thousands of 'ordinary' people, in support of a political cause. We often discussed the Middle East and I was impressed by the depth of her knowledge and her understanding of the Palestinian predicament as well as her general demeanour which was never haughty or arrogant but completely natural and relaxed. I don't think Vanessa Redgrave ever wore make-up except on a stage or film-set but her piercing blue eyes, once met, made an indelible impression. After one march in 1979 I asked her for an interview and she warmly invited me to her home near Chiswick.

The movie star's home was modest and comfortable, a far cry from Hollywood, yet her little boy, ten-year-old Carlo, who came downstairs to greet me so politely, was the son of the Franco Nero (whom she would marry, in a romantic twist, on New Year's Eve 2006, thirty-seven years after their first split); Redgrave's partner at that time was Timothy Dalton, who would later star in the James Bond films. Vanessa Redgrave made me a cup of coffee and we sat in the kitchen chatting; she asked me about my own family history and listened with great interest and such empathy that I almost forgot the professional purpose of my visit.

The problem with many of my acquaintances who espoused far-left political views in their youth is that, unlike Vanessa Redgrave, they haven't stayed the course. As soon as they accumulated a little wealth or standing of their own, all their socialist ideals were tossed into the bin. I have observed numerous political chameleons: Iraqi communists who are political exiles one moment and working for the CIA the next; British journalists who are radical socialists in their youth and end up writing for the *Daily Mail*, and Arab Marxists who overnight switch to Islamic fundamentalism. My own political belief in the principles of justice and the fair distribution of wealth, while definitely left-wing, are pragmatic and were never so radical as to be untenable. Perhaps this is the secret of a long-lived political creed.

Among my favourite far-left characters were Ken Livingstone and Tony Benn. Livingstone, twice-elected mayor of London and formerly leader of the Greater London Council (GLC), was dubbed 'Red Ken' and described by the right-wing newspaper, *The Sun*, as 'the most odious man in Britain'. Coming from a political climate where a 'Red Ken' would never be tolerated for one second by the authorities, I watched his antics with wonder. He antagonized Margaret Thatcher's Tory government by mounting hoardings displaying London's soaring unemployment figures on the roof of the GLC building, which was almost directly opposite the Houses of Parliament across the Thames. He also declared London a 'nuclear free zone' and invited Gerry Adams, the leader of Sinn Fein, to visit him at the GLC in 1982. Unfortunately, Adams was refused entry to the country under the Prevention of Terrorism Act, leading Red Ken famously to declare that Britain's treatment of the Irish over the past 800 years was worse than Hitler's treatment of the Jews. On Arab affairs he has been no less controversial, stating that the Saudi royal family should be 'swinging from lamp-posts' and describing Ariel Sharon as a war criminal (citing the massacres at Sabra and Shatila). Inevitably, he has been accused of anti-Semitism, a charge he rebutted by hosting a Jewish Hanukkah ceremony at City Hall in December 2005.

In the early 1980s, Tony Benn was an isolated figure on the extreme left of the Labour Party. Now, in his eighties, he is a powerful and popular figurehead for the anti-war movement. I have long admired him for the obvious strength of his personal convictions and his tremendous power as an orator in and out of the Houses of Parliament where he held a seat for more than forty years. The first time I heard of him was in 1963; I had bought a second-hand *Times* in Rafah and read about this extraordinary

British aristocrat who had renounced his title under the new Peerage Act, so that he could remain in the House of Commons. This humility and disregard for wealth and status resonates with the Arab sensibility and deeply impressed me. Tony Benn was guest of honour at the 2006 launch of my first book, *The Secret History of al-Qa'ida*.

Also branded 'loony left' by the tabloids, MP George Galloway has long been an outspoken critic of British and American policies in the Middle East. He has championed the Palestinian cause for many years and told me recently that he spent several months with the PLO in Beirut in 1967. I first came across him when his constituency city, Dundee, twinned with the West Bank town Nablus in 1980. In 1981, the Mayor of Nablus, Bassam Shaka, lost both his legs in an Israeli bomb attack. A delegation from Dundee, led by George Galloway, went over to Palestine to condemn this atrocity and in 1982 invited Bassam Shaka to Scotland where they provided him with medical treatment, including prosthetic legs.

In March 2003, just before the outbreak of the Iraq War, I started to meet George Galloway on a more regular basis as we were both speaking out against an illegal, unwarranted US invasion. He is an impressive commentator on Middle Eastern politics and holds crowds spell-bound with his fiery rhetoric at demonstrations. He has drawn a lot of very public criticism for his personal life, of which I know little. I did once ask him, jokingly, what had drawn him to his Palestinian wife, Dr Amineh Abu-Zayyad, whom he had married in 2000. He replied that, among other attributes, he liked Dr Amineh's innate discretion. 'Arab women don't gossip to the press,' he said. 'They are concerned with honour.' It was with some surprise, then, that I opened the *Sunday Times* on 1 May 2005, the eve of elections, to discover a remarkably candid interview with Dr Amineh by Nick Fielding in which she announced the couple's imminent divorce.

Perhaps the most publicly vilified of all the 'loony left', Arthur Scargill, was leader of the National Union of Mineworkers (NUM), 1981–2000. I watched his career with fascination because trade unions in the Arab world tend to be limp organizations that more often represent the interests of their government than the workers. As leader of the Yorkshire miners, Scargill had already established a fearsome reputation and his use of 'flying pickets' – workers who would travel to join pickets at striking coal mines – ensured victory for the miners in their 1972 and 1974 strikes. Arthur Scargill's name became synonymous with industrial action in the minds of the British public and comedians like Jimmy Tarbuck and Mike Yarwood often made jokes about him, such as this one: 'Manchester United are buying the best striker on earth.' 'Who's that?' 'Arthur Scargill.'

The late 1970s will be remembered as the era when trade unions lost a lot of public sympathy. The political climate was confrontational, and while I sympathized with the left, I could see that the more radical elements went too far and pulled the rug out from under the feet of socialist progress. The endless strikes that blighted British society and the economy for several years towards the end of that decade eased Margaret Thatcher's ascent to power. These culminated in the so-called 'Winter of Discontent' in 1978–9, when London's streets and parks were teeming with uncollected rubbish. I can remember the stench and the sight of rats scuttling among piles of refuse. Even the gravediggers went on strike, with corpses left unburied while the unions haggled over money.

The unions were top of Margaret Thatcher's hatchet list when she took office. Arthur Scargill and the Iron Lady were destined for a head-to-head confrontation and that came about with the bitterly fought 1984–5 miners' strike. I remember Scargill announcing in 1983, when Ian MacGregor was appointed as head of British Coal, that the government had a plan to destroy the mining industry, along with a list of the mines it would close on a year-to-year basis. Scargill's thesis was that, by dismantling the heavy industries whose workers formed the most militant unions (mining, shipbuilding, iron, and steel), the government would simultaneously destroy the far-left in the Trades Union Congress (TUC). Many ridiculed these assertions as paranoia but history shows that, of 170 working pits in 1984, only fifteen remained when privatization went ahead in 1994. The end of the miners' strike in 1985 was seen as a major defeat not only for the NUM but the trade unions in general. Margaret Thatcher had torn out the heart of that mighty beast, the TUC, forever.

Academia

In December 1978 the publication of *The Times* and the *Sunday Times* was suspended until the management and unions could agree on the introduction of new printing technology and the reduction in manning levels that this would imply. I decided to interview Harold Evans, then editor of the *Sunday Times*. He gave me an hour of his time and talked about how British newspapers are run and organized. He was frank about the internal politics going on at the time which would ultimately result in the split that saw the founding of the *Independent* seven years later. What I learned helped me in my own career and in particular when I came to set up my own newspaper.

Discussing what made a top-flight journalist, Harold Evans had emphasized academic excellence and this jolted me into resuming a long-held personal ambition. I applied for a Master's degree in Middle Eastern Studies at SOAS, to start in the autumn of 1980. Five days after I submitted the application form, I received a rejection letter from SOAS which I found rather strange. I asked a friend who was studying in that department to find out the reason and he learned that SOAS had had several bad experiences with arrogant, ill-informed young Arab journalists who considered it a matter of honour to argue with their non-Arab tutors and lecturers. I went straight to SOAS and asked to see Professor Yapp, the head of the department.

Professor Yapp was in his late fifties and his office was crammed with books, on shelves, in piles on the floor, and in leaning towers on his desk. I thought I knew a lot about the Middle East but this professor grilled me with obscure questions and seemed almost triumphant whenever I foundered, which was most of the time. 'Tell me, Mr Atwan,' Professor Yapp said when the humiliation was complete, 'Why do you want to study here?'

'I want to learn about the British mentality,' I replied. 'I am sure the key lies in your education system, in the way you teach your students. I want to know why a British expert is calm and unruffled on television while an Arab commentator will be screaming and shouting and putting people off ...'

Professor Yapp laughed. 'You have a lot of enthusiasm,' he said. 'And I think you have potential, but you are lacking two essential things: knowledge and proper academic experience.'

'What would you recommend?' I asked him. By now it had become a matter of pride. I could not accept an outright rejection and I wanted to leave with the door still open, or even slightly ajar. Professor Yapp opened a drawer in his desk and produced a list of about forty books. 'This is the reading list for the MA. I suggest you go away and read all of them and then come back to see me in a year's time. Maybe then we can offer you a place.'

I had no intention of reading all those books. It would have taken every waking hour and by then I was the London bureau chief for *al-Madina* newspaper, a job that took up most of my time. Looking for an easy way out, I applied for a similar MA course at the London branch of the University of Southern California but left after a few sessions, realizing the course was not what I was looking for. I still had my heart set on SOAS and a year later made another appointment with Professor Yapp. I had settled on a strategy – or rather a gamble – for getting onto the course. I had done some research on Professor Yapp's academic background and discovered that he was particularly interested in Arab nationalism. If I read up on this one subject, I reasoned, I might be able impress him enough to get a place. By chance, I had been sent a review copy of a new book on the subject by a key Arab commentator, Zein Nour Eldin Zein, in which he reversed his earlier Marxist stance, and now opined that nationalism can and should be based on Islam alone. I read it the night before the interview.

The next day, I turned up to meet the professor. We talked about Mrs Thatcher, whom I had recently interviewed, and I acquitted myself well in discussing current affairs with him.

'Well now,' said the Professor, 'did you manage to get through the reading list?'

I chose the path of blunt honesty. 'I am afraid not,' I announced. 'If I had read all those books why would I need to do your course? I would already know almost everything you are going to be teaching. But I have studied Arab nationalism in depth, perhaps you could interview me on this subject to see if my potential has improved?'

Professor Yapp took to this approach. The interview went well until he asked me a question about Zein Nour Eldin Zein which I answered in detail, referring to his new book. Of course, Professor Yapp didn't know about the book because it had only just been published in Beirut, and in Arabic, and he refused to move from his position that Zein was a Marxist. Fortunately, I had the book in my briefcase and produced it, summing up its contents as concisely as I could. He was finally impressed and told me I could start in October.

Atwan the Married Man

Among the friends I made at SOAS was a Canadian woman called Deborah Pugh. She was a born comedian with a natural antipathy towards authority. Deborah was left-wing and involved in Middle-Eastern politics and pressure groups. Having completed her degree, she decided to go to Gaza to teach English in the refugee camps and I was delighted when she said she would like to visit my mother in Rafah. In order to let my mother know Deborah was coming I had to first call her better-off neighbours who possessed the only phone in that part of the camp. One of their children was then dispatched to find my mother and let her know that I would be calling back in half an hour.

When Deborah got to Gaza, she asked people what she should take as a gift for my mother when she went to our house. Someone suggested chickens and, having bought four, she set off for the Rafah refugee camp. Her entry into this shanty town caused a great stir. Deborah is a tall woman, nearly six foot, with long red hair; she was wearing shorts and a T-shirt and held a pair of squawking chickens firmly by the legs in each hand. Within seconds, she had a chaotic entourage of ragged children running along to keep up with her as she searched for my mother's house. In the confusion she managed to let go of the chickens and this was an excuse for the whole camp to get involved, with people running around chasing the birds all over the place.

A few days later, I received a phone call from my mother: 'She is perfect,' she said.

'Who? What do you mean?' I asked.

'Dayboorah,' said my mother. 'You want my blessing and you have it, my son.' I was horrified. Stupidly, and because nothing was further from my mind, it hadn't occurred to me that my mother would think of Deborah as a prospective wife for me.

'No, Yamma,' I said. 'She is just a friend.'

'Don't be bashful, my dear, marry her, it is good. She is beautiful and has fine strong legs. You are lucky. I am proud of you.' Nothing could sway her from this opinion and it was not until Deborah returned to Rafah some time later with her new husband, the Anglo-Egyptian playwright Kareem al-Raoui, that my mother accepted my denials. Even then, she remained dissatisfied with the success of the man she considered my rival in love and grumbled, 'Why did he get to marry her and not you?'

Having accepted that Deborah Pugh was not my betrothed, my mother went on a mission to get me married off as soon as possible. With my new job as London bureau chief for *al-Madina* and attendant elevation in status and income, my mother was convinced that I was the most eligible of all Palestinian 'bachelors' (with the possible exception of Yasser Arafat). 'You can get any girl you want,' she declared, 'Please, you only have to look.'

What my mother did not know was that I had made a pact with 'the bachelors' that we would all remain single. We had seen the havoc marriage wreaked with colleagues' lives, the instant surrender to routine and domesticity, the lack of freedom to travel at a moment's notice. Celibacy, we reasoned, was much more compatible with a career in journalism.

I had bought my first house in December 1982; it was a modest little terraced house in Chiswick but it mattered a great deal to me. My family had never had their own home since they were forced to leave Isdud, and I had spent my life as a refugee and a stateless person. As soon as I moved in, I planted a fig tree and some vines in the little garden to remind me of Palestine. Neither produced much fruit due to the cold English climate and the grapes were sour, but the fig blossomed every spring and gave me much happiness. Where 'the bachelors' were concerned, this terraced house was party headquarters, somewhere we could stay up late and play music with no risk of being told off by landlords or neighbours or wives. I was also the official bachelor chauffeur, picking the others up and driving them around in my Ford Fiesta. So long as I was single I was valuable to my friends and I determined not to let them down.

Over a period of months, in 1982 and 1983, I was submitted to a constant barrage of telephone calls from Gaza alternately pleading and furious. 'I want to see your children before I die,' my mother wailed on one occasion, even though she already had scores of grandchildren. Then I heard her say to my brother, thinking her hand over the mouthpiece made her inaudible, 'This bastard is just fooling around. I'm going to find him a wife if it's the last thing I do.' Another time, she called me, having wound herself up into a state and said, 'Come on, admit it, you don't like women, do you?'

'Mum, I do like women, I'm just useless. I have no idea what to do with women. I have tried but nothing ever comes of it. If I like them they don't like me and vice-versa.'

I thought I had heard the end of the marriage saga when there was a lull for a few months but I should have known that my mother was not going to give up on her dream so easily. I thought I was comparatively safe, since she refused to come to London where she could have really started meddling, saying she would rather die than go to a *kafir* (infidel) country. Like many Arabs, she was afraid of the lands beyond the Muslim world where she believed strange languages, religions and customs reigned. In former times, the Arabs used to call the Atlantic 'the Ocean of Darkness' and conceived of it as a vast wilderness. My mother still felt like that.

However, I was due to go to Saudi Arabia for a family reunion (the Israelis consistently refused me a permit to visit Gaza) in December 1983, and it was there that my mother struck. No sooner had she wiped away her tears of joy at seeing me again, than she got out a set of glossy photographs and announced, 'I have found the perfect bride for you.'

I must admit that the young woman in the photographs was beautiful and seemed qualified for the job in every respect. Basima was Palestinian and a graduate. Her mother was from Jaffa but her father was from Isdud and, like me, Basima had been born in a refugee camp although the family had fled to Kuwait, where they still live, when she was seven years old.

To all intents and purposes this was an arranged marriage, and having spent several years in the West I still harboured some romantic notions of a chance meeting with the perfect partner who could have been of any nationality as far as I was concerned. I had to admit, however, that I hadn't yet encountered anybody even remotely suitable and realized that, since our respective families knew each of us so well, their judgement on our potential compatibility could not be dismissed; I could also see that a good arranged marriage obviates cultural differences and is built on common ground.

However, I still had no intention of marrying and was secure in the knowledge that my mother's project was doomed to failure because a recent series of bomb attacks on the US and French embassies in Kuwait had resulted in a state of emergency and no visas were being granted. My mother knew nothing of these circumstances and I didn't enlighten her.

'Go and meet her,' she urged and, certain I would be refused, I promised to go to the Kuwaiti embassy the next day.

I was pleased to find a surly bureaucrat at the visa desk, who was in the process of telling me how crazy I was to even think of going to Kuwait, when I heard a rich voice behind me announce, 'You are Abdel Bari Atwan!' It was the ambassador, returning from his lunch. He shepherded me into his office where he complimented me on my column in *al-Madina* which he said he read every day. He asked me why I wanted to go to Kuwait and so I told him that I wanted to meet my prospective bride, adding hastily, 'But it is all under pressure from my mother. I am happy being a bachelor.'

'I don't understand,' the ambassador said. 'Do you want to go to Kuwait or not?'

I couldn't resist making a joke in reply: 'Look,' I said. 'I want to alleviate your "Palestinian problem". If I go to Kuwait, marry one of your 400,000 Palestinians and bring her back with me to London you will have one fewer over there.' Before I knew it, he had issued me with a visa, backdated to before the crisis.

I met Basima several times in the company of her family. The name Basima means 'the smiling one' and suits her well. From the outset I felt drawn to her and my allegiance to 'the bachelors' began to seem absurd compared with the prospect of such a lively, intelligent (not to mention beautiful) life partner. I was persuaded that it was time for me to have a family and that this was a wise move. In my youthful arrogance it hadn't occurred to me that Basima would be anything other than delighted to have me as a husband, so when she expressed doubts I was amazed. Basima was not keen to live in London, she didn't want to leave her family and some of her relatives were actually opposed to her marrying me. Now my pride was involved, and far from being downcast I started to make a concerted effort to appear irresistible; always smart, I was constantly armed with bracelets, flowers or chocolates. Fortunately I succeeded and by the last day of my visit we were engaged to be married. It wasn't until I got on the plane to go back to London that I remembered I was going to be in hot water with the gang.

On my first day back, I invited 'the bachelors' out for dinner to a Lebanese restaurant after work. As the table groaned under countless *mezzes* and grills, I took the opportunity to recommend the idea of marriage.

'How marvellous it would be to eat like this everyday at home,' I ventured.

Hafiz paused, a lamb kebab halfway to his mouth. 'Better to have it in a restaurant where nobody's going to pester you about the washing up,' he said, and the others nodded their agreement.

'And we can go out to listen to some music afterwards. We're free, not like those bloody husbands,' Eyad added. I could see I wasn't going to get anywhere with the diplomatic route and I placed my right hand on the table, so that the ring Basima had given me glinted in the candlelight.

'What's that?' asked eagle-eyed Hafiz, touching the gold band.

'I'm getting married.' I told them. All three put down their cutlery and gaped at me in silent astonishment and horror. I gave them a few moments to absorb the shock. 'She's very nice,' I said lamely. No response. 'Clever,' I added. 'And pretty.' Osman wiped his mouth with his napkin and got up. 'Abdel Bari, I never thought I would live to say this but you are a traitor,' he declared, and left the table.

'Who is going to drive us around now?' asked Hafiz. 'And where will we hold our parties?'

'Well, you can do as you wish. You be a fool if you must but we're never going to marry,' said Eyad and the others agreed.

'And we're not coming to the wedding,' Hafiz said. 'It's certain to end in divorce so it would be hypocritical to come. You're far too eccentric for any woman to put up with for long.'

'You will only have bad luck in this foolish venture,' said Eyad. 'You'll never make a suitable husband.'

The conversation turned to what a lousy husband I was going to make which occasioned a great deal of mirth and merriment. Osman returned and the evening ended much better than I had anticipated.

Of the four original 'bachelors', two stayed true to their word and never married. They now like to blame me for their celibate state and claim that I robbed them of their marriageable years. Eyad was the only other one who found a bride. 'The bachelors' were later joined by Bakir Oweda who, having married and divorced twice, readily converted to celibacy and they remain a gang of three.

Meanwhile, Basima and I wrote to each other and spoke often on the phone and romantic feelings blossomed. After six months we fixed the date for our wedding. Just two days before I was due to fly to Kuwait the borders were closed again after the emir had been the subject of a failed assassination attempt in which many of his bodyguards were killed. Once more, the embassy made an exception for me and I was allowed to travel. None of my family or friends, however, were able to get visas to attend the wedding; the perpetual exile, I was a one-man tribe among Basima's family of hundreds, but it was a very special day and I was exceptionally happy.

I have been surprised by the proliferation of 'lonely hearts' columns even in the most respectable British newspapers and, more recently, these have been joined by computer dating systems which perform a similar, if more basic, function to family matchmakers (without the human touch). No other method of couple-making has drawn as much criticism as arranged marriages in the Western media yet, as it turns out, more than twenty years on, no amount of money, research or yearning could have turned up so perfect a match for me as Basima.

Changes

Basima had not been to a European country before and she wasn't pre-pared for the grey London weather and darkness falling at 4 PM in winter, something that still makes her depressed. I was the only person she knew in London and she didn't know me that well yet. Some friends of mine set up a wedding committee and surprised us with a large party at the Foreign Press Association to celebrate our marriage and welcome Basima. I was delighted to discover all three of the remaining 'bachelors' among the guests.

Those early days of marriage were a time of change and adjustment for both of us but I could see it was more difficult for Basima; I worked unpredictable and often long hours and she was alone at home with little to do. For a clever and spirited young woman it was a frustrating existence. Things slowly improved for her after she enrolled on an English course and started travelling around her new home city on the bus. I was proud of the way she faced the challenges of her new life.

After years in the pipeline, my application for British citizenship reached the top of the pile in 1985 and was accepted. I still remember the enormous pride I took in being able to vote for the very first time in my life in the

1987 general election. I had never been part of the democratic process and woke up early, putting on my best suit and polishing my shoes before setting off for the polling-station.

In 1985 too, our first child was born; we were at the hospital for two days waiting for Khalid to arrive. He was a breech presentation but to our relief, he was delivered naturally, bottom first, and with no complications. I made light of this once the anxiety was over, joking that he knew he was a Palestinian, to come into the world in this manner, demonstrating his defiance from the start.

We had decided not to impose our cultural beliefs and practices on the children except in one small matter: as Muslims we believe it is our duty to have our sons circumcised. Unfortunately, this operation is imbued with memories of pain and disaster for me. Because my father was impoverished he couldn't afford a celebration for each of us boys but decided to wait until there were three and have us all circumcised together, rather like the three-for-the-price-of-one bargains on offer in supermarkets nowadays. Although the operation is usually carried out shortly after birth, when it is relatively safe, I was eight years old when we were taken to visit 'Dr' Khalil in Deir al-Balah refugee camp. 'Dr' Khalil had a glass eye and was a jack-of-all-trades, functioning as a barber, vet and dentist. In fact, he was more accustomed to pulling out rotten teeth and treating animals than performing this delicate surgery. The operation was agonizing and afterwards the wound became infected. It was painful for months and I couldn't wear trousers, only a *jalabiya*, which I had to hold out in front of me all the time so it wouldn't touch the wound. There were no doctors to treat me but eventually my immune system summoned up the wherewithal to conquer this infection and it healed. But I could have ended up being impotent for life, or dead.

When Khalid was born I had no intention of putting him through a similar trauma and decided to have him circumcised as early as possible. We asked the hospital if they could arrange this and were delighted when they told us it could be done immediately. We were sitting marvelling at the infant, when a bearded figure wearing a skullcap walked into the ward. He made his way over, introduced himself as the local rabbi, and said that he'd come to circumcise the baby. This ritual being one thing we have in common with our Jewish cousins, Khalid became one of very few Palestinians to have been circumcised by a rabbi and he was fortunate, because the man was good at his job and the experience was relatively painless.

In 1987, we had another child, a little girl called Nada, and I considered that my obligation to contribute to the global population had been fulfilled with these two, but thirteen years later, in 2000, I was at the BBC studios, waiting to take part in a panel discussion about al-Qaʻida and Osama bin Laden, when my mobile phone rang. It was Basima telling me that she was expecting another baby. I was amazed and must have looked shocked. The BBC researcher looked at me in a concerned manner and asked me if I was alright. 'Considering that I am fifty years old, I am more than alright,' I beamed. 'Still fully functioning it seems.'

I have a number of regrets where my children are concerned. I love them all but know that I have not been able to spend enough time with them, due to the demands of my job. A few years ago Basima was talking to Khalid, who was twelve at the time, about what career he might follow. 'Anything other than journalism', he answered. 'I don't want to be like my father, I'd like to enjoy my children's company and see them grow up.' When Basima told me this it was deeply wounding because family life is such an integral part of our heritage. Gradually, I made more effort to be a better father. Nowadays on my one day off a week – usually Saturday – I turn off my mobile phone and dedicate this time to them, although Nada and Khalid now have their own lives, their own friends and they don't want their old father hanging around. When Khalid received his degree, I made sure I was at the graduation ceremony even though it was the day after the Mumbai rail bombs and I was being interviewed by Sky News, the BBC and CNN, as I was being driven to it.

Khalid has an additional reason to be bitter: when he was eight I used to take him to watch football whenever I had time on Saturdays. Our local club was Queens Park Rangers, so I bought him a season ticket for all their matches and he became an ardent fan of that ill-fated team. Poor Khalid had to watch his team tumble down the premier division, shoot through the first, and land with a bump, shell-shocked, in the second division. I wish I had taken him to watch Chelsea or Arsenal or any club that he could have supported safe in the knowledge that they would win the occasional game. I recently bought another QPR season ticket for Kareem and now he will have to go through the same suffering as his brother.

It has been a challenge raising our children in Britain, trying to keep their sense of what it is to be Palestinian whilst encouraging them to fully integrate into British society. I have avoided talking to them about politics because I want them to form their own opinions about these matters. English is their first language, complete with London accents, but we speak Arabic at home and from an early age they have all been regular visitors to the Arab Club in London, which was founded in 1980 and organizes concerts and other cultural events, as well as running a Saturday language school. I am happy that I was able to take Nada and Khalid to see Jerusalem and visit my mother in Rafah refugee camp three times before her death in 2003. Sadly, she was never to meet Kareem.

Nada and Khalid have reached a stage now where they are trying to work out their identities. Are they Arabic or British? Is it possible to be both? When they were younger, they wanted to fit in with their peers, as all children do, and over the years the family home has been shaken and rattled by various forms of American and British pop music. We didn't interfere or comment in any way, and independently they have become interested in their roots. They are keen to know about the refugee camps and our childhood days in Palestine, researching for themselves the history of the Arab–Israeli conflict. Nada discovered Nancy Ajram, the Lebanese singer currently taking the Arab world by storm, which was also a treat for Basima and me. Both Nada and Khalid are exploring Islam in their own way, and I am glad to report that Khalid is following in his father's footsteps by being the designated driver on nights out with his bachelor friends.

I sympathize with my children's situation. Even after thirty years in Britain, I am culturally confused and my thoughts and dreams are played out half in English and half in Arabic. I feel that my cultural identity has become blurred with time and that to some extent I have lost my roots, a situation that troubles me whenever it is thrown into relief as it was, for example, when I visited Gaza and initially experienced alienation rather than a sense of homecoming. Basima has spoken of similar feelings and I sometimes wonder if history has condemned us to a permanent state of psychological exile.

7

Beirut-on-Thames

Although I had chosen to explore British culture and integrate as much as possible, any Arabs wishing to ignore the fact that they had left the Middle East would have been able to do so in London in the late 1970s. The British capital was well on its way to becoming the microcosm of the Arab world it is today, with its oil sheikhs, fundamentalists, belly dancers, Lebanese chefs, freedom fighters and exiled politicians of every persuasion. I believe that the reason so many Muslims are drawn to London lies in the ancient struggle between the colonizers and the colonized; the paradoxical tension between resentment and admiration on the part of the latter, and the latent guilt of the former which resulted in a more open immigration policy than that of many other Western governments. Wealthy Arabs were in possession of such quantities of money that they felt able, in some ways, to subjugate their erstwhile conquerors and buy their servitude. The poorer workers, meanwhile, mostly came to London to service their wealthier fellow Muslims in one capacity or another.

While there had always been Arabs in London, from the Yemeni sailors who lived around the docks in the nineteenth century to the Iraqi exiles who began arriving in the 1930s, significant large-scale migration started in the 1970s. The 1973 oil crisis[1] produced an economic boom in the oil-producing

---

1.   In 1973, OAPEC (the Arab members of OPEC) decided to cut exports to the US

countries of the Middle East; many newly rich Gulf Arabs decided to flee their politically unstable homelands and seek new investment opportunities in London. The British media at the time abounded with stories of outlandish purchases by Gulf visitors, some of which were true: a prince from the obscure Arab emirate of Ras al-Khaimah bought the Dorchester Hotel in Park Lane and sold it on in 1985 to the Sultan of Brunei; Mahdi al-Tajir, the London Ambassador for the UAE at the time, purchased Mereworth Castle and later added an 18,000 acre country estate in Perthshire and the Park Tower hotel to his property portfolio; the less ostentatious snapped up rows of houses in Mayfair and Kensington. In a 1976 article, David Hirst, writing in the *Guardian*, noted that 10,000 properties in London had been acquired by Middle Easterners at a cost of £100 million in that year alone.

The civil war in Lebanon, which started in 1975, and the Israeli invasion seven years later, saw new waves of migration to the British capital. Beirut had been the hub of the Arab press as well as the favoured holiday spot for an estimated 800,000 Arabs; London now hosted both and became known as 'Little Beirut' or 'Beirut-on-Thames'. London hoteliers and entrepreneurs were swift to cater for these new tourists' bulging wallets, recruiting Arabic-speaking staff and chefs. Arabs from different countries identified and colonized their favourite hotels: Saudis preferred the Grosvenor, for example, whereas the Lebanese were usually to be found at the Hilton. The resulting juxtapositions of cultures produced some comic moments. Once I was in the piano lounge of a Park Lane hotel where a group of robed men were sharing a hookah pipe, while all around European men in suits and well-dressed women took their afternoon tea and chatted discreetly. After about half an hour, the smoke generated by these gentlemen smelt like a bonfire and had become so thick that it set off the fire alarms. The fire brigade arrived, followed by the police, who decided to turn a blind eye to the nature of the substances being smoked and simply asked these exotic visitors to hubble-bubble less vigorously.

Harley Street was a popular destination and the phenomenon of surgical tourism began back then. Tests and examinations were undergone for

---

and its Western allies in retaliation for their support of Israel in its war against Syria and Egypt. At the same time they decided to exploit their monopoly of the oil market to engineer a four-fold hike in oil prices, resulting in rampant inflation in the West.

just about every imaginable illness and routine operations such as a tonsil-lectomy, which can be performed in any Arab hospital, were purchased in London just for the kudos. It was not unknown for claustrophobic members of Gulf royal families to fabricate illnesses in order to justify a trip to London accompanied by a chaperone who would enjoy an all-expenses-paid trip. Most Gulf embassies enlisted the services of a medical attaché who was charged with making arrangements for would-be patients. Several clinics in Harley Street fell prey to the kind of corruption that is commonplace in the Middle East; at least one medical attaché was recalled when he was caught banking his cut of the inflated bills charged to his countrymen by certain doctors. This entrepreneur was arrested on his return and given a lengthy prison sentence.

Wards in the private clinics and hospitals were luxurious, with deep carpets and extravagant flower arrangements wherever you looked. Recovering patients would host jolly gatherings for friends and relations who, staying in nearby hotels, had come to provide emotional succour. Food would be delivered by top London restaurants and a variety of entertainment was available, from films to fashion parades. It sometimes happened that the nurses were drawn into these festivities and more than once a male patient fell in love and went home not only cured but with a British fiancée.

A less-noticeable Arabic presence – and for the average British newspaper reader, less interesting – were the thousands of North African workers slaving behind the scenes in hotels and restaurants, and the many Arab students who attended British universities. Then there were people like me, ordinary, run-of-the-mill professionals from Arab lands like Syria, Palestine and Jordan, seeking to make our way through life and enjoying the new challenges and opportunities London had to offer.

It was curious how certain London boroughs attracted different Middle Eastern nationalities and classes as ex-patriot communities developed: Edgware Road was full of Gulf Arabs, as well as being an upmarket pan-Arab holiday resort; Knightsbridge hosted the ultra-rich, major and minor royalty, and the upper classes – we used to call them the sheikhs of Knightsbridge; Queensway was home to poorer Arabs from North Africa while the northern boroughs became a magnet for Islamists.

Of all of these, the most colourful area was, and remains, Edgware Road. Here, Arabs from many nations still come for a break, escaping the summer heat in their own countries and relishing the culture, freedom and fun the city has to offer. Edgware Road was so thoroughly Arabized when I arrived that I wrote a spoof story in *al-Madina*, claiming that the British government had decided to open an embassy there to represent its interests. A huge industry mushroomed around these tourists and resident Arab businessmen benefited as much as their British counterparts. There were local Arabic-language magazines divulging the latest gossip, advertising the services of translators and interpreters (who were earning a small fortune facilitating business and property deals, as well as accompanying clients to Harley Street), and listing an array of live performances by Middle Eastern entertainers, from singing stars to low-class belly dancers.

I would go to the Edgware Road area often in the early days just to watch my fellow Arabs enjoying themselves as if they were in Beirut or Cairo. Girls from the Gulf, who spent most of their lives covered up, drenched themselves in perfume and took to the streets replacing the veil with a small headscarf over their hair. Young men responded to this display of beauty with alacrity and you'd hear their whispered attempts at seduction, 'You're beautiful, you're lovely, why won't you talk to me?' and the girls would only smile and giggle and hurry on. Sometimes, you'd see one giving her suitor a telephone number and that would be cause for celebration by the young man and his friends even though it was highly unlikely he would ever dare to call her.

Exploitation of these visitors was rife. There were shops all along the Edgware Road selling pirated cassettes of Arabic music which the proprietor would copy in front of you on a tape to tape machine. In a bid to keep their costs down these pirates would use tapes that were shorter than the original recordings with the result that side one would end five minutes earlier than it should. I bought one by Umm Kulthoum and just as she embarked on the climax of one of her most moving songs, having built up to it in stages for the past twenty minutes, she was cut off by the click of that side of the cassette coming to an end. Restaurants sprang up all over the place with the word *halal* emblazoned on their windows and menus. One day, we noticed a newly opened restaurant selling Arabic food and the owner had put up a notice boasting '*Halal Falafel*' which caused hilarity for some, and indignation for the more fervent Muslims, as *halal* is, of course, the correct Islamic method of killing animals for meat and has nothing to do with *falafel*, which are made primarily of chickpeas. We later discovered that the man behind this clever idea was an Arab Jew who thought *halal* was the same as *kosher*.

The pickpockets' grapevine buzzed with stories of wealthy Arabs carrying around thousands of pounds in cash and many of these Middle Eastern tourists were robbed at one point or another. They were sitting targets because they didn't understand the way London streets worked and had little experience of crime. It was not considered unusual to be barged into by a passer-by and it wouldn't have occurred to these visitors that they had just been relieved of a wallet. I often saw men and women leaving their bags outside a phone booth to make a call, oblivious to the fact that a thief was standing by waiting to snatch them the minute the door swung shut.

There was a Palestinian journalist called Abdullah Shiti, who was a colourful character, well known at this time for his satirical writings. Based in Kuwait, he came to London for a visit and was mugged in broad daylight in a street near Marble Arch, losing all the money he had for his trip. He related this incident in his daily column and was astonished when rich Arabs sent him large amounts of cash by way of compensation for his misfortune. Abdullah ended up with more money than he had lost.

There were around twenty Arabic nightclubs and most of the popular musicians and singers from the Middle East came to London to perform, including the Lebanese singer, Sabah, whose life was as compelling as her voice. We flocked to see this notorious wedding-addict, who would end up being married ten times, though at that time she was only on husband number six. One of her marriages – to Rushdy Abaza in 1967 – lasted just three days. Faiza Ahmed of Egypt, Sadoun Jaber of Iraq, and the Lebanese Walid Tawfik all sang in London clubs in their heyday. When the singer Fairouz came to the Albert Hall in the mid-1980s, crowds of Arabs willing to pay hundreds of pounds to see their idol were queuing round the block for two days before tickets even went on sale.

Greeks throw plates on the ground to show their appreciation but Arabs throw money. It was common for members of the audience in Arabic nightclubs to be so drunk that they became indiscriminate and would toss money at the feet of even the most appalling performers. When it was a question of belly dancers things would get completely out of hand, particularly if there were people from nations which were at political odds, such as Saudis, Kuwaitis and Libyans. If the Libyan tucked £100 into a belly dancer's belt, the Kuwaiti would wedge £200 on the opposite hip. Not to be outdone, the Saudi would wrench out £300 in crisp new notes and scatter them on the stage. Once I saw a member of a royal family from the Gulf, who was so intoxicated he could hardly stand, swaying next to the stage where a mediocre dancer was giving a few bored swishes of her hips while staring into space. The young prince beckoned the nightclub owner over and gave him his credit card, 'I want a thousand pounds in cash,' he insisted. The owner obliged and brought the cash which was then placed, adoringly, if unsteadily, at the feet of the dancer whose face at least became more animated thereafter.

Many top-notch musicians and dancers would make clandestine trips over to these London clubs because they could make so much money in one evening. Whoever they were, however, the performers had to split their tips three ways – a third for them, a third for the musicians and a third for the nightclub owner. The peak of all this madness was in the early 1980s, and it subsided when the price of oil fell dramatically and even Gulf princes realized they did not have bottomless financial resources.

The Middle Eastern clubs rewrote the timetables for British nightlife, often staying open until nine in the morning. For their Arab clientele, the daily schedule would run something like this: breakfast at noon, lunch at five in the afternoon followed by a nap, with dinner at around 11 PM. Nobody went out much before midnight, and it is still the case that restaurants and clubs in Edgware Road don't get busy until one or two o'clock in the morning.

I was commissioned to write an article about Arab tourism which took me to a nightclub called The Nile. There was a bouncer called Mustafa Kamel Mustafa, who appeared to enjoy his work inspecting potential customers as they passed his bulky form. Many of the women who went to these clubs were prostitutes although you would never know it if you saw them outside the venue. They would be wearing coats and full-length skirts, or trousers, with their heads and part of their faces concealed by a scarf. The minute they got inside, however, they would enter the ladies' toilets only to reappear half an hour later plastered in make-up and perfume, with curly hair, tiny miniskirts and plunging necklines. They were mostly from North African countries and had come to London on tourist visas organized by pimps based in London. Some of the prostitutes acted independently, and there were also British students who'd heard that tens of thousands of pounds could be procured to boost their grants, if they spent just one night with a rich man from the Gulf.

Mustafa Kamel Mustafa stood outside The Nile every night until his Catholic wife, Valerie Fleming, complained that he was flirting with the female club-goers and gave him an ultimatum. Mustafa took this to heart and in 1984 started going to the mosque and there experienced a radical conversion to Islam. Less than a decade later, he returned from Afghanistan where he had been fighting in the *jihad* against the Russians, minus an eye and with a hook instead of a right hand. This was Abu Hamza al-Misri who became the *imam* of Finsbury Park mosque, and was sentenced to seven years in jail in February 2006 for inciting murder and racial hatred.

Some Arabic countries, especially the Gulf States, grew worried about the decadent and extravagant antics of their nationals while on holiday in London. There were several magazines and small tabloid papers that published all the gossip, with scandalous accounts of the behaviour of well-known Arabs, often members of Gulf royal families. The sources of most of these stories were chauffeurs or servants who would talk of millions lost gambling in casinos and recount salacious tales of their employers' sexual escapades: princes cruising for blondes while their wives, according to the moles, were driven to discotheques where they too would seek out lovers for the night.

As time went on, less scrupulous journalists started to use these stories for blackmail and several were paid large sums of money not to publish them. Some of the embassies of more conservative countries sent spies to the clubs to see what was going on and issue whispered reprimands where necessary. Reports would be sent back home and kept on record. On occasion, the spies would enjoy their mission too much, forgetting the reason they were there and start joining in with the debauchery themselves.

The British newspapers had a field day with their Arab visitors' extravagant behaviour. There were stories of waitresses being tipped hundreds of pounds by appreciative Gulf diners and millionaire Saudis shoplifting in Harrods; there were derogatory cartoons like the one of a fat man in white robes and a *keffiyeh* leading a camel down Edgware Road with four veiled wives behind him. It is true that some of the Arabs were illiterate, inexperienced and unsophisticated, but they were the minority.

I don't want to give the impression that every Arab who came to London was extravagant. Far from it. The majority were families, and Edgware Road would be full of people out strolling in the evenings, meeting old friends and acquaintances, stepping into cafés and restaurants for some mint tea or coffee, or organizing picnics and barbecues in Hyde Park.

A highpoint of any visit to 'Beirut-on-Thames' was Speakers' Corner on a Sunday afternoon. Middle Eastern regimes do not generally encourage free speech, so the idea of a place where anyone can stand up and say whatever he or she wishes was both novel and exciting. There was one speaker called Haroun, a Muslim who came from Mauritius, and who addressed his audiences in English. His fame spread through word of mouth and he became a cult figure among Middle Eastern visitors. He was sarcastic and cracked disrespectful jokes about the British, their government and their queen, always ending with anti-Zionist slogans at which point he would pull out a Palestinian flag and wave it to massive cheers from the crowd. Though enjoying his rants, the Middle Eastern listeners would look anxious; used to muscular state intervention, they felt he was in imminent danger of assassination by MI5. He was offered all kinds of help and support, from money to a safe haven in the Middle East if ever he had to flee for his life.

Abdel Bari's Citizens' Advice Bureau

From November 1979, as London bureau chief of *al-Madina* newspaper, I had my own small suite of offices in the International Press Centre. Friends and acquaintances from the Middle East would often drop in or call me; after a few months I noticed that the claims to acquaintanceship were becoming increasingly tenuous, until it got to the point where the visitor wouldn't bother saying he was a 'friend of so-and-so who you once met in Cairo' and would instead enter my offices and announce himself as a complete stranger. Naively, I responded to this presumptuous behaviour with typical Arab courtesy and hospitality. News of my open-door policy spread like wildfire and I came to be regarded as a sort of tourist office for visiting Arabs. They would pop in or phone me up to find out the best restaurants and clubs, or where they could buy a certain type of linen suit. Worse than that were the many who used me as a citizens' advice bureau and brought me their problems: one wanted me to find him a job; another, accused of a crime, requested my services as interpreter at the police station; once a man burst through my door in a terrible state, shouting that he had just woken up on the floor of his hotel room and had lost £10,000. I still don't know what he thought I could do about it since I was neither an insurance company nor a bank.

One day someone phoned me from a pay-phone. I looked at my watch after the opening conversational courtesies had continued for an inordinately long time, accompanied by the sound of coins being constantly fed into the machine. After I had answered his enquiries into my health and well-being for the fifth time and accepted his congratulations and listened to him praising God for my strong constitution, I wondered what this uninvited caller really wanted. Since I had a cab waiting outside to take me to a television studio, I was pressed for time and, feeling impatient, asked him what he wanted. 'Ah, Abdel Bari,' he said. 'The problem is that I am bored.'

'Bored?!'

'Yes, I am in hospital in Harley Street, my wife has gone shopping and there is nothing here, nobody to talk to, no entertainment, just a lot of ill people.'

I had many calls and visits from Arab men who had married British women, who for some reason were often of Irish extraction. Some of these Arabs had fallen in love but there were also some who had married to gain British citizenship. While I was never sympathetic to the latter, I did try to help those who wanted to make things work, explaining that British women had different expectations from many of their Arab counterparts and would not necessarily be satisfied with a domesticated life. The complaint I heard most commonly was that their British partners were not 'like mother'. Mother, of course, had done everything for these men: cooking, cleaning, washing and nursing them. A more serious issue was to do with domestic violence. It is regrettable that some Arab husbands beat their wives, and young men who had grown up with this in their families thought nothing of trying the same with their British wives. While I am sure that some women suffered this kind of ordeal in miserable silence, quite a number of them gave as good as they got. I had calls from men choking back tears as they described how strong their wives had turned out to be. One told me that his wife had punched him, 'With an upper cut, like a boxer'. I had little sympathy for these battered husbands, nor was I sorry when wife beaters ended up in police cells.

There were other cultural difficulties to overcome in even the most harmonious Anglo-Arab marriage. One was how to raise the children, especially where religion was concerned: Muslim, Christian, a combination of both or none at all? Children hate to stand out as different and so there were agonies over what to name them. The Arab community in London discovered a whole range of dual-nationality names, for example Sami and Sara.

In Muslim culture, being cuckolded is the most shameful thing that can happen to a man. Not only does it mean the end of the marriage, it is also a mortal blow to his pride and honour. Unfortunately, British wives seemed to be more likely to subject their husbands to this torment than their Arab sisters, or perhaps they were just worse at hiding it. I would advise men in this position to go to the mosque and talk to the *imam*; one positive effect was that a number of men found solace in religion and deepened their understanding of it. The practical and legal side of divorce British-style was an alien concept, and some reached breaking point when they discovered that they were likely to lose custody of their children, as well as having to pay a maintenance allowance to a woman who had betrayed him.

Finding a suitable wife was often a problem for Muslim newcomers to London. When the late Dr Zaki Badawi was *imam* at Regent's Park mosque, he came up with a novel solution to this problem. In the latter part of the 1970s, he asked his staff to set up an informal marriage bureau. A catalogue of suitable, single women was drawn up with photographs and a short personal description. Men would look through this catalogue and discuss suitability and compatibility with members of the mosque. If a match was deemed suitable, the couple would be introduced, accompanied by chaperones, and matters would proceed from there.

Yusuf Islam

The well-known British pop star, formerly known as Cat Stevens, converted to Islam in 1977 and took the name Yusuf Islam. He met his Afghani wife, Fawzia Ali, the daughter of an accountant from Surbiton, at Regent's Park mosque and they were married on 9 September 1979. I was the first person to interview Yusuf Islam after his conversion. Dr Badawi arranged for me to meet him at the mosque. I was fascinated that such a successful young man, who had everything most people only dream of, would give it all up to devote himself to Islam. Yusuf Islam was humble, softly spoken, and proud of his religion. He wanted to start a new chapter to his life and was ashamed of his former drug-taking, drinking and womanizing.

It turned out that even Cat Stevens wasn't his real name. He was born Stephen Demitri Georgiou and brought up by his Cypriot father in the Greek Orthodox faith. The name change happened when he embarked on his musical career as a teenager. He admitted to me in our interview that he had treated women as 'goods' before his conversion. 'They had to be beautiful and that was it,' he said. He had had many girlfriends, including Patti d'Arbanville who later went out with Mick Jagger. Yusuf Islam described how he began to feel disillusioned with all the trappings of fame and started on his search for deeper meaning in life. In 1977, he almost drowned in the Pacific Ocean and shortly afterwards his brother, David, brought him an English translation of the Qur'an which he at once felt was the 'spiritual truth'.

Dr Badawi described to me the first time Yusuf Islam went to Regent's Park mosque to worship. 'I told him I hoped he wasn't going to give up music,' Dr Badawi recalled, 'but he was adamant, insisting that musical instruments were considered *haram* in the Qur'an. I tried to dissuade him from such a radical standpoint but he auctioned all his instruments and gave the money to Islamic charities.' In 1983, Yusuf donated a substantial amount of money towards the founding of a Muslim school in London and he remains a key figure in London's Muslim community.

I saw him again at an Islamic conference in Khartoum in 1992. The President of Sudan, Omar al-Bashir, hosted a banquet for some of the participants including myself and Yusuf Islam. Yusuf had not sung in public since his conversion but at President Bashir's request he agreed to sing an

Islamic song that was popular in the Prophet Muhammad's time. It was a wonderful performance, sung in Arabic with no accompaniment, and received a standing ovation.

Yusuf went back into the recording studio in 1995 after an absence of seventeen years to make *The Life of the Last Prophet*, a CD of songs, verses and recitations from the Qur'an. Some time later, he played guitar on a Dolly Parton album and released his first commercial record since 1978, *An Other Cup*, in late 2006. He appears to have overcome his qualms about instruments – he carries a small piano around with him in a briefcase on which he composes his songs – but his faith is just as strong and his songs reflect that.

In 2004, Yusuf Islam was a victim of the current wave of Islamophobia when he was refused entry into the US on the grounds that he might be a terrorist, an assumption based solely on suspicion of his name and the fact he had a beard. The plane he was on was diverted to a military base in the US, from where he was sent back to Britain. I telephoned him afterwards and he was furious, saying he would seek compensation and an official reversal of the decision.

Jihad *Comes to Neasden*

If Yusuf Islam softened his radicalism to some extent, the early 1990s witnessed the arrival in London of thousands of Muslims for whom such compromise was not an option. These were the returning *mujaheddin* from Afghanistan and Bosnia. Many of these Islamists were unable to return to their homelands and sought political asylum in Britain, cutting dramatic figures in the leafy northern suburbs of London, with beards and Islamic clothing. They included men who had fought with Osama bin Laden against the Russians and remained crucial to the evolution of al-Qaʻida. Osama bin Laden had established the 'Advice and Reform Committee' (ARC) and this organization had offices in London from 1994, headed by Khalid al-Fawaz. Al-Fawaz, who was known among the Arab ex-patriot community as 'bin Laden's Ambassador', was imprisoned in 1999, accused of having played a role in the 1998 al-Qaʻida US embassy bombings in Nairobi and Dar es Salaam. For a curious journalist like myself, these men represented a portal into the fascinating hidden world of the *jihadis* and Khalid al-Fawaz was to be the first stepping stone when I went to interview Osama bin Laden in Afghanistan in 1996.

Finsbury Park and Neasden were popular with the Islamists, who established mosques and Muslim schools in these areas. Having spent the 1980s in *mujaheddin* training camps, living in tents or mud houses, they were grateful when they arrived with their, often large, families for state provision of substantial houses, schools and the National Health Service. For some of these characters the comforts of the West proved more compelling than *jihad* and they settled here permanently, entertaining the youth in the mosques with colourful tales of their past heroism.

This was a situation that Osama bin Laden had foreseen. He issued a *fatwa* (ruling) against settling in an 'infidel' country and told me when I met him that he would 'rather die than live in a European state'. Dr Ayman al-Zawahiri (who together with bin Laden had formed the World Islamic Front for Jihad against Jews and Crusaders) also voiced the fear not that his peers would be corrupted, but that their children would become 'Europeanized'. Bin Laden's *fatwa* represented an obstacle for *jihadis* preparing for flight to the West and was only overcome when the *Mufti* of *al-Jihad*, Dr Said Imam, issued individual *fatwas* allowing people to 'go to Europe and live with the atheists on a temporary basis until a Muslim country applying true Shari'a is established for you to move to'. The presence of the ex-*mujaheddin* in Britain may well have contributed to the radicalization of a segment of British Muslim youths who see in them the fighting spirit wanting in their parents, whom they perceive as passively accepting a low social status and the humiliations of racism and Islamophobia.

Among the high-profile Islamist figures in London are Dr Muhammad al-Massari and Dr Saad al-Fagih, both leading Saudi dissidents and founts of useful information. Dr al-Massari, with an eye to irony, likes to meet interviewers and colleagues alike in Mcdonald's, an incongruous figure sitting at a formica table surrounded by the gaudy paraphernalia of the fast-food outlet, dressed in a long white robe and sporting a full beard. Dr al-Fagih lives in north London where he runs the Movement for Islamic Reform in Arabia from the front room of a suburban home. London has played host to people with closer ties to al-Qa'ida, several of whom I have met. One of them was Abu Qatada, often described in the media as 'al-Qa'ida's spiritual leader in Europe' and who had lived in London since coming to Britain on a forged UAE passport in 1994. I had seen him on television and had the impression he was not only radical but violent: he was championing the Algerian Armed Islamic Group (GIA) at the time and was reported to have issued a 1995 *fatwa* legitimizing the killing of the wives and children of 'apostates'.

I was surprised in the summer of 2005 when the receptionist at my paper, *al-Quds al-Arabi*, told me 'a guest is waiting in your office'. I tend to invite guests into my office, and not the other way around. My surprise turned to shock when my visitor turned out to be none other than Abu Qatada who was under house arrest at the time and electronically tagged.

Abu Qatada, whose real name is Omar Uthman Abu Omar, is a Palestinian born in 1960 in Bethlehem. He was different from how I had imagined, with a good sense of humour, and not as extreme as I had anticipated, although still radical in his political and religious views. Abu Qatada kept me entertained the whole of his visit, talking about poetry, literature and other cultural matters, as well as theology. I remained mindful, however, of just how dangerous this man might be, if the accusations against him are true.

Abu Qatada had gone on the run in December 2001, having been accused of involvement with planning the 9/11 attacks on New York and Washington, as well as being a mentor of the 'shoe bomber' Richard Reid. I asked him what had led to his recapture and subsequent imprisonment in HMP Belmarsh from where he had emerged, tagged, in March 2005. Abu Qatada said he had become tired of moving from one house to another, inconveniencing and endangering the friends and acquaintances who were hiding him. 'I was careless and phoned my family,' he recalled. 'I knew my phone was tapped and they arrested me.'

Abu Qatada distanced himself from the horrifically violent way the GIA had developed and said that he believed they had been infiltrated by Algerian intelligence services. Hearing I was writing a book about al-Qa'ida, Abu Qatada told me that he personally had accepted al-Zarqawi's *bayat* (pledge of allegiance) to Osama bin Laden when he became the Emir of al-Qa'ida in the Land of the Two Rivers (Iraq) in October 2004. This was quite a scoop. Not long after his unexpected visit to my office, Abu Qatada was arrested again and he has been in prison since August 2005 awaiting extradition to the US.

Another top-ranking al-Qa'ida figure I met in London in the mid-1990s was Abu Mus'ab al-Suri (al-Suri means 'the Syrian' and forms part of his *nom de guerre* his real name is Mustafa Setmariam Nasar). Al-Suri was captured in Pakistan in September 2005 and is accused of involvement in several major atrocities including the Madrid and London bombings, in 2004 and 2005 respectively. I first met him in his capacity as a journalist in London in 1995. Like Abu Qatada, he was involved with the GIA and was editing their radical newsletter, *al-Ansar.* He told me he was planning to move to Afghanistan and offered his services as a correspondent for *al-Quds al-Arabi* which I declined, having read some of his radical outpourings in *al-Ansar.* Displeased, he asked if I would at least write him a letter of accreditation to ease his path. Again I refused.

I thanked God a thousand times that I had not done as al-Suri asked, for when I arrived in Tora Bora, Afghanistan, in November 1996, where I was to spend three days with Osama bin Laden, he was the first person I met. He told me that he had joined al-Qa'ida and I later discovered that he had trained in various *mujaheddin* camps as a young man and had been a Muslim Brotherhood commander in Iraq. He is also accused of training elite fighters for al-Qa'ida in military strategy, explosives and urban guerrilla warfare between 1988 and 1992. If US intelligence had found letters of accreditation from me on him when he was arrested I would have had a lot of explaining to do.

Al-Suri is a tough character and I remember him being often agitated in manner and opinionated – I watched him openly disagree with bin Laden during my stay in Tora Bora. Many have commented on his dourness and the only time I saw a smile on his face was when I complained about the food Osama bin Laden gave me in the caves.

Despite his lack of personal charm, Abu Mus'ab al-Suri is respected among *jihadis* for his formidable intellect and has been a key al-Qa'ida strategist for a number of years. In August 2005, a wide-ranging article by al-Suri was published on several *jihadi* forums on the internet, which I translated into English. It includes a colourful insight into the lives of *jihadis* in London during the time I am describing:

> The *jihadis* who were in London from 1992–1997 were active in the Muslim community in Britain and set up mosques, Islamic institutes, lectures, educational facilities, and published newsletters. I,

myself, set up a study centre for Islamic world conflict in London and acted as a media contact for Osama bin Laden. When television teams went to Jalalabad to interview our Sheikh [Osama bin Laden] I accompanied them, and I also acted as interpreter for Robert Fisk of *The Independent* when he met our Sheikh.

London was the centre for communications between Islamist groups and ones opposed to the governments of their own countries. We maintained communications with *jihadi* leaders outside Britain, in particular Dr Ayman al-Zawahiri [al-Qa'ida's second-in-command] whose regular calls I would take in a telephone box in the London suburbs. He used to give us his advice from his hiding place in Caucasian countries. We were also in touch with Sheikh Osama bin Laden who was in the Sudan, as well as *jihadi* leaders in Europe and Chechnya, Bosnia, Turkey, Egypt, North Africa, Lebanon, and Yemen. On a regular basis, we would meet with these leaders and study the situations. Since I had a Spanish passport I could move freely.

All these activities were taking place right under the noses of the government and security services during John Major's government and that's what encouraged me to live in London for three years. Most of the organizations were above ground – for example Osama bin Laden's Advice and Reform Committee had an office in London where he issued all his communiqués ... The Major government was clever and served the security of Britain and the interests of its people by accepting our truce; which meant that we would never target the country or use it as a base to attack any *jihadi*'s country of origin, so long as the security forces left us alone.

Most of us *jihadi*s and Islamists were interviewed by the British security forces between 1994–7 but this was done in a polite and reasonable manner. When Tony Blair came to power in 1997 he tore up the unwritten understanding and stabbed the *mujaheddin* in the back by changing the laws and harassing us. I believe this showed early on that Tony Blair already had the intention of attacking the Muslim world under the American umbrella.

In the past, interrogations by the security forces had been a political and theological dialogue. There were indirect threats of deportation as a maximum punishment but there was no violence and the officials were courteous. This we could bear to live with but after 1997 it became tough and threatening.

I went to Afghanistan in 1996 and again in 1997. I met Osama bin Laden and he gave me a letter for the *mujaheddin* in London urging them to come to Afghanistan, because life in London was becoming unbearable and Britain was no longer a safe haven. Many left at this time and I can find no excuse for those who didn't. They must have been too keen on the good life in Britain or else they were deceived by the trick of democracy and the idea that they were protected by the law.

Peacocks

If the majority of Londoners, including most of its journalists, were oblivious of what was going on in *jihadi* circles, the British press were entranced by other larger than life Arab characters living in London, such as Egyptian-born Muhammad al-Fayed, who owns, amongst other businesses, Harrods, and the Palestinian publisher, Naim Attallah.

In early 2004, I was at the Harrods sale, looking for new ties, when I saw the unmistakable figure of al-Fayed himself. He was showing Colonel Gaddafi's cousin, Ahmed Qaddaff al-Dam, around his store with a degree of pride befitting his assimilation into this 'nation of shopkeepers'. The two men spotted me and came over to say hello. Hearing that my son, Khalid, was mad about football, al-Fayed reminded me that he had bought Fulham football club in 1997 and very kindly suggested that I bring Khalid to watch them play as his personal guest. His next offer astonished me. He brought out an ornamental pillbox from his inside pocket and tapped out two tablets. 'You should try these, my friend,' he smiled. 'It is a new drug especially for us men – it is called Viagra.' I have no idea if this was just one of al-Fayed's practical jokes, they might have been mints for all I know because I declined his offer.

The next time we met, I was lunching with a Lebanese politician in the Harrods restaurant. Al-Fayed came in while we were there and greeted us with great charm. 'Why don't you ever call me?' he asked me. 'We have plenty to talk about.'

'I thought you were living in Geneva,' I explained. 'I thought you'd moved there as a protest for not getting your British passport.'

'I am back now,' he said. 'As you know, in our tradition the younger should call the older out of respect, so I will be waiting.'

I know that al-Fayed wanted to discuss the death of Princess Diana.

His allegations of a conspiracy leading to the death of Princess Diana were aired at length in the recent inquest, with the coroner ruling that there was no evidence to support them. There are several precedents, however, including the 1944 murder of the celebrated singer Asmahan. Born Amal al-Atrash, she was a Syrian princess, though she spent most of her adult life in Egypt where she rivalled Umm Kulthoum as a singer. Strapped for cash due to a chronic drink problem she was easy prey for the British security services and spied for them throughout the Second World War, until her death in a 'car accident' that coincided with the discovery that she was a double-agent. Asmahan drowned in a ditch while her chauffeur escaped with minor injuries. In the US too, such deaths are not uncommon: during the Watergate scandal, thirty key witnesses were mysteriously killed between 1972 and 1975, three of them in car crashes. I had some sympathy with al-Fayed's point of view.

Why would the British establishment seek the death of the most popular member of the royal family? Diana was in love with, and possibly about to marry, Dodi al-Fayed, who was a Muslim. I voiced my assassination theory on ITV and, in the course of the televised debate, found myself at loggerheads with Bernard Ingham, who had been Margaret Thatcher's press secretary. I suggested that the British establishment, of which he was a member, found the idea of the heir to the throne having a Muslim step father completely unacceptable. It ended in a heated argument and as soon as the cameras were turned off, Mr Ingham marched off muttering, 'This is not British television,' without shaking hands or saying goodbye to anyone.

During the same show we debated the issue of arranged marriages which the British media was up in arms about at the time. One of my fellow guests was the daughter of a disgraced Tory MP who had had a child with his mistress. This lady had been married and divorced more than once, leading me to point out that people don't always make the right choice for themselves. I jokingly suggested that if she let me arrange a good Muslim husband for her, I might make a more successful match. She laughed and refused my offer but I was amused to see, two years later, that BBC2 launched a series called *Arrange Me a Marriage* based on the same premise. The irony was that Princess Diana's marriage to Prince Charles was itself, to all intents and purposes, an arranged marriage.

Naim Attallah is a self-made millionaire, who has occupied the head of the boardroom table at Aspreys and Mappin & Webb, published *The Literary Review* and *The Oldie* magazines, and had his own publishing house, Quartet Books. Like me, Attallah is Palestinian, but there the resemblance stops. He is an active older man who, even now, in his seventies, surrounds himself with beautiful young women. I interviewed him several times in the 1980s when he was at his most flamboyant, famed for throwing the 'best parties in town' in his offices, which were housed in a spectacular Mayfair penthouse with a stuffed tiger in a glass case in the middle. Platinum-haired, Attallah's fingers and lapels glittered with jewels and bright colours; he favoured yellow shirts and his ties were as loud as his voice. His staff seemed to be composed entirely of the daughters of the British upper class, who populated the pages of *Hello!* magazine when it entered the scene in 1988, and whom he collectively referred to as his 'girls'. One such 'girl' was the now-celebrated chef, Nigella Lawson. I once asked him about his choice of staff and he laughed, saying, enigmatically, 'It is very nice for all of us.'

Attallah is an energetic man who likes to try his hand at a variety of enterprises, some successful, some less well-judged. As a publisher, he produced two of my favourite books, David Hirst's *The Gun and the Olive Branch* (an objective history of the Palestinians) and *The Palestinians* by Jonathan Dimbleby with wonderful pictures by Don McCullin. Even his failures are sensational, however, in keeping with his flamboyant persona. He turned his hand to writing some years ago and authored several books, including novels that featured erotic passages so gratuitous and unrealistic in their detail that *Private Eye* named him 'Naim Utterly Disgusting'. According to ghost writer Jennie Erdal, some of those earlier works were not written by him at all. In her book *Ghosting*, she claims to have written some of his novels in addition to many of his articles. If Erdal is to be believed, she also penned letters on Attallah's behalf to his long-suffering Polish wife, Maria.

In 1979, Attallah decided to produce a film about Ibn Saud, the founder of Saudi Arabia. As London correspondent for a Saudi paper, this was of interest to me and I went along to interview him. Preparations for the film were not going well and Attallah was in a terrible mood, throwing tantrums and barking down the phone or at his 'girls'. He was obsessed with the idea that the king should ride on a black camel, the rarest type there is, but no one could track one down. They'd been trying for days and everybody was 'useless, utterly useless'.

'Why don't you just dye one?' I suggested. He halted in his tracks and glowered at me, 'Abdel Bari Atwan, that is the most idiotic ... ' He stopped in mid-sentence, reconsidering. 'Yes. Good idea!' he shouted, tapping a number into the phone on his desk. 'Just dye one!' He snapped as soon as someone answered. 'Yes ... get a normal brown one and dye it black!'

Attallah had already spent a lot of money on this film. He had paid a prominent screenwriter to adapt an Arabic biography of Ibn Saud into an English script, and he told me that he had almost finished a reconstruction of Mecca in the Moroccan desert. I wrote about the camel in a humorous article for *al-Madina* and was surprised when I learned the film was not, after all, to go into production. Rumours abounded that the Saudi royal family had lost their confidence in the project and arranged for it to be quietly dropped, but made sure that no one was out of pocket.

8

Osama bin Laden

I was in Yemen in 1998 when the car I was being driven in was besieged by a crowd of people who recognized me and blocked our path. 'Sheikh!' they clamoured. 'Talk to us about the Sheikh. How blessed you are to have spent time with him.' They were talking about Osama bin Laden, who is particularly revered in Yemen since his father originally came from the Hadramaut region in the south of the country. Because I had interviewed him and spent three days with him, I found myself in the awkward position of being viewed as an Islamist and religious authority – a Sheikh – myself. During my short stay I was even approached to lead prayers in mosques and give sermons although I have no theological credentials, apart from being a practising Muslim.

A publisher in Sanaa sought to make more canny use of my fleeting association with Osama bin Laden. 'Please, Abdel Bari,' he begged. 'Just write one tiny little booklet about the Sheikh, we will put the picture you have of you and him together in the mountains on the cover and we will both become very, very rich!' I refused because I was certain this man did not desire the kind of balanced account of the al-Qa'ida leader that I eventually published in my book, *The Secret History of al-Qa'ida,* in 2006.

This phenomenon is not limited to Yemen. I seem to have developed a following of sorts throughout the Arab world. When I gave a talk in

Tunis at the end of 2006, for example, the police had to cordon off the street because of the crowds. Even in London, I am constantly stopped in the street by people wanting to shake my hand or have their photograph taken with me. My children are appalled, muttering: 'It's not as though you're a pop-star.'

When I went to Tora Bora in 1996 to meet with Osama bin Laden and his men in their hideout, I had no idea how dramatically the resulting interview would change my life and my career. The edition of *al-Quds al-Arabi* in which it was published sold out within minutes of hitting the news-stands. I was bombarded with calls from all over the Middle East begging me for copies. One Saudi friend who claimed not to be speaking to me broke his silence to phone me, asking for five copies, one for a member of the royal family. Entrepreneurs made blackmarket photocopies of the article which exchanged hands for ridiculous sums. The Muslim world was fascinated by Osama bin Laden.

Few would approve of the violent methods the al-Qa'ida leader endorses, and the majority of Muslims would probably not wish to live under the strict Shari'a form of governance he aspires to, but the West still fails to understand that the man himself has become a figurehead of iconic status in many Muslim countries. It is worth briefly reviewing his biography in this context and identifying exactly what it is about the man that resonates so strongly with his peers.

Osama bin Laden was born in Riyadh, Saudi Arabia, on 10 March 1957. His father, Muhammad bin Laden, had started out as a labourer when he first moved from Yemen to Saudi Arabia but soon demonstrated that he possessed all the shrewdness and daring for which his countrymen are famed throughout the Arab world, starting his own construction company and rapidly accumulating a fortune on the back of the Kingdom's petro-dollar-fuelled building boom. Muhammad was introduced to Osama bin Laden's mother, Alia Ghanem, while on a business trip to the Syrian coastal region of Latakia in 1956. When he made her his fourth wife shortly afterwards, it was his tenth marriage, as he had divorced six times. By all accounts Alia was a great beauty and when Osama bin Laden was born a year later, he inherited her good looks. Alia and Muhammad were divorced while Osama bin Laden was very young but Alia was soon married again, this time to Muhammad Attas with whom she had three sons and a daughter.

Though he was the forty-third of fifty-three siblings, Osama bin Laden was favoured by his father who died when he was only ten years old. Members of the family have told me that Osama bin Laden didn't play with the other children but preferred to sit quietly with his father and was often to be found reading the Qur'an. When I asked him about his childhood Osama bin Laden recalled how he had often accompanied his father to construction sites and from a very early age had joined the labourers, working on roads and buildings as his strength permitted. He was particularly proud of the fact that his father had been in charge of the mosque building and maintenance programmes in Mecca and Medina (the most holy places in Saudi Arabia) and had won the contract to restore the Dome of the Rock mosque in Jerusalem. For Osama bin Laden, it was the nature of his father's work, 'God's blessing', rather than the reward, 'Allah's bounty', that mattered. This is important in the context of the complete disregard for wealth or material comfort that Osama bin Laden would exhibit in later life.

Muhammad bin Laden was a billionaire by the mid-1960s and had gained considerable influence with the royal family. When King Saud and his brother Crown Prince Faisal fell out, Muhammad bin Laden was among those who persuaded Saud to abdicate in favour of Faisal. It must have been immensely distressing for the ten-year-old Osama bin Laden when Muhammad was killed in a plane crash. King Faisal told the children they were in his charge from now on but Osama opted to spend more time with his mother and his stepfamily. Perhaps this demonstrates an early antipathy towards the House of Saud who would later become his mortal enemy.

I have rarely met an Arab man who speaks well of his stepfather so I was particularly struck by the affection Osama bin Laden expressed for Attas during the time I spent with him. Bin Laden's love for his mother is quite exceptional, and she, too, adores her son and follows his outlaw career almost obsessively, recording his television broadcasts and cutting out newspaper stories about him. The Saudis would later exploit this when they were trying, in the latter half of the 1990s, to persuade Osama bin Laden to return to the Kingdom and apologize to the royal family whom he had accused of being un-Islamic. Alia, together with a delegation of senior male relatives, was dispatched to Sudan and Afghanistan in a private jet on at least nine occasions, according to bin Laden, but he refused to oblige. 'I apologized to my family,' he told Peter Arnett in a CNN interview broadcast on 10 May 1997, 'because I knew they were driven by force to come to talk to me.' The CIA are also aware of the close ties between mother and son and, for this reason, the two have been unable to meet for nearly a decade.

Osama bin Laden married his cousin, Najua Ghanem, when he was just seventeen and they have eleven children. He subsequently married four more times, divorcing one wife, Um Ali, at her request because she felt unable to live the austere lifestyle he expects his family to share with him. Bin Laden's eldest son, Abdullah, also returned to Saudi Arabia following an argument with his father during which he asserted his right to enjoy the luxuries their family wealth could procure which he viewed as 'the blessing of Allah'. Bin Laden told me that this had deeply wounded him. When I met him he had a total of eleven sons and thirteen daughters, Najua had returned to her native Syria with his blessing and he told me that his remaining three wives lived harmoniously under one roof.

Osama bin Laden studied economics and business administration at King Abdulaziz University in Jeddah and continued his religious development. His mentors were renowned Islamic figures such as Muhammad Qutb and Dr Abdullah Azzam. The latter also introduced Osama bin Laden to politics and in particular the situation in Afghanistan which had been invaded by the Soviet army in 1979. Azzam emphasized the religious obligation of *jihad* to liberate fellow Muslims from foreign occupation and by 1982 Osama bin Laden had moved to Afghanistan more or less full-time where he fought with the 'Afghan Arabs' alongside the *mujaheddin*.

Back in London, I began to hear reports about bin Laden's activities in Afghanistan and realized that something extraordinary was afoot. By now a millionaire in his own right, he had arranged (and paid) for a whole fleet of heavy construction equipment to be delivered to him in the remote mountains of the Hindu Kush. The arrival of bulldozers, drilling equipment and excavators took the *mujaheddin*'s campaign onto another level. Now we heard of the creation of routes over hitherto impassable mountains and hidden labyrinthine camps like the one at Tora Bora I would visit in 1996. This undoubtedly contributed to the defeat of the Soviet invaders in 1989.

Something else fascinated me: visiting *mujaheddin* started to talk about a new school of thought among the Afghan Arabs. Osama bin Laden was among a group of Islamists who were developing a wider vision whereby *jihad* would not only be about, or end with, the local war in Afghanistan. By 1986, Osama bin Laden had started setting up his own training camps in Afghanistan and 1988 saw the establishment of an embryonic al-Qa'ida whose headquarters moved to Sudan, with Osama bin Laden, in 1991.

After the Afghan war, Osama bin Laden had briefly returned to Saudi Arabia in 1990 and was initially fêted as a returning hero, gracing the front cover of several magazines. Things turned sour, however, when the Saudi government invited half a million US soldiers onto their soil to defend Kuwait against Saddam Hussein's army. Osama bin Laden was dismayed – his offer to assemble an army of 100,000 Afghan Arab veterans to assist the Kuwaitis rather than allow an 'infidel' army on 'holy land' had been dismissed. His implacable hatred of the US (and his overt opposition to the Saudi regime) stems from this period and he started making anti-American speeches in Saudi mosques, linking the US with Israel's continued oppression of the Palestinians. Saudi cleric Sheikh bin Uthaymin issued a *fatwa* urging Muslims to prepare for battle with the 'invaders' and bin Laden broadcast this call, encouraging Saudi youths to seek military training in Afghanistan. Bin Laden was now viewed as a security threat within Saudi Arabia and he was placed under house arrest. His passport had been confiscated, but on the pretext of attending to some business affairs he left for Pakistan, never to return.

The Islamic National Salvation Revolution Party had taken control of Sudan in a 1989 military coup and bin Laden set about establishing a safe haven there for Afghan Arab veterans who, like him, were unable to return to their homelands. Word went out that al-Qa'ida was providing homes and jobs in Sudan and hundreds of *jihadis* moved with their families into the houses the organization rented for them. Al-Qa'ida also purchased several farms where some of the land was used for military training.[1] Al-Qa'ida carried out their first attacks on US targets during this period: the first was in 1992 when it bombed US troops in transit at the Goldmohur Hotel in Aden, Yemen, killing three people and wounding five; the second took place in Mogadishu, Somalia, and was immortalized in the 2001 Hollywood film *Black Hawk Down,* directed by Ridley Scott. Until my interview with

---

1.   Statement by Jamal al Fadl, in *The Osama bin Laden I Know,* compiled by Peter L. Bergen (New York: Free Press, 2006), p. 121.

Osama bin Laden in 1996, nobody knew about al-Qa'ida's involvement in the Mogadishu battle which saw the destruction of two US Black Hawk helicopters and three others seriously damaged by rocket-propelled grenades (RPGs). Osama bin Laden confirmed that Abu Ubaydah al-Banshiri (al-Qa'ida's military commander who would later drown in a ferry accident on Lake Victoria) had led the al-Qa'ida men who participated in the attack which they had planned in cooperation with the Somali warlord General Muhammad Farah Aideed. Seventeen US airmen died in the battle and seventy-three were wounded; President Clinton's administration responded with a rapid withdrawal of all remaining US military in Somalia. Osama bin Laden told me that he was sorry they had 'run away' because he had had 'further plans for them'.

Osama bin Laden's men had demonstrated that they were capable of taking on, and beating, the world's greatest superpower in a local battle. Nevertheless, most of bin Laden's time in Sudan was spent developing the organization's political ideology and on various construction and agricultural projects which he financed himself in good faith but which were to leave him out of pocket to the tune of $165 million when President al-Bashir proved unable to repay the loans. Osama bin Laden told me that the Sudanese had offered him compensation in the form of cattle and grain and I was amazed by his good humour when he laughingly wondered what he was supposed to do with such goods. He was already on the CIA's most-wanted list when he was forced to leave Sudan in 1996; President al-Bashir could not withstand the increasing pressure from Egypt, Saudi Arabia and the US to rid himself of this dangerous guest.

Osama bin Laden returned to Afghanistan where he formed an initially uneasy alliance with the ruling Taliban and established his base and hiding place in the mountains of Tora Bora. To me, as to many Muslims, he was already becoming the legendary figure he is today. Here was a man who, a billionaire in his own right, had shunned all material comfort for a life of hardship and privation in pursuit of an ideological vision. And this vision was pan-Arab, inclusive, incorporating disenfranchised individuals and disparate nations into one *umma*, the collective Muslim nation. Many of those who have been drawn to al-Qa'ida have mentioned the fact that it 'doesn't matter what nationality you are' as one of its attractions in a world all too easily split by ethnicity or race.[1] Furthermore, bin Laden was a warrior, and stories of his bravery in battles in Afghanistan were widely circulated. Since the US, after years of self-interested meddling in the region's politics, is viewed by many Muslims as the source of their problems, al-Qa'ida's ability to launch successful attacks against the military superpower was inspirational for many and Osama bin Laden's call to arms has been taken up by thousands of young men.

In the West, meanwhile, Osama bin Laden, while definitely on the CIA 'terror' radar, remained relatively obscure through the 1990s, though some journalists were picking up on his burgeoning status and significance in the Arab world. From the outset bin Laden was media-savvy, hand-picking the very few journalists to whom he would offer an interview on the basis of their previous work and political understanding. Robert Fisk was the first to interview him in Sudan in 1993 and he met him again in Afghanistan in 1996; the American writer and broadcaster, Peter Bergen, conducted the first television interview for CNN in 1997. I was known among the small group of specialists in the West and while I was often approached for comment, information or contacts, my own profile remained relatively low.

All that changed in the aftermath of 9/11; the *Guardian* newspaper revived the story of my trip and published an English translation of my interview with bin Laden. A picture of me with the al-Qa'ida leader filled the front page of the second section and the text was syndicated throughout the world. I have related elsewhere in this memoir how I had the world's press camped outside my offices for several days after the attacks on New York and Washington. Overnight I became an international media figure and 'world expert' on al-Qa'ida.

The Secret History of al-Qa'ida has been translated into fourteen languages and is a best-seller in several countries. While my trip to Tora Bora has undeniably been good for my career it has also got me into quite a lot of trouble. In February 2003 I was invited as guest speaker to the Commonwealth Writers' Association in Sri Lanka. In the question and answer session that followed my talk, I was asked by an Asian journalist to describe what bin Laden was like as a person. I compared him to the Buddha because he renounced all his wealth and possessions, or Mahatma Gandhi who

---

1. See, for example, the FBI report of their interview with Muhammad Sadiq Odeh, ibid., p. 138.

spoke up for the poor and lived a very humble life and added, 'But a violent Buddha or a violent Gandhi obviously.' The next day, headlines across the subcontinent screamed: 'Arab Editor compares bin Laden to Buddha and Gandhi'; the journalist had dropped the crucial word 'violent'. To make matters worse the story was picked up by the wires and sent all over the world within twenty-four hours. I had to do a lot of damage control, reiterating that I had qualified the comparison, but I am still sometimes challenged over this unfortunate statement which I have never repeated. While any association with Osama bin Laden, however short-lived or tenuous, often generates admiration in the Muslim world, in the West it is dangerously open to misinterpretation.

I did not approach al-Qa'ida for an interview with Osama bin Laden – nobody would be able to breach the sophisticated security measures the organization employs – but they approached me. It seems that the leadership approved of *al-Quds al-Arabi*'s independent stance, which was unique in the Arab media at that time, because in 1994 we received the first in a series of communiqués from Osama bin Laden, criticizing Gulf regimes and alleging that the rulers were embezzling oil revenue that should benefit the people. Few other papers in the Arab world would even consider publishing such things. I still have a collection of these communiqués, which were sent by fax and signed by bin Laden, including the August 1996 'Declaration of Jihad against the Americans Occupying the Land of the Two Sacred Places' which we received shortly before the first tentative approaches were made with regard to my visit to Tora Bora. Until they turned to the internet, al-Qa'ida sent all their communiqués to us; the last we received claimed responsibility for the Madrid train bombings. Nor were they alone; Saddam Hussein also faxed us lengthy communiqués both during and after the 2003 US invasion of Iraq. For me, this was the role of the free, uncensored, objective press I aspire to, but not everybody saw it that way.

At the beginning of 2004 I was invited onto the O'Reilly show on Fox News. Bill O'Reilly favours the highly adversarial interviewing style of a Jeremy Paxman, usually holding back the biggest punch until the end hoping for a knock-out. In my case he suddenly asked me why my paper had been the vehicle of choice for al-Qa'ida and Saddam Hussein (who was on the run at the time) to issue statements, accusing me of sympathizing with fugitives and radicals. 'Saddam is secular and to the left on the political spectrum,' I answered. 'Osama bin Laden is Islamist and conservative. If I receive communiqués from both these extremes that means I am in the middle, doesn't it?' For once O'Reilly backed down. I pursued my advantage, 'If Fox News received a video tape from Osama bin Laden tomorrow with exclusive pictures, a real scoop, are you really telling me that you would say to the courier, "No thanks, we don't want it"?' O'Reilly responded with a mumble and the interview was over.

The Eagle's Nest

So how did it happen that, in November 1996, I became one of the few Western-based journalists ever to interview Osama bin Laden and the only one to be invited to spend a significant amount of time with him in his mountain-top lair, the 'Eagle's Nest'? I wrote at length about my time in the 'Eagle's Nest' and the remarkable conversations I had with Osama bin Laden in *The Secret History of al-Qa'ida* and do not intend to reproduce the account here but I will briefly describe that momentous trip and my subsequent dealings with bin Laden and al-Qa'ida.

I am still not quite sure why Osama bin Laden and his right-hand men chose to invite me from among all the Arab journalists for this exclusive and unique access. I had certainly never expressed any kind of sympathy for their aims, although I must admit I was rather fascinated by the global vision which they were already beginning to develop and express even in 1996. I realized that here was a brand-new, unexpected and totally committed opposition to burgeoning American global hegemony. I later found out that bin Laden and Dr Ayman al-Zawahiri admired my outspoken criticism of certain Middle Eastern regimes and my opposition to the 1991 Gulf War. In addition my paper was the only truly independent voice in the Arab media at the time and they believed that I would accurately and even-handedly report on what I found – they were not disappointed.

The initial contact was made by Osama bin Laden's bearded and robed London representative, Khaled al-Fawwaz, who very casually dropped his query as to whether or not I would like to meet 'the Sheikh' into another conversation altogether. Osama bin Laden wasn't as infamous then as he is now but he was still being hunted by many of the world's intelligence agencies, including the CIA, and had a $5 million price on his head. I knew the journey would be hazardous and difficult since Afghanistan was probably the most dangerous country in the world at that time. I knew that I could be in danger both from the CIA – if they tailed me and then attacked – and bin Laden's men if I were to unwittingly betray the location of al-Qa'ida's headquarters through some carelessness on my part. I told al-Fawwaz to give me twenty-four hours to decide and wrestled with nightmare scenarios whereby my children would be left fatherless, my wife a widow and my paper with no editor. However, as a journalist with more than twenty years' experience I knew I had to go.

There was another reason I took this risky assignment. We Arab journalists have long criticized ourselves for our reluctance to quit the comfort of a five-star hotel in any danger zone and have always admired our Western counterparts who readily put themselves on the front line. I wasn't a young reporter with anything to prove but I wanted to pioneer a braver kind of journalism and set an example for my staff at *al-Quds al-Arabi*.

I knew that secrecy was imperative and that I wouldn't be able to tell my family or colleagues where I was really going. I have always maintained that luck plays a very important role in journalistic success and it so happened that al-Jazeera television invited me to Qatar to participate in a television debate at exactly the right time. I told everyone I was going to Qatar and onwards to Dubai 'to relax' for a few days. Since I never 'relax' and everybody knows it, this occasioned some mild interrogation and I was sometimes obliged to be uncharacteristically curt and brusque to stave off any further enquiries. My wife, Basima, was not so easily deflected. Although I travel regularly, a situation she usually accepts without demur, on this occasion she must have intuited that something unusual was afoot.

'What shall I pack for you?' she asked, opening the small suitcase I usually take on my travels. I had been given strict instructions not to bring anything, presumably for security reasons in that I might conceal a weapon or a tracking device.

'Nothing,' I replied.

'Nothing?' Basima shot me an interrogative look.

'Well ... A few shirts,' I conceded. 'And maybe a couple of ties.'

'Trunks?' asked Basima, getting out my bathing costume.

'No!' I replied. Basima put them down on the bed and turned to me.

'You said you were going to Dubai to relax,' she pointed out. 'Aren't you going to sunbathe and swim then?'

'Maybe...' I allowed the item to be put into the case, grimly imagining myself arriving at the HQ of the world's most dangerous *jihadi,* deep in the mountain cave systems of Afghanistan, wheeling a neat little suitcase behind me.

Basima's suspicion was not blunted by this exchange and when I left the next morning she gave me a very quizzical look and said, 'Be careful', in a meaningful voice. When she later discovered the truth about this trip she was so angry that she didn't speak to me for several days.

I had been given absolutely no inkling of how the interview was to come about. All I knew was that I had to be at the Hotel Pearl Continental in Peshawar, Pakistan, on such and such a date and that on arrival I was to telephone a man called Faisal whose number had been given to me written in pencil on a scrap of paper. Incredibly the logistics of the trip worked perfectly. I travelled disguised in Afghan clothing to avoid suspicion – a long shirt, baggy trousers and a turban which looked completely ridiculous on me as I do not possess the proud bearing and aquiline features of the Pashtun who usually wear it. We crossed several mountain ranges in an assortment of the world's most antique vehicles guided by a succession of rash drivers, miraculously surviving hairpin bends, hair-raising precipices and rock falls to arrive, more than thirty-six hours later, at the 'Eagle's Nest' camp deep in the mountains of Tora Bora.

It was dark when we got there, but I could dimly make out the forms of armed men moving briskly around, steam rising from their mouths and noses in the freezing night air. There were several armoured vehicles around the entrance to the caves bristling with RPG launchers and machine guns.

It was just before midnight on 23 November when I entered the cave where Osama bin Laden was sitting cross-legged on a carpet with some of his followers, among whom I recognized his lieutenant, the renowned military mastermind Abu Hafs al-Misri, and Abu Mus'ab al-Suri. It was a rather strange moment because I had only ever seen this well-known face in photographs before. 'The Sheikh' had his beloved Kalashnikov rifle in his lap (indeed I never saw him without it the entire time I was there) but he put it to one side as he got up and came to greet me with a warm smile. He laughed a little as he took in my absurd outfit and his eyes lingered on the turban before he shifted into a more business-like mode and led me to sit with him, enquiring about my journey.

We talked for some time over an unappetizing dinner of fried eggs and hard bread. I was saving my more political questions until the next day when I would be sharper after a good night's sleep, but I started a light-hearted conversation about how these men spent their spare time in such a harsh environment. Osama bin Laden loves horses and managed to keep quite an impressive stable even in hiding; apparently he sometimes took some time away from the camp, riding into the wilderness accompanied by his three wives and children for horseback racing and target practice. I was surprised when the men told me that Osama bin Laden was a great volleyball player. 'It's because he's so tall,' Abu Hafs volunteered and described how he was the captain of one team while the 6 feet 3 inches tall bin Laden headed the opposition. There were regular matches which would be enthusiastically watched by the entire camp.

Since we were all laughing, Osama bin Laden was obviously inspired to relate the hair-raising but funny story of their flight from Sudan to Jalalabad in May that year. One of his most trusted lieutenants, Sayf al-Adl al-Misri, was co-ordinating the trip, which was conducted in such secrecy that not even the Russian pilot knew where they were going. Not only was the pilot kept in the dark about their destination, he didn't speak a word of Arabic and had no idea of the identity of his passengers – all heavily armed al-Qa'ida men. Sayf al-Adl sat in the cockpit with the pilot throughout the entire flight, his machine gun across his knees, scouring maps and checking the navigation instruments, issuing loud verbal instructions accompanied by sign language. Somehow the plane got to Afghanistan where they were greeted by a small Islamist delegation.

I asked them why they had chosen such an austere lifestyle. Osama bin Laden told me that his ambition was to live a life as close to that of the Prophet's companions as possible. Although he was a billionaire he had no interest in luxury or even comfort: 'It is better to live under a tree on these mountains,' he said, 'than in great palaces having compromised our religion' (a reference to the Saudi royal family). He portrayed life as a test of faith, steadfastness and obedience to Allah; he aspired only to Paradise and said that the quickest route was by martyrdom (he often referred to his desire to die as a 'martyr' during our time together). He also reflected on the military failures of organizations whose leaders are fond of extravagance and whose foot soldiers are incapable of enduring great hardship. There was something incongruous, but empathetic, then, when my hosts insisted in considerate tones that I must be tired after my arduous journey. I was offered a bed, sharing a cave with Osama bin Laden himself. This 'bed' was a mattress lying across several crates of grenades, with an arsenal of rifles and machine guns suspended from the ceiling, which – together with a cockerel outside who wouldn't stop crowing – did not make for an easy night's sleep. Bin Laden had no such problems and slumbered like a baby until dawn, his Kalashnikov at his side.

The next day we walked alone together in his beloved mountains and he told me about his personal past, clarified several mysteries (for example, the involvement of al-Qa'ida in the Black Hawk attacks in Mogadishu referred to above) and outlined the long-term strategies of his organization, developed over time with several highly intelligent and well-educated strategists, not least among them Dr Ayman al-Zawahiri and Abu Mus'ab al-Suri. In retrospect I can see that this careful planning and far-sightedness has been key to the success of the organization and I am amazed by how much of what the al-Qa'ida leader told me has actually come about. At the time it seemed unthinkable that al-Qa'ida could inflict any real and lasting damage on the mighty US. Osama bin Laden stated that he wanted to fight the US in Muslim lands where his *mujaheddin* would have the advantage; to do this he would have to 'provoke' them into sending troops to the region. This is exactly what subsequently happened: in the aftermath of 9/11 the US first launched a full-scale attack on Afghanistan and then invaded Iraq. In order to increase the numbers in a burgeoning pan-Arab Islamic army, al-Qa'ida's rhetoric would focus on Muslim unity and a sense of belonging to the Muslim nation, the *umma*. According to the al-Qa'ida master-plan, the US would be stretched militarily, fighting wars on several front, and then engaged in a long battle of attrition (as has indeed come about in Iraq and Afghanistan where the insurgency continues unabated). Economically astute, bin Laden then outlined how these costly wars would drain the US coffers, forcing it into a downward economic spiral resulting in bankruptcy and fiscal implosion. We now know that the war in Iraq alone has cost the US $3 trillion and the nation faces a full-blown recession.

I asked Osama bin Laden what the final outcome of this confrontation with the West would be and he looked towards the snow-capped mountains with a serene smile as he described how the 'hated and corrupt' Arab regimes would be overthrown, releasing the Muslims to 'fight the Pagans all together'. Finally, according to his vision, a global Caliphate would be established.

Osama bin Laden has immense personal charisma and speaks softly and gently, constantly offering a reassuring smile. Though I do not agree with his interpretation, I do consider Osama bin Laden a religious authority and leader who exhibits an extraordinary understanding and knowledge of theological matters. For this reason, when I wrote my account of this trip, I referred to him as 'Sheikh' and I was the first to do so in print. Sheikh is a term of respect which we use for older people, religious leaders or very wealthy men. Osama bin Laden, in fact, is all three and I stuck by this appellation despite vociferous objections from the Gulf Sheikhs who felt he was usurping their position and credibility.

Our conversation continued into the night and through another inedible dinner. In the morning I had to break the ice on a bucket of water to perform my ablutions but despite the hardships of life in the Eagle's Nest I was almost sorry when it was time to leave and we said our goodbyes.

I have not spoken personally to Osama bin Laden again, but his men kept in touch with me until the US developed such sophisticated surveillance methods that any kind of telephone communications became too dangerous for them. Shortly after my account of my time in Tora Bora was published in *al-Quds al-Arabi* I received a call from one of the Eagle's Nest men who did not give his name. 'When he got to the bit about the horrible dinner you had, the Sheikh burst out laughing,' he told me. 'He has promised that if ever you go to him again he will put on a large banquet with a stuffed lamb for you.'

The Aftermath

In 1998, Osama bin Laden and Dr Ayman al-Zawahiri announced the formation of the World Islamic Front for Jihad against Jews and Crusaders in the pages of my newspaper. When the umbrella group carried out its first attacks against the US embassies in Dar es Salaam and Nairobi on 7 August 1998, it claimed responsibility in a statement released to us. The US administration responded by bombing bin Laden's bases in Afghanistan and shortly afterwards I received a personal telephone call from Abu Hafs al-Masri, who told me that the US mission had failed: bin Laden and all the key leaders were still alive. He then added: 'Sheikh Osama bin Laden has a message for US President Bill Clinton: he will avenge this attack in a spectacular way and will deal a blow to America that will shake it to its very foundations, a blow it has never experienced before.' I published these comments but neither I nor any other al-Qa'ida watcher would have believed the organization capable of the level of destruction inflicted on New York and Washington just three years later.

As a result of my three days in Tora Bora and the publication of my book *The Secret History of Al-Qa'ida* it seems my name is now inextricably linked in the public mind to that of the world's most wanted man. There have been some strange and totally unexpected ramifications: in January 2008, for example, I received a puzzling telephone call from CBS concerning Omar bin Laden, one of Osama bin Laden's nineteen children who had been the object of much press attention after he married a British woman, Jane Felix-Browne, who has now taken the Islamic name Zaina. Omar, it appears, had told CBS researchers that he would not give them an interview without my 'blessing' which they now sought. 'But I have never met either of them,' I told my contact at CBS. 'I'm not an agent for the bin Laden family!'

Since my book was published in 2006 I have had numerous problems entering the US and was unable to get to Washington, DC, when I was invited to give a seminar at the New America Foundation; when I subsequently went to the US Embassy in London to apply for another visa, this time to participate in a debate with Richard Perle at Harvard University, I was taken into a small room and finger-printed as if I were a criminal. In September 2007, I was invited to speak at the Brisbane writers' festival; despite applying for a visa well in advance, I had still not received it by the date I was due to fly to Sydney. It was only when the Australian press took up the story which they widely portrayed (correctly, I believe) as an example of Islamophobia that the Embassy suddenly found they were able to process a visa for me in twenty-four hours. I attended the festival but was two days late for my talk which the organizers obligingly rescheduled.

It appears the British intelligence services were bugging Muslim MP

Saddiq Khan and I am certain that I too am a candidate for surveillance. Friends and colleagues have suggested I should have my home and offices 'swept' for bugging devices but I assure them that I would rather be listened to than be the object of baseless suspicion and conjecture.

I was twice offered the opportunity to visit bin Laden again. In April 2001 I received another telephone call from Abu Hafs al-Masri. He suggested that I should come to Afghanistan and interview not only Osama bin Laden but also the Taliban leader, Mullah Omar, who had hitherto refused to speak to the press. I went as far as getting my visa at the Pakistani Embassy before I changed my mind. The whole trip would have been too risky – even applying for the visa may have alerted the US and British secret services and I did not want to be the person who led them to bin Laden. If they attacked his hideout I would be killed, if they failed to capture or assassinate him he and his men would think I'd colluded with the intelligence services and kill me themselves. While it is true that I might go to heaven, I am not in any hurry.

I was approached again after 9/11. Abu Hafs al-Masri had been killed in the 16 November 2001 US bombardments of Tora Bora but I received three telephone calls from another person who didn't give his name. I presume it was Khaled Sheikh Mohamed, who was very close to bin Laden at the time. He said, 'The Sheikh is waiting for you', and invited me to go somewhere to meet him again. I would very much like to have gone and I would be fascinated to meet Osama bin Laden again, but I can't imagine it will ever be safe to do so.

9

Yasser Arafat and the PLO

I knew Yasser Arafat, the Chairman of the PLO, who died on 11 November 2004, for many years and, though I frequently disagreed with him, he remains a uniquely significant figure in my life and, indeed, the lives of all Palestinians. Although his political career was fraught with controversy and he attracted a great deal of criticism from friends and enemies alike, he died without having compromised the Palestinian position, without concession, without surrender. First besieged and then, as I believe, poisoned by the Israelis, he conducted himself with dignity to the end and is now remembered and revered by his people as a truly great Palestinian.

When I was starting *al-Quds al-Arabi*, I asked Arafat what advice he could give me about leadership. Referring to the Qur'an he told me, 'First, avoid anger and choose forgiveness instead; second, never be unkind or hard-hearted.' Failure to abide by these principles, he said, would result in disloyalty and even desertion. Arafat had founded Fatah in the late 1950s and was already a legendary figure when I was growing up. Under Arafat, Fatah developed its military wing, al-Asifa, and, unlike his predecessors such as the more intellectual Ahmed Shukairy, the PLO's first leader, Arafat looked very much the fighter in his trademark camouflage trousers and jacket, and distinctive *keffiyeh*. To us, Arafat was a hero and our spokesman. People liked him because he spoke their language, and didn't indulge in the rhetoric of Marxist ideology, theology and Arab nationalism. He had one cause: to liberate Palestine from occupation.

Arafat's populist approach inspired and galvanized the entire Palestinian nation in those early days. The PLO set up a short-wave radio station that broadcast revolutionary songs and these became the backdrop of my teenage years in the refugee camps of Gaza. I remember lyrics like, 'I am the son of Fatah, I never shout any name but its name,' and 'Guerrilla war, guerrilla war, oh land of our fathers.' These songs were often sung at parties and even in school.

Actually, the man who wrote many of these songs was a relative of mine called Sayeed al-Muzien, the ex-Palestinian ambassador to Saudi Arabia. He had the distinction of having been involved in a fist fight with Yasser Arafat in the 1970s. The two of them were in the middle of an ideological disagreement regarding the direction Fatah should be taking when al-Muzien, who was more conservative, made the big mistake of trying to slap Arafat's face. The ensuing brawl would have ended badly for al-Muzien had Arafat's bodyguards not intervened. Sayeed al-Muzien fell out with Arafat once and for all in 1990 over his stance against the Gulf States during the invasion of Kuwait and was removed from his post.

I little imagined, as a teenager in the refugee camps, that my future self would frequently meet this brightest star among Palestinians, let alone discover that this idol was not only fallible but, often, downright wrong.

Mohammed Abdel-Raouf Arafat al-Qudwa al-Husseini was born on 4 August 1929. He was always known in the family as Yasser, since it was said he resembled Yasser al-Birah, a Palestinian fighter in the Arab revolt against the British in the 1930s. Arafat was cagey about his place of birth but the general consensus is that it was Cairo, Egypt, and not Jerusalem as he would have liked us to believe. His father was a businessman from Gaza who had little to do with his children; indeed, Yasser Arafat didn't attend his funeral when he died in 1952. His mother, Zahwa, was from a highly influential Palestinian family; her uncle, Haj Amin al-Husseini, was appointed Grand *Mufti* of Jerusalem by the British in 1921, remaining the most prominent Arab figure during the period of the Mandate. Zahwa died when Arafat was just five years old and he was sent to live with an uncle in Jerusalem, travelling frequently between Cairo and Palestine in a pattern of restlessness that would characterize his entire life. His Fatah movement started an armed struggle against the Israeli occupiers in 1965, a year after the umbrella Palestinian Liberation Organization was founded. He went into hiding in 1965 and re-emerged after the 1967 Six-Day War with the *nom de guerre* Abu Ammar.

In 1969, he became chairman of the PLO executive committee and was driven out of Jordan, where Fatah was based, along with thousands of other Palestinian freedom fighters in the Black September massacres of 1970. His new headquarters were in Beirut but even though he won recognition for the PLO as the sole and legitimate voice of the Palestinian people at the UN in 1974, he was unable to rest in one place. In 1982, he was forced to flee again when the Israelis invaded Lebanon. PLO headquarters were briefly established in Tunis before another move, this time to Syria. In 1983, he was expelled from Syria, and returned to Lebanon where he was besieged by the Syrian army and forced to return to Tunis. In 1987, the First Intifada broke out in the Occupied Territories but it was not until 1994, in the wake of the Oslo Accords and in receipt of the Nobel Peace Prize, that Arafat returned to Palestine where he established the Palestinian Authority (PA) in Gaza. Sadly, Arafat's presidency did not usher in a period of peace and stability and the discontent that had been brewing in the interim erupted again with Ariel Sharon's uninvited entry into the al-Aqsa mosque compound in 2000. Sharon initiated a personal vendetta against Arafat and became his mortal enemy. The Palestinian leader spent most of his last two years confined to his bombed-out offices in Ramallah, besieged by the Israeli army and air force. He was stricken by a mysterious 'illness' at the end of October 2004 and moved to Paris where he died on 11 November 2004.

I knew Arafat for more than twenty-five years and I admired and liked him as a person. We enjoyed periods of closeness – for example during the first Gulf War and its aftermath when he found himself very isolated – and times when a fundamental disagreement over policy matters would set us at odds. My inclination is more towards Islamic pan-Arabism but Fatah, according to Arafat's vision, was resolutely nationalistic. For Fatah, the Palestinian question was only about the Palestinian people, to be resolved by us alone. For me, the matter concerns the entire Arab and Muslim world, the *umma*. Arafat guarded his relations with the Gulf and other Arab leaders carefully (although he fell out with many of them due to his support for Saddam Hussein during the first Gulf War): they provided him with generous funds after all. To me, many of those same leaders were corrupt dictators who had contributed to our downfall, if not through active collaboration then by the absence of military back-up in our fight or by strategic silence.

Arafat was loyal to his friends and I was careful not to burn my bridges with him. This required some effort since he was often infuriated by the fierce criticisms I levelled at him both in print and in conversation. Most of my differences with the PLO leadership were to do with their peace negotiations with Israel, mediated by the US and first encompassed in the Oslo Accords in 1993. I was against this and every subsequent round of negotiations because they did not satisfactorily resolve the issues that most concern the Palestinians: sovereignty over Jerusalem, the right of return and compensation for up to six million Palestinian refugees, the dismantling of illegal Israeli settlements, control over security and the establishment of final state borders.

Mahmoud Abbas (also known as Abu Mazen), now the Palestinian president, disliked me for what he perceived as my refusal to compromise. He thought I was ruining the show for the PLO leaders and decided to sideline me. Arafat took a different tack and often tried to woo me over to their side by incorporating me into the PLO political machine. Back in 1989, for example, I received a strange phone call from our correspondent in Amman. 'Congratulations, Abdel Bari,' he said.

'Why?' I was baffled.

'You have been elected to the PNC.'[1]

'Have I?' I was astonished by this news since I wasn't aware I had even been a candidate. 'Which party am I in?' I joked.

'You are independent.'

'Thank God,' I laughed. I saw the hand of Arafat in this and on reflection considered it an honour. As an independent member I would sit beside eminent Palestinians like Muhammad Darwish and Edward Said whose company I greatly enjoyed and it is fair to say that this was the most interesting and enjoyable aspect of my time in the PNC. I attended nearly every annual assembly until the organization stopped convening in 1996. It

---

1.   The Palestinian National Congress, a sort of parliament-in-exile that met annually, headed by Yasser Arafat.

was a good opportunity to have my say and be heard by the most influential of my people as well as to listen to other points of view.

In 1993 Arafat invited me to accompany him to Washington for the 'historic' signing of the Oslo Accords. I had no difficulty in refusing that offer. Arafat tried again, in 1994, to win me over with an offer to join his cabinet in the Palestinian Authority as minister for culture and information but I had no desire to become a politician. Two years later, he sent an envoy, Ghibril al-Roujoub (his security adviser in the West Bank), to meet me in London, suggesting I move to Gaza and act as an under-secretary in the ministry for a six-month period. Taking a lower profile post, he reasoned, would give me the chance to see how things worked, meet the right people and see how I liked it prior to accepting a ministerial appointment. Although this compromise offer was slightly more realistic and better tailored to my temperament (Arafat was perceptive) I didn't waver and again refused. When he visited London a few months later he again offered me a ministerial post; I promised to think seriously about it because I didn't want to offend him, but again refused.

Many of us were opposed to the Oslo Accords but even seasoned observers were amazed when Arafat first revealed that he had held secret talks with Israeli Premier Yitzhak Rabin. What many people don't know is that the waters of direct negotiations between Israel and the PLO had been tested as much as a decade previously by Issam Sartawi, a PLO moderate. I met him in London in 1983 and was shocked when he told me he had held face-to-face talks with senior Israeli politicians. 'The decision was taken by Arafat and Fatah,' he claimed, 'but they are distancing themselves from it because it is a huge gamble.'

I felt that Arafat's new-found 'political pragmatism' concealed an increasingly egocentric agenda. It was well known that the US had been looking to replace him as the representative voice of the Palestinians in the peace process due to his support for Saddam Hussein's invasion of Kuwait in 1991. They had already made inroads with other key Palestinian figures who had emerged during the Intifada including Faisal Husseini and Hanan Ashrawi, now the leader of the independent 'Third Way' party. Perhaps it was because he sensed that he was in danger of losing his position that Arafat agreed to the 1993 secret talks with Rabin in Oslo. He benefited from the Oslo agreement in that his PLO was acknowledged as the legitimate voice of the

Palestinian people and the Palestinian Authority, which he would head, was established to exercise administrative control in Gaza and Jericho.

With the Oslo Accords, Arafat had recognized the right of the state of Israel to exist and condemned all forms of terrorism as well as brokering an end to the First Intifada, all immense concessions, but had procured very little in exchange. In my view, Arafat had sold six years of Palestinian bravery and sacrifice cheaply and played all his cards just to get the game started.

I could see that Arafat had made the mistake of behaving with Western leaders according to the Arab mentality which assumes that if you manifest goodwill the other side will reciprocate. This doesn't wash with the US and Europeans who expect diplomacy to be a form of barter. History is full of examples of misguided Arab political generosity. In 1972, during the Cold War, President Sadat of Egypt decided he would be better off being backed by the US and was discussing the possibility of dismissing the Soviet military advisers in his country with King Faisal of Saudi Arabia. Faisal understood the Western mentality well and advised him to ask the US to negotiate the return of the Sinai (from the Israelis) in exchange. Needless to say, Sadat did not heed this advice and duly received nothing in exchange for his shift of loyalty.

I remember going to visit Arafat in his Tunis office in late June 1994. It was just a few days before his triumphant return to Gaza but he was alone and sullen. Some of his entourage had abandoned him for ideological reasons, refusing to be party to the Oslo Accords; others, perhaps the majority, had left for financial reasons. Economic support from Kuwait and Saudi Arabia had been cut off as a result of the PLO's support for Iraq in the first Gulf War and the organization's coffers were temporarily empty at this point. We talked for many hours and at 3 AM, just as I was leaving, Arafat said to me, 'Listen Abdel Bari, I know you are against the Oslo Agreement but never forget what I am about to tell you: one day the Israelis will flee Palestine in their thousands. I won't see this in my lifetime but you surely will, and the Oslo Agreement will have been a contributing factor.'

The Israelis have not yet fled Palestine in their thousands as Arafat predicted, but they have withdrawn from Gaza. There is evidence of some increase in reverse migration, from Israel to Europe, the US and Canada. I believe the Israelis are experiencing a weakened sense of national security and a general feeling of exhaustion due to constant domestic and international strife, most recently the 2006 war in Lebanon. The war with Hezbollah, which lasted thirty-four days, was the first in which they failed to achieve a definitive victory.

Most Palestinians had lost faith in the Oslo Agreement by 1995 but the PLO had committed itself to 'final status negotiations' and these were convened at Camp David in July 2000. I had seen little of Arafat in the mean time and was not party to his thoughts either before or during the talks. Besides, the participants were not allowed access to either mobile or landline phones, to ensure that the outside world knew nothing of what was going on. However, Mahmoud Abbas excused himself and his entourage from the talks in order to attend the wedding of one of his children. He stopped over in London and sent Ahmed al-Khaledi (who was one of the Palestinian negotiators) to let *al-Quds al-Arabi* know what was going on in Maryland. Al-Khaledi revealed that Muhammad Dahlan,[1] Hassan Asfour[2] and Muhammad Rashid[3] were all in favour of accepting the final draft President Clinton had put forward which included giving Israel partial sovereignty over Jerusalem and compromising the Right to Return. Abbas and Arafat, however, would not surrender on these points. I don't know if this leak was Abbas's personal initiative or if he was prompted by a despairing President Arafat, but when we published this information it created an uproar among the Palestinians and an international controversy. Some believe that this intervention by Abbas played a significant role in relieving the pressure on Arafat and bringing about the failure of the Camp David negotiations.

Enjoying the privilege of private conversations with Arafat, I was often party to his hidden agenda and strategic machinations. Post-Camp David, he told me that he had signed the Oslo Accords as a manoeuvre to buy time and break out of the isolation that had been imposed on the PLO after the first Gulf War. He had never, he said, intended to give way on the refugees' right to return and he had resisted immense pressure to concede partial Israeli sovereignty over Jerusalem during the Camp David negotiations. He was particularly upset that this pressure came not only from the US but also from other Arab leaders; despite the ban on telephone calls, he had

---

1. Chief of the Preventive Security Service (PSS) – the PA's police force.
2. Palestinian co-ordinator of peace negotiations.
3. An Arafat adviser.

been allowed to take one from Prince Abdullah bin Abdul Aziz of Saudi Arabia who urged him to be 'flexible' on the matter of Jerusalem.

With regard to the failure of the Camp David talks, there is a postscript. One of Arafat's aides later told me that the PLO leader had called Clinton three days before he was due to leave office in January 2001. 'You are a great man,' Arafat told him. 'The hell I am,' Clinton is said to have replied. 'I'm a colossal failure and you made me one.'

The US effectively decommissioned Arafat after the Camp David talks and the Fatah leader told me that it was in direct response to this that he personally oversaw the formation of the Fatah suicide-bomber wing, the al-Aqsa Martyrs' Brigade which carried out its first attack on 29 November 2001 and was very active throughout 2002. Arafat had previously condemned the use of 'human bombs' which Hamas had employed since 1994 but now he had given up all hope of a negotiated settlement. As his rival George Habash once said, 'the nature of the struggle is determined by the nature of the enemy'. Arafat didn't want Hamas to hijack the vanguard of armed struggle with their martyrdom operations, either. Arafat always wanted to compete.

I managed to get on the wrong side of Arafat early on in my career, which could have been disastrous for me. This falling out was not to do with politics but humour. It was back in 1984, when I was covering the Palestine National Council in Amman for *al-Sharq al-Awsat*. I couldn't help but notice two stout, elderly ladies wearing full Palestinian dress sitting in the balcony seats. As soon as Arafat entered the hall they started ululating; when he opened his mouth to speak they would ululate; and when Arafat rose to leave, the same thing: 'Lalalalalalalalalalalalal', in chorus, as if they were in a musical. It seemed as if he had brought them there as part of his entourage and I found this rather cheap.

On my return to London, I wrote an article about these ladies for *al-Sharq al-Awsat* under the title *Muezzins* (those who call the faithful to prayer). It was a funny piece but Arafat was not amused. He phoned the newspaper and asked to speak to the editor-in-chief, complaining about the article and claiming that I had insulted him personally. My editor told me that Arafat was shouting and had threatened never to allow me to interview him again; I admit I was worried I had gone too far.

It was not until 1988 that I needed to test the waters with Arafat again. In July of that year, King Hussein announced that Jordan was relinquishing sovereignty over the West Bank, a major step with enormous significance for the Palestinians since this meant, in effect, that it was now their territory. I telephoned Arafat with some trepidation. He was in Baghdad at the time having backed Saddam Hussein in his war with Iran. I disagreed with this stance but avoided the subject in our brief conversation. My caution paid off and a cordial exchange ended with me being invited to meet the PLO leader in Bulgaria a few days later.

I was in a taxi going to the airport when there was huge bang. The next thing I remember was waking up in hospital in agony. When I touched my head, my hand came away covered in blood; I looked down and my white shirt was also blood-stained. A nurse was cleaning me up and I asked what had happened.

'You were in a pile-up on the M4,' she told me.

'What's the damage?' I asked. 'I'm meant to be somewhere.'

'Well, you've got a lot of cuts, whiplash, a broken nose and a head injury,' she said cheerfully. It turned out that I had been catapulted through the windscreen from the back seat because I hadn't been wearing a seat belt. It was a miracle that I wasn't more seriously hurt and apparently several had been killed, so I felt blessed rather than unlucky. God obviously still intended me to interview Arafat. I told the astonished nurse that I was discharging myself. Fortunately, my suitcase had come with me in the ambulance so I was able to change my blood-stained clothes before leaping in a taxi and heading for the airport again where, by another lucky chance, my original flight had been delayed and I could still make it.

The hostess at the British Airways check-in desk looked at me askance. 'Are you sure you're fit to travel?' she asked. I nodded. She called over a supervisor and I heard snatches of their whispered conversation, the supervisor murmuring, 'Maybe we should call the police?' They appeared concerned and I realized that with my swollen face and broken nose I must have looked as though I was running away from something. I explained as best I could, determined to get to Sofia and do the interview; I didn't intend to lose face with Arafat and knew this was going to be an important and historic interview. They eventually gave me my boarding pass and I had just enough time to buy a newspaper before going to the plane. In the newsagents, I was amused to see that *Playboy* magazine was carrying an interview with Arafat. There was a tiny picture of him on the top right-hand corner of the front cover and a good eight pages of text about him inside. I bought a copy and stuck it in my bag.

I was greeted with similar suspicion in Sofia and on leaving the airport I was tailed by the secret police. I checked into a hotel but found it difficult to sleep because I was in such pain. Early in the morning, there was a knock at my door and I stumbled, bleary-eyed, to open it. An unsmiling hotel worker was standing there. 'You vacate your room now,' he said.

'Vacate the room? But it's only 7 AM. I've never been to any hotel where you have to leave before midday,' I replied in disbelief.

'This is Bulgaria,' he insisted. I was exhausted and needed more sleep to recover from the trauma of my accident and be fresh for Arafat. 'Okay – look,' I said, getting my wallet out of my jacket. 'I'll pay for another night. How much is it?'

'You leave now, you come again after midday. Receptionist come then.' I was flabbergasted and angry. Covered in bandages and plasters, it must have been obvious I was in pain and in need of rest.

'What am I supposed to do? Stay in the street?'

'If you want; that is your problem,' said my persecutor.

'Well, I am not leaving. You can do whatever you want to do about it. I am waiting for people and they are coming at ten.' I shut the door and crawled back into the bed. I had just drifted off when there was a loud knocking at the door. This time I found two vicious-looking uniformed police, who informed me, arms crossed, that if I didn't comply with the 'regulations' I would be arrested. I was still arguing with them when two Palestinians arrived. This is unheard of – a Palestinian who was early for an appointment, let alone two of them – but in the middle of this surreal scene anything seemed possible. They managed to calm me down and sort out my problem with the police and ten minutes later I was sitting between them in the back of a cab, heading back to the airport to get a plane to Varna, by the Black Sea, where Arafat was waiting.

Arafat (whom we more usually addressed as Abu Ammar in person) greeted me warmly. He was impressed by my bruised and bloodied state. Holding my chin and turning my head from one side to the other, examining my array of cuts and bumps, he said, 'Abdel Bari, you are a true guerrilla now!'

As we settled down for a chat we were joined by one of his right-hand men, Jamal al-Sorani (Abu Omar), who was a humorous man and enjoyed a good joke. 'By the way, Abu Ammar,' I said, opening my bag and grinning at al-Sorani. 'I didn't know you were fond of *Playboy*.' Arafat raised his eyebrows and looked alarmed. 'What are you talking about?' he said, looking at al-Sorani reassuringly and glaring at me. 'Of course I'm not.' I got out the copy of the magazine that I had bought at the airport, staring at the cover, holding it so that he couldn't see it. 'Oh Abu Ammar, you are the cover model. You look very beautiful. I didn't know you had such assets.' Al-Sorani took it from me and joined in the joke. 'Wow, Arafat,' he chuckled. 'You've got the body of a 20-year-old!' Arafat got up and snatched the magazine from us. He stared at the cover where the little picture of his head with his trademark *keffiyeh* floated above a topless blonde girl in a mini-skirt. 'That American bastard!' he choked. 'I didn't know it would end up in *Playboy*. It was an American freelance journalist who came and interviewed me. He said he was doing it for a respectable newspaper!'

This was a turning point in my relationship with Arafat. He was touched that I had travelled all the way to Varna to meet him despite my injuries. He opened up and gave me an interview which, in retrospect, was one of the best I conducted with him.

Although he wasn't exactly a 'playboy,' Arafat was fond of women. He started young; his brother Dr Fathi Arafat told me that when they were growing up in the impoverished Sakakini district of Cairo, he was already in love at the age of fifteen and he used to meet a girl discreetly and send her romantic letters. Arafat kept a careful eye on his reputation but liked to have a discreet female companion most of the time. One of his entourage told me that he had secretly married several times under a temporary arrangement called an *orfi* which is permitted under Islamic law. Contracted for a specific period before two witnesses there is no obligation to make such a marriage public. Rachida Mahran was one such wife and I met her on several occasions. She was the widow of a Palestinian fighter and at first I enjoyed her company. I once told her an anecdote from my own life, which had already been published as part of a short story I wrote for a Saudi newspaper and which I have related in this book, about how I was the only person who couldn't give his friends a forwarding address when leaving university because a Palestinian refugee doesn't know where he or she will wander to next. Rachida subsequently wrote a novel that was based on a similar anecdote. Whether it was a coincidence or not I can only guess.

Rachida was discreet about her relationship with Arafat but had her subtle ways of seeking recognition. I remember seeing her at the PNC meeting in 1987, looking at him tenderly and handing him hankies to wipe his brow when he was speaking. I was not alone in noticing this and the Middle East's most famous cartoonist, Palestinian Naji al-Ali, infuriated Arafat by caricaturing the situation. Shortly afterwards, al-Ali told the *Index on Censorship* that his life was in danger and he was assassinated two weeks' later on 22 July. A colleague on his newspaper, the Kuwaiti daily *al-Qabas,* told the BBC[1] that he had received a telephone call from a senior member of the PLO warning him to 'correct [his] attitude' but al-Ali had ignored the warning and published another cartoon lampooning Arafat. I must point out, though, that his killer remains unidentified and some Arab press speculation pointed, instead, at the Israelis.

Rachida wrote a biography of Arafat called *Al Raq'am al Sa'ab* which translates as *A Difficult Number.* I was keen to read it, thinking that it would be full of interesting things he'd told her during their intimacy; I hoped it would reveal the secrets of his birthplace and the first five years of his life which have always been shrouded in mystery but, although well written, it was essentially a hagiography and I lost interest.

Arafat did eventually publicly declare a marriage, to Suha, who is now his widow and to whom I will refer later. At one point, I went to Tunis to meet him and found all the hotels were full. His people put me up in a small villa and when the bodyguard showed me around he opened the door on a modest room and said, 'You can stay in here – that's the bed where Arafat used to sleep with Suha in secret before they declared their marriage officially.' I didn't mind at all and was pleased to sleep in such a historic bed.

The Gulf War

At the end of December 1990, I travelled to Tunis to visit Arafat. He was sitting at his desk signing papers and giving orders; Arafat was bureaucratic

---

1. http://news.bbc.co.uk/onthisday/hi/dates/stories/july/22/newsid_2516000/2516089. stm

and had a centralized concept of power. He would check each receipt before paying expenses. I sat with him while he finished his mountain of paperwork and we talked about the Iraqi invasion of Kuwait on 2 August 1990. He put down his pen and animatedly described his last-minute negotiations with both Saddam Hussein and the Kuwaitis. He had wanted to find an Arab solution to the crisis and avert the full-scale confrontation between Iraq and the US which he, at that time, believed was inevitable. He didn't like the idea of 100,000 US soldiers gathering on the Arabian peninsula and said, 'When the conflict is over they are not going to simply pack their bags and go home'.

The immediate cause of Baghdad's ire and subsequent military threat against Kuwait was oil. At a meeting of Arab Petroleum Ministers in Saudi Arabia which took place on 10 July 1990 at Iraq's insistence, Saddam Hussein demanded a ceiling on OPEC oil production. Prices were falling due to overproduction by some states and this was further damaging the already beleaguered Iraqi economy. Kuwait was one of the main culprits and furthermore stood accused of slant-drilling into the Iraqi side of the disputed al-Rumaila oil fields. Saddam claimed that the Kuwaitis were siphoning off 300,000 barrels of Iraqi oil a day in this manner and described their whole attitude as 'economic warfare'. Meanwhile the US had started a military build-up in Saudi Arabia.

Arafat told me that he had gone to Baghdad on 29 July 1990, just four days before Saddam invaded Kuwait. He had successfully intervened before when Arab leaders seemed intent on conflict with each other and hoped to broker a peace deal.

On this occasion Arafat was accompanied by Jamal al-Sorani (Abu Omar) who was known for his sarcastic humour. Arafat described how Saddam sat looking haughty and arrogant at his neatly ordered desk while the PLO delegation sat crouched over a coffee table. As Arafat told the story their conversation went like this:

'President Saddam, can I ask you a question?' al-Sorani began.

'You may.'

'Do you realize that the Americans are massing half a million troops on your border as we speak?'

'Of course.'

'The Americans are the strongest superpower on earth. Have you done your calculations correctly?' al-Sorani continued. Arafat noticed the Iraqi leader's brow furrowing and his eyes beginning to smoulder. Everyone, even the leader of the PLO, feared Saddam's temper (with good reason) and he pressed al-Sorani's foot with his own under the table.

'There is no question about it,' Saddam stated with forced calm. 'Iraq will win the war.' Despite Arafat's non-verbal entreaties, al-Sorani continued on the same path: 'But surely you must think about defeat, to consider all your options. Imagine if even one percent of your plan goes wrong – ' Arafat now struck his colleague under the table while smiling at Saddam to whom he said, reassuringly, 'Oh Iraq is strong, very strong.' But al-Sorani was on a roll: 'Do you have a secret weapon, President Saddam? Something that no one else has? Not even the mighty US? If you do, just tell us about it please.' At that point, Saddam reached for one of the many telephones on his desk, his eyes 'spurting fire', as Arafat described them to me. Finally silencing al-Sorani with a fierce kick, Arafat got to his feet and shook hands with Saddam, bringing the interview to a hasty conclusion.

Having failed to make any inroads with Saddam, Arafat now flew to Kuwait, where he went straight to see the emir, Sheikh Jaber al-Ahmad al-Sabah. Arafat had his own grudge against the emir at that time: Palestinian workers in Arab countries paid a *D'am* (the nearest English equivalent is a 'tithe') to the PLO which was levied at source by their employers and administered by the various governments. At the Baghdad summit in May 1990 Arafat claimed that Kuwait had frozen the *D'am* and started paying some of it to the Hamas. However, it seems Arafat was prepared to put this behind him in the interests of brokering peace at this crucial moment.

Arafat had always been well received by the emir in the past, and he expected to be listened to as he emphasized how dangerous Kuwait's situation was. The emir however, according to Arafat, hadn't listened to a single word, but had constantly interrupted him and tried to change the subject by asking him about the Intifada and the 'heroes of the stones'. The meeting lasted just twelve minutes.

Arafat then approached Sheikh Saad al-Abdullah, the Kuwaiti crown prince. The two men had been friends for a long time and Saad al-Abdullah had been part of the Arab League delegation that had rescued Arafat during the Black September purges of the PLO by the Jordanian security forces in the early 1970s. 'Sheikh, how many days will your troops remain steadfast if the Iraqis invade you?' Arafat asked him. Sheikh Saad al-Abdullah replied that the Kuwaiti military chief of staff had told him they might hold out for six days but that the deputy chief of staff had said only six hours. Obviously the Kuwaitis did not expect to be standing alone for very long.

I was still mystified by Saddam's confident refusal to withdraw from Kuwait. The whole world could see that America stood poised to attack Iraq. Arafat agreed; not only he, but also the Yemeni Vice-President Salim al-Beed and King Hussein of Jordan, had visited Saddam in the past few days. Saddam had refused to consider a withdrawal, Arafat told me, saying that 'a bigger world power' had assured him that if he stayed in Kuwait there would not be a war. I questioned Yasser Arafat about the identity of this power. He refused to answer.

On 14 January 1991, three days before America launched its attacks on Baghdad, Arafat's second in command, Abu Iyad – who had been outspoken in his opposition to the Iraqi invasion of Kuwait – was assassinated in Tunis by a member of the ANO (Abu Nidal Organization), a Palestinian group, opposed to the PLO but close to Saddam. Arafat was in Baghdad at the time and he telephoned me on 16 January. I was amazed when he announced that he had come round to Saddam's way of thinking: 'The US are not going to intervene,' he said. 'There's not going to be a war, don't worry.'

'Of course there's going to be a war,' I argued, wondering if the PLO leader had lost his mind. 'It's going to happen any minute.'

'I have it on the best authority,' he insisted. 'I am now flying to Tunisia to Abu Iyad's funeral and hope to see you there.' The next day 'Operation Desert Storm' began with US planes blitzing Baghdad. I still hadn't any idea why both Arafat and Saddam were convinced that there wouldn't be a war and that Saddam would win the game of brinkmanship he was playing with the US. My hunch was that it was a conspiracy: the US wanted the war to further their agenda in the region and if Saddam pulled out of Kuwait they'd lose their excuse to attack him. The US had a highly placed double-agent at work, convincing the two Arab leaders that they were only bluffing.

It wasn't until 1996 that a possible answer to this mystery surfaced when an Israeli newspaper published a lengthy interview with Yitzhak Shamir who had recently been replaced as Likud premier by Benjamin Netanyahu and was ready to make some disclosures. Shamir explained how he had held a series of talks with King Hussein of Jordan about the future of the region back in 1988, in the aftermath of the Iran–Iraq War. He spoke of one meeting in particular, on 2 August 1990, the day Saddam invaded Kuwait. According to Shamir, he had travelled to the king's Aqaba palace to discuss the crisis. The king told him that he was obliged to side with Saddam Hussein and outlined his reasoning: 95 percent of the Jordanian population supported Saddam; if the Jordanian ruler opposed Saddam he would, in all likelihood, swiftly invade Jordan; the Jordanian people, supporting Saddam, would depose the ruling Hashemites, and Iraqi troops would be on the Israeli border within hours. In this version of King Hussein's logic, support for Saddam was entirely for the benefit of the Israeli state.

I, and many other commentators, had been surprised when King Hussein came out in full support for Saddam Hussein when he invaded Kuwait, because he usually adopted a position that suited the American agenda or, at least, remained neutral. The king had also made a point of being photographed next to Arafat and gave every indication that he was against the Americans on this occasion.

Whilst it offered an explanation for the king's support for Saddam, I always believed that Shamir had exaggerated this story until I later met Adnan Abu Odeh who had been King Hussein's political adviser at the time. I was placed next to him at a magnificent dinner hosted by Tahir al-Masri, a former Jordanian prime minister. Abu Odeh had been the Jordanian representative to the UN from 1992 but 'retired' in early 1995, spending the next two years in American academia, which could be considered something of a demotion. I had a sense that there was a feud between him and King Hussein and thought it a good time to ask about the past and mentioned Shamir's claims.

'I was at the Aqaba meeting,' he confided. 'Everything Shamir has said is absolutely correct.' He asked me not to publish this information because he was writing a book and this would be one of his main disclosures. Meanwhile King Abdullah succeeded to the Hashemite throne in 1999, and Abu Odeh was appointed as the new monarch's political adviser. When Abu Odeh's book, *Jordanians, Palestinians and the Hashemite Kingdom in the Middle East Peace Process* was published in 1999, I scoured its pages and found no mention of King Hussein's meeting with Shamir. I phoned and asked him why he had failed in what I considered to be his duty to history. He gave me an evasive answer from which I inferred that a request not to talk about this had come from the highest level in the Jordanian government.

In a further twist, King Hussein was invited to Washington to meet President Bush Sr in the wake of the Gulf War, and US financial aid to Jordan continued without disruption. This is hardly the way a leader who had sided with the enemy would be treated and suggests that the US had been well aware of King Hussein's complicated diplomatic manoeuvrings. Unfortunately the governments of Saudi Arabia and the Gulf states, as well as Hosni Mubarak of Egypt, were fully convinced that King Hussein had backed Saddam for political and military reasons and turned against him, with serious economic repercussions. I was told by the editor of *al-Sharq al-Awsat*, Osman al-Omeir, that the king was so eager to effect a reconciliation with his erstwhile benefactors that he asked al-Omeir to mediate on his behalf with King Fahd (with whom the editor was on excellent terms) but to no avail.

His Friends among Leaders

Arafat often spoke to me off the record and confided that of the Muslim leaders, the closest to his heart were the Yemeni President Saleh and President Ben Ali of Tunisia, adding that he had never had a particularly good rapport with Syria's late President Hafez Assad. Whenever we discussed the Egyptian President Mubarak, Arafat would recall Sadat with some nostalgia, as having been the lesser of two evils.

I remember the time I went to meet Arafat in East Berlin where he had been invited by Honecker to take part in the fortieth anniversary of the republic in 1989. When Arafat came from the celebrations he was ashen; he went directly to the suite in an official residence and shut himself in. An hour later he asked me to come up and I found him frowning and depressed, staring at the German TV screen with his protruding eyes. After some time I asked him, 'Are you fluent in German?' He answered with a terse 'No' and silence reigned for several more long minutes while he continued to stare at the screen. Then his face relaxed and his smile returned. 'Come and look!' he said, pointing to the screen. 'There I am, shaking hands

with the Soviet leader, Mikhail Gorbachev. I want you to be a witness.'
He sent for the correspondent from the Palestinian news agency, WAFA,
and dictated a statement to the effect that he, Arafat, had met his Soviet
counterpart Mikhail Gorbachev together with President Honecker, and
that they had had a lengthy discussion about the situation in the Middle
East and global politics. He added that the men had agreed to continue
these talks in Moscow and that the Soviet president had extended an official
invitation to Arafat to visit the Russian capital for this purpose. I pointed
out to President Arafat that the handshake had lasted just a few seconds.
'Yes,' he agreed, 'but I don't want people in Syria to say that Gorbachev
ignored Arafat. Now I have the evidence that Arafat was the first Arab
leader to meet the new president of the USSR, and that I shook his hand
and talked with him.'

The reason that Arafat and President Hafez Assad remained at odds
for many years was the latter's expulsion of the PLO leader from Syria in
the most humiliating manner. Arafat told me that he wasn't given any
notice to quit Damascus and that President Assad had sent a low-ranking
intelligence officer to escort him from his residence to the airport without
even allowing him enough time to collect his personal things. He added
that he felt so angry that he nearly pulled out his pistol and shot the officer
but changed his mind because he understood that he was just carrying out
orders. I think Arafat forgot many humiliations but this one stayed with
him to his grave.

Assad was also behind the removal of the PLO from southern Lebanon where they had set up what amounted to a state within a state. Yet
despite their history, Arafat never missed an opportunity to travel to Syria
in the hope of establishing more cordial relations. In Arab culture, when
somebody dies there isn't any need to wait for an invitation to attend the
family home to offer condolences; so when Assad's mother died in 1992,
Arafat set off for Qurdaha (Assad's home town) and went again in all good
faith when Assad's son, Basil, was killed in a car crash in 1994. He told me
how disappointed he had been by the cool way he was received on both
occasions. Despite the fact that no love was lost between them, Arafat
respected Assad and generally spoke well of him, commenting on his lack
of materialism. 'The sofas at his family home were the same ones I sat on

twenty years ago,' he told me approvingly. 'And they haven't changed any of the furniture at the Republican Palace in Damascus either.'

Among the People

There are countless stories about Arafat's concern for his people and of these, one stands out in particular. I had been invited to have dinner at his offices in Tunis. There was little on the table, partly because there were few guests and also because the quality of food available at that time was poor. In any case, Arafat's meals tended to be tasteless and very plain, much like hospital food. The point is that he asked his aides to go and invite all the people who were outside waiting to see him to come and share the food with him.

One of those invited was a teacher who had lost his job in Algeria. He asked Arafat if he would appoint him as an official at the Palestinian embassy in Algiers. Arafat took a written application from him and signed it, approving him as the third secretary at the embassy. He then told the man to go to the finance department to have his application endorsed and put into effect. I knew that Arafat was all but bankrupt at the time and after dinner when we returned to his private office, I chided him, saying, 'Abu Ammar, you have ruined this man. You have given him a job but he will never be paid a penny because you don't have the money. I know about it because one of my colleagues at *al-Quds al-Arabi,* Adli Sadiq, was posted to the Palestinian embassy in Algeria. He didn't get paid once in six months and he was the ambassador!'

Arafat fixed me with his gaze and said, 'Yes, I know that. But this poor man has a family to feed, he has children. He came to the President of Palestine with such high hopes and it is impossible that I would send him away empty-handed. If Allah opens the way for us to overcome our financial problems we will be able to pay him; if the situation stays as it is, his situation will be no worse than his colleagues' in the embassy.'

Arafat liked to break the fast on the first day of Ramadan at a special home he had built in Tunisia for the children of martyrs. In 1993 he asked me to accompany him and I went with two other guests – the popular singer, Walid Tawfiq, and Georgina Rizk, the former Miss Universe. When he arrived at the home, Walid Tawfiq was mobbed by children – teenage girls in particular – who wanted to shake his hand or get his autograph. Arafat was a little embarrassed by this situation. Press and television cameras were there, set up to record the arrival of the Palestinian president, but Walid Tawfiq had stolen the limelight. After a moment's reflection Arafat turned to me and said, 'I can understand how those children feel. He is a very impressive person.'

Everyone in the Arafat camp had been surprised by Walid Tawfiq's persistence in getting this meeting. He had been obliged to wait a whole week in Tunis before seeing Arafat. He had told Arafat's aides that he wanted to discuss 'an art project concerning the Palestinian question', which was obviously not considered a priority. We later discovered that what he really wanted was to ask Arafat for Georgina Rizk's hand. As the widow of the martyr Ali Hassan Salameh, a close comrade of Arafat, Georgina had stipulated that she would not accept Tawfiq's proposal without Arafat's blessing.

Arafat and Osama bin Laden

Although both men had iconic status in the Arab world, they disliked each other enormously and were very different on a personal level, Arafat having a huge ego and Osama bin Laden being a more humble type. I suspect they both experienced some rivalry, however, and were not slow to voice their criticisms of each other. Historically they had taken opposite sides in the Afghan war which lasted from 1979 to 1989 and Arafat accused Osama bin Laden of being a creature of the Americans. Arafat was close to the Soviet leadership and the PLO backed the USSR whereas, of course, Osama bin Laden was with the *mujaheddin*. Osama bin Laden, meanwhile, accused Arafat of betraying the Palestinians and the whole Arab nation when he signed the Oslo Accords in 1993.

When the attack on the World Trade Center and the Pentagon occurred on 11 September 2001, Arafat was devastated. He considered this a disaster for the Palestinian people since it could provoke widespread Islamophobia and a paranoid backlash against any organization the US cared to label 'terrorist'. He condemned Osama bin Laden and al-Qa'ida unreservedly.

Suha Arafat

The first time I realized something was going on between Arafat and Suha – who was one of his secretaries at the time – was in April 1990. Arafat was on an official visit to India and I travelled to New Delhi to meet him. He was accompanied by Jawid al-Goussain, then head of the Palestinian Fund, Taysir Quba'h and Khalid Salam, his economic adviser. Suha was also there, and something about her self-assurance suggested she may have meant more to the PLO president than a normal employee.

Matters came to a head when Arafat's entourage demanded that the Palestinian ambassador to India add Suha's name to the list of official delegates, enabling her to attend all the meetings. The Indian prime minister was hosting a state banquet for President Arafat whose aides further requested that Suha be seated at the top table. The ambassador refused point blank on the basis that Suha was not of sufficient rank for such an honour. Arafat's entourage tried a thousand ways to get him to change his mind but he would not be swayed. Arafat made no attempt to intervene in this crisis, but what the poor ambassador didn't realize was that the person he'd dismissed as a 'mere secretary' was in fact already the president's wife. But how could he know? The news of the marriage had not yet been announced. Nevertheless I followed this particular dignitary's subsequent career with interest and noted that he never got another promotion.

On the way back from India via Abu Dhabi, I travelled on the same plane as Arafat. He sat opposite Suha exuding contentment and his eyes gave away the romance. We all looked at each other in surprise. I was moved to ask Jawid al-Goussain if maybe I was imagining things but he confirmed that he had noticed it too.

Shortly afterwards Arafat made the marriage permanent and official, something we all found surprising since he always used to say he would never wed. 'I am married to the Palestinian cause,' he often repeated.

When the Second Intifada broke out in 2000, Suha left Gaza – where she had been sharing an ordinary house with her husband – and moved to Paris with her five-year-old daughter, Zahwa (who had been named after Arafat's mother). Her luxurious lifestyle following Arafat's death has been the source of bitterness and criticism among the Palestinian people. Arafat told me how much he regretted the absence of his daughter after they left;

it wasn't until two days before his death that he saw her when she visited him in hospital in Paris just before he went into a coma.

An Old Mule

Arafat used to joke that it was a shame there were no Air Miles for private jets because he was the world's most travelled man, spending more time in his plane than on the land. I flew in his plane many times myself and was not surprised when it crashed in the Libyan desert during a sandstorm in 1992 because it was so old, with the plodding, faltering gait of a mule on its last legs. It used to rattle and shake the whole way, whether there was turbulence or not. Travelling in it was a real ordeal but Arafat was oblivious to his fellow passengers' terror and considered his plane the best, even better than King Fahd's golden Jumbo Jet.

The danger of his plane lay not only in its age and constant need of repair but also in the way it was used. It was a compact aircraft, intended for ten passengers, but Arafat used to transform it into a cargo plane. He filled it with the heavy presents he carried with him everywhere he went. Not jewellery or ornamental daggers but numerous replicas of the Dome of the Rock, made from shells and plaster. Then there was his luggage and on top of that, the surplus passengers he invited along. On one of my trips, I needed to use the toilet, which was situated at the tail end. I discovered that not only had the seats at the back had been turned into beds for his entourage to sleep on, but so had the aisle. Somehow, I managed to lurch over the slumbering bodies, stumbling and tripping on all the rifles and pistols under my feet, and made it to my destination. I opened the door with a sigh of relief only to find that this tiny cubicle too had been requisitioned as a makeshift bedroom. Mission unaccomplished, I slowly returned to my seat.

As soon as he got into the safe haven of the plane, Arafat would take off his battle fatigues in front of everybody, revealing trendy boxer shorts, undo his *keffiyeh* and change into a comfortable blue tracksuit for the duration of the flight.

A Modest Lifestyle

Much has been said about Arafat's irregular personal financial activities but nobody has produced any proof. Indeed, Said Aburish, whom I know well, told me that he spent two full years investigating alleged corruption for his book *Arafat: From Defender to Dictator* but found nothing that suggested Arafat's personal finances benefited from any misuse of funds. That is not to say that Arafat was above using money to influence other people and the allegation that he set up accounts in other people's names is true, but his intention was to conceal the PLO's financial affairs, not his own.

My own experience of the man was that he had little interest in money except to fund the struggle. He told me once about the first time he was given money by King Faisal during a visit to Riyadh in 1968. The king sent an envoy to him with a cheque for $5 million and said, 'This is for your own personal expenses.' Arafat took the cheque and put it in Fatah's funds, and wrote to the king thanking him, explaining what he had done with the money. Arafat said that since taking up guerrilla warfare he hadn't had a personal bank account in his own name. He didn't carry money with him and I never saw him invite anyone to a restaurant or buy as much as a coffee. Arafat died without owning anything, either property or land. The house he rented in Tunisia was a two-storey property, with three bedrooms, one of which was converted into an office, and whilst he had an armour-plated Mercedes Benz, that was for protection not ostentation.

In fact, the only luxury he permitted himself were sweets, of which his favourite was *halwah*, made from ground sesame seeds and honey. He used to take a chunk and put it in one's mouth; I have disliked any kind of confectionary since my days delivering Turkish Delight in Jordan, but I swallowed the cloying goo, because I didn't want to insult him. He was also fond of chocolate caramels and usually had some in his pocket to pop in his mouth when no one was looking. Once we were attending a conference and he offered me some sweets which, unusually, were very nice. I asked him what they were.

'Don't you know?' he said, as if surprised by my ignorance. 'They call it Marron Glacé.'

'And what is Marron Glacé?'

He looked at me and shrugged. 'I don't know. But it is delicious.'

I asked around and discovered it was a French delicacy. The next day I teased him about this, certain he had been introduced to such things by Suha's family – wealthy, bourgeois Palestinians from the West Bank who spent a lot of time in Paris. 'This Marron Glacé is an upper-class thing, Abu Ammar,' I pretended to chide him. 'You are getting spoilt indulging yourself with such luxuries.' 'Shhhh!' he said, looking around like a child caught in the act of doing something naughty. He reached for the tin which was by now nearly empty. 'Shut up and have another one,' he said.

Arafat was a strict Muslim. He never missed his prayers, and didn't smoke or drink alcohol, yet he wasn't judgemental about the way other people chose to live and had secular people around him. I accompanied him on a charter flight sent by the Romanian President Ceausescu; members of his entourage were ordering gin and tonics but Arafat turned a blind eye. He was more concerned with loyalty and trust; during the same flight he leaned over to me and joked, 'I'm dying to go to the toilet but I daren't because those people will stab me in the back if I do.'

Dublin

One of the strangest personal experiences I had with Arafat was in Dublin, the capital of the Republic of Ireland, where he was invited on an official visit in 1996. I met him late at night when he'd finished his preparatory talks and we then agreed to meet again for breakfast at 7 AM the next day.

I arrived punctually at his hotel suite and found his entourage in an agitated state. They asked me to wake the president up myself, stressing that he did not have long before his meeting with his Irish counterpart, Mary Robinson. I was baffled as to why one of them didn't wake him. But they insisted that the job was mine, saying that I had a special place in Arafat's heart. Not convinced, but curious, I went to his bedroom and knocked on the door nervously. Arafat opened it wearing a tracksuit, his eyes flashing with anger. He was taken aback to see that I was the one waking him up but he understood straight off: 'You know why they got you to do this job?' he asked. I replied, 'No, how could I?' Then he told me how he had got up in the middle of the night and found the bodyguard who was meant to be on duty fast asleep. 'I even took his weapon from his hands and he didn't so much as twitch.' He started shouting, 'These people are idiots. They haven't got a clue what their duties are. It's the middle of the night and Arafat's personal bodyguard is drooling and snoring!'

Arafat had a fear of assassination and there had been many attempts on his life. I can reveal a secret now – the reason he was so reluctant to go to Gaza and kept on postponing his return after signing the Oslo Agreement was that there was credible intelligence that the Abu Nidal Organization had smuggled five rocket launchers into Gaza and were planning to blow up his armoured car and kill him. Since they had already assassinated numerous PLO representatives and officials, everyone knew this wasn't an empty threat.

India

Arafat had long-standing ties with the Gandhi dynasty and he took me to visit Rajiv Gandhi and his wife Sonia, who would later lead the Congress Party. Rajiv Gandhi treated Arafat as if he was part of the family and wanted to enlist his help during his presidential campaign. He proposed an unusual mission for the PLO leader. Among India's many gurus was one, greatly revered by his followers, who had Palestinian origins. Rajiv wanted Arafat to visit him: 'You're the leader of the Palestinians,' he reasoned, 'so he should be open to your persuasion. I am sure you can convince him to get all his disciples to vote for me.' Arafat duly obliged and set off to the *ashram* where the guru was housed. The guru was humble and welcomed Arafat in Arabic. Arafat soon got to the point and in a rather undiplomatic manner said, 'Look, I am asking you as leader of the Palestinians to support Rajiv Gandhi.'

'Excuse me,' said the guru, 'What is the population of Palestine?'

'Five million, six million,' said Arafat.

'Well, my followers number forty million,' said the guru. 'So I don't think you are in any position to order me about!' Arafat always remembered this encounter and joked about it a lot. It wasn't so amusing for Rajiv Gandhi though because he lost the election.

The next day Arafat asked me to accompany him to Calcutta and to arrange for a photographer to come with us. 'What are you going to do there?' I asked. 'I am going to give a speech to a large crowd in the Netaji Stadium,' he said. Arafat did indeed give a speech at the stadium which was filled with tens of thousands of people but this was not the real reason for his visit. That afternoon, we were driven into the heart of the slums of Calcutta where Arafat was to meet Mother Teresa.

Arafat was a master of PR. He knew how to get the headlines but this was publicity genius even by his standards. The Nobel Peace Prize-winning nun greeted the guerrilla leader who kissed her hands. Both wearing their own distinctive head-gear – Mother Teresa with her white nun's habit edged with blue and Arafat with his *keffiyeh* – they sat on a dusty bench, engaged in deep conversation about the plight of the Palestinian people. Mother Teresa spoke with passion and sympathy and the world's press went mad! They were bathed not in divine light but the light from a hundred flash bulbs. The pictures were beamed around the globe and appeared in every newspaper the next day. Four years later, in 1994, Arafat received the Nobel Peace Prize himself.

End Game

The last time I met Arafat face to face was at the end of 2000. Between then and his death I had several telephone conversations with him. He used to call me from time to time to talk about the latest situation or because he was angry about a critical editorial I had written about the Palestinian Authority. He complained about the way the US was systematically side-lining him in order to promote Mahmoud Abbas, whom they considered more flexible. He believed the US wanted him to sign a final peace treaty, which would surrender Jerusalem and the right of return, and then retire. 'They want me to be like a male bee,' he mused. 'To mate with the queen just once and then die.'

Arafat's nemesis, Ariel Sharon, was elected prime minister in 2001 and initiated his persecution of the Palestinian leader. There was no denying it was personal. In January 2002, the Israeli army launched a major offensive in Ramallah and in March 2002, tanks and soldiers surrounded what remained of Arafat's bombed-out compound and placed him under house arrest. Sharon mockingly announced that Arafat could leave any time he wanted, on condition that he never return to Palestine. I spoke to Arafat during the period he was under siege and he told me that he was certain Sharon would assassinate him; he thought the most likely method would be poisoning. He had put a combination padlock on his fridge and ate only tinned products. (The Israeli forces, it should be said, are no strangers to assassination by poison. On 25 September 1997 in Amman, Khaled Meshal of Hamas was jabbed in the ear with a syringe containing poison by a Mossad agent. King Hussein insisted that an antidote be provided instantly unless Netanyahu wanted an international incident to ensue, and threatened to break the peace treaty between Jordan and Israel. The Israelis complied.)

A brief truce in May 2002 saw Arafat emerge to rapturous public demonstrations and with permission to roam relatively freely in Gaza and the West Bank; but when the US-sponsored 'road map' for peace was produced in 2003 Sharon wanted Arafat exiled. By April 2004, Sharon had become all the more daring in his desire to crush Arafat and announced that the ageing leader was a 'legitimate target' for assassination. Two weeks earlier, Israeli helicopters had fired rockets at a car carrying the wheelchair-bound religious leader, Sheikh Ahmed Yassin, who was killed in the attack.

Arafat was isolated, once again under siege in his compound and ostracized by many of his fellow Arab leaders. Two months prior to his death, he asked one of his trusted aides to phone me with a story: the Egyptian intelligence chief, Omar Suleiman, had been to visit him and had laid his cards on the table. Suleiman said that the Israeli agenda was to kill him, while the US favoured permanent exile. The Egyptians proposed a third way, offering Arafat their protection if he would relinquish government and control of the Palestinian security forces to Prime Minister Ahmed Qorei. According to the Egyptian plan, Arafat would become a figurehead but retain no actual power. Suleiman gave Arafat six weeks to effect these changes but nothing happened.

A while later, he telephoned me personally. His voice was quiet and demoralized. 'They have all abandoned me,' he said. 'Not one of those Arab leaders has been in touch even to say hello.' He said he knew that his days were numbered but he was defiant. 'I am a man of faith, Abdel Bari. I will never give up the Palestinian cause. I want to die a martyr,' he said. He saw Sharon as his mortal foe, 'He wants me to die before him,' he confided.

'And I am afraid that he will succeed. That's why I would never shake his hand.' Arafat's last days were spent in expectation of assassination. As well as his precautions against poisoning, he had iron poles mounted on the roof to prevent Israeli helicopters from landing on it and slept with a gas mask beside him.

On 25 October 2004, Arafat experienced excruciating abdominal pains and vomited during a meeting. His doctors were unable to find anything wrong but suggested it could be a 'bug'. Then on 27 October, the Palestinian leader fell unconscious for a full quarter of an hour but aides managed to bring him around. Doctors from Egypt and Jordan were as baffled as Arafat's own physicians and suggested he should be moved to Paris. As he was taken from his compound to board a plane for France he whispered to his aides, 'This time they got me.' When Arafat stopped over in Amman, King Abdullah did not so much as pay him a courtesy visit.

French doctors ruled out the presence of any kind of life-threatening illness, yet by 3 November Arafat had fallen into a coma from which he would never emerge. He died on 11 November 2004. Religious leader, Sheikh Taissir Tamimi, who was at Arafat's deathbed, told of blood oozing from the pores all over his face at the end. His doctor Ashraf al-Kurdi stated that his symptoms were typical of poisoning. This opinion is also shared by Arafat's brother Muhassen who is a medical doctor in Abu Dhabi and who is convinced that Arafat was assassinated by someone in his own entourage. He told me that he could have been poisoned by a handshake. Arafat died before Sharon, it is true, but the latter didn't have much time to enjoy this victory, because two months later he suffered a massive stroke and has been in a permanent vegetative state ever since.

Arafat wanted to be buried in Jerusalem, near the al-Aqsa mosque, but the Israelis refused permission for this. Instead he was buried in the courtyard of his ruined headquarters at al-Muqata'a in Ramallah, where a large memorial has been erected and which still inspires the Palestinian people today.

I was unable to attend his funeral because it took place in Cairo and I am barred from Egypt. Nor could I pay my respects in Palestine because I was not able to get an entry permit there either. But as I watched the burial in al-Muqata'a on television, I remembered the first time I visited him in his beachside Gaza headquarters after the interim agreement had been implemented. He was uncharacteristically quiet. It was night-time and after a while he said, 'Listen carefully,' but did not speak.

'Listen to what, Abu Ammar?' I asked.

'Listen to the sea,' he said. 'Can you hear it?' I could smell the salt and I listened to the steady rhythm of the waves breaking on the sand. I knew what the leader was thinking as he continued. 'Without the Oslo Agreement I would still be in exile,' he said. 'My dream is to be buried under Palestinian soil and now that I am home that may yet come true.' And while I still disagreed with him politically, on this point he was right. I hope his soul is at rest now.

10

Right to Return

In 1995, the Palestinian Authority had been in administrative control of the Gaza Strip for more than a year and I decided to take the family to visit our homeland. I hadn't been back since 1968 except for a brief stay in 1973 when I escorted my brother's bride, Camilla, to Jordan. Basima had left Palestine aged seven, an absence of twenty-seven years. She was overwhelmed by the prospect of going 'home' and recalled all the names of her primary school friends and the places where they used to play in al-Nusairat refugee camp. 'Wherever we moved those memories came with me,' she told me as we sat planning our trip. 'I remember more from those times than any other period of my life.'

Much of my family had not moved far: my mother still lived in the same little house in Rafah but she shared it now with my brother Jalal, his wife and six children. My older sister Souad was still in Gaza, in Khan Younis refugee camp, and my youngest sister Amal had moved to the Gaza Beach refugee camp where she had married a distant cousin Souhail, producing several children in quick succession. Whenever I feel low I telephone Amal, who has a biting sense of humour and refuses to let anything get her down for long, as befits her name which means 'hope'. I remember one call I made to Amal in 1989 at the height of the First Intifada after the telephone lines had been cut for several months.

'So, are you delivering or expecting?' I asked her. 'Or both?'

'I just had a baby,' she replied. 'Three months ago.'

'I knew it,' I laughed. 'And is it a boy or a girl?'

'It was a boy,' she said. 'But he's dead.' Shocked, I changed my tone and asked what had happened.

'He was a lovely fat baby with beautiful green eyes,' said Amal. 'We called him Abdullah and he was happy and healthy. I put him in his cot one afternoon and went to sit outside. Suddenly some kids came tearing towards me with five Israeli soldiers after them. The boys went around the back of our house and started throwing stones at the soldiers who opened fire with a tear gas gun. I ran indoors to get away from the gas and went straight to the baby. He was suffocating, the canister had landed right under the open window of the room where he was sleeping. I rushed him to the doctor but it was too late.'

Deeply upset, I murmured my commiserations, reflecting how petty my problems were compared with the life my family was forced to endure in Gaza. Amal shed a few tears but soon spoke again. 'But don't worry, brother,' she said. 'I am pregnant again and I will compensate for him.' True to her word she later gave birth to twin boys.

Now Basima and I busied the Rafah refugee camp telephone network with the news of our intended trip that summer and my mother went into organizational overdrive. My other brothers were living abroad but the whole family agreed to travel to Rafah in August for a reunion.

A Beautiful Country

We were flying British Airways and I had a British passport but I expected some kind of problems at Tel Aviv airport since my name and appearance clearly identify me as a Palestinian. I asked my family to wait until the rest of the queue had gone through passport control because I didn't want to cause a long delay for our fellow passengers while we were quizzed. To my surprise the woman at the desk simply glanced at us, put red cards in our passports and waved us through.

'Well, that was alright,' said Basima, visibly relieved, and gathering children and belongings we walked on, chatting about what we would do and who we would see. A young woman approached us, dressed in civilian clothes, but with the air of an official. She can't have been more than twenty-two. 'Excuse me,' she said. 'Would you mind following me for a moment?'

In the interview room she scoured her computer screen. 'How long have you been away, Mr Atwan?' she asked.

'Twenty-seven years,' I replied. 'Except for a brief trip in 1973.'

'Why is that?' she asked.

'I am sure you know why,' I said, trying not to become agitated.

'Do tell me,' she looked away from the screen and scrutinized my face.

'Because our country is under occupation ...'

'You have brothers,' the young woman interrupted. 'Where are they now?'

'One is in a refugee camp,' I told her, 'the others are abroad.'

'Why?'

I didn't know if she was trying to provoke me or if she was genuinely igno-rant, but I did know I had to be careful. 'We are stateless,' I answered calmly, 'because you Israelis have taken our country!' Her computer now informed her that I was a member of the PNC and she asked me a little about this and how often I attended the meetings of this parliament in exile before wishing us a good holiday. 'A good holiday? In a refugee camp?' I asked her.

'Our country is beautiful,' she smiled.

We took a taxi from Tel Aviv to Gaza, hugging the Mediterranean coast as we headed southwards through cultivated farmlands and orange groves. The August sky was deepest azure and the air was permeated with the crisp scent of hot earth. The children were excited, enjoying the sunshine and the glimpses of beaches, imagining no doubt that this journey would end in a five-star hotel with a choice of swimming pools as all our previous holiday flights had done. As we entered a large city, I noted that the sign was in Hebrew. Our driver was an Israeli of Moroccan origin who spoke fluent Arabic and I asked him where we were.

'Ashdod,' he said. 'The biggest port in Israel.' My heart thumped in my chest. I was speechless for a moment, gazing out of the window as I composed my emotions. 'This is where Basima's father and both my parents came from,' I told the children. 'Isdud. It was only a village back then, before the *Nakba*.' I had read about the mass immigration of Soviet Jews into this area after 1991, boosting the population to more than 200,000, but I was still overwhelmed by this transformation. 'Is there anything left of the original village?' I asked the driver. 'What do you mean?' he said. 'There was nothing here before. Ashdod was established in the 1960s by the Israelis.'

As we travelled along the dusty main road through Isdud I saw a ruined building to the left in front of an orange grove. There was Arabic graffiti painted in white on the broken red walls. I asked the driver to stop and I got out. The graffiti said, 'Here stood Café Gaben.' I couldn't believe my eyes. Café Gaben: how often I had heard my father talk about this place. It had been the focal point of village social life, the only café where the youth could meet, the place where men would gather after a day's work to play backgammon or cards and drink strong tea. I stepped over the broken wall and went inside the ruin; it was full of weeds and broken bottles and passers-by had used it as a toilet. Yet I could make out the remains of mosaic tiling where the counter would have been and the café reassembled itself in my imagination; the walls still contained the sound of men talking, a steady murmur broken now and then by laughter or a voice raised in irritation or protest, the clanking of coffee cups, the odour of hashish smoked in a hookah.

This strange communion with the past was broken by the sound of real footsteps in the present. I turned to find an Israeli settler standing on the other side of the broken wall staring at me. He was carrying an Uzi machine gun and addressed me in Hebrew at first, of which I didn't understand a word. 'What are you doing here?' he then asked me in broken, heavily accented Arabic.

'It's Café Gaben,' I said.

'It's a ruin,' he replied. 'You'd better get out. For your own safety.'

'My brothers were born in Isdud,' I told him. 'A Palestinian village.'

'Well, that is the past.' He seemed nervous, even embarrassed.

'No, it is also the future,' I walked to the wall and climbed over it, pointing at the taxi where Khalid and Nada's little faces were peering out. 'My future and my children's,' I said.

Homecoming

We took the taxi as far as the Eretz checkpoint at the northern tip of the Gaza Strip. My brothers were meeting us there since they were forbidden to drive outside the Occupied Territories. On 17 July 1994 – only a year before – Eretz had been the scene of a terrible massacre when Israeli forces opened fire on Palestinian workers on Sunday 17 July. A six-hour battle ensued, during which IDF (Israeli Defence Force) soldiers were joined by Israeli settlers from within the Gaza Strip, as well as four Israeli tanks and a helicopter; by the end, eleven Palestinians lay dead and up to 200 had been wounded. I had this in mind as we took our luggage from the back of the taxi and walked the dusty road towards the checkpoint. Several armed Israeli guards watched our approach with their fingers on the trigger of their machine guns. Basima gripped little Nada's hand so tightly that she complained it hurt; I realized that Basima was battling with the phobia she had developed as a child and which had sent her scuttling behind her mother's skirts every time she saw an Israeli soldier. 'Look!' I said, trying to distract her. 'There are my brothers!' I pointed at the four men who were waiting for us by an ancient taxi on the other side of the checkpoint, hands by their sides.

'Why don't they wave?' Khalid asked me, clinging to my arm and jumping up and down excitedly.

'Because the soldiers might think they are making a signal,' I said. He had no idea what I meant. 'Never mind, we will be there soon,' I said. The soldiers glanced at our passports and let us through. 'You see,' I reassured my family. 'Everything's fine.'

We had a warm reunion by Jalal's seven-seater Mercedes taxi. The children had never seen such an old vehicle though it is typical for a Gazan.

'You should send it to the Mercedes company for their museum,' I told Jalal. 'It's living proof that they can create an indestructible car.'

'Actually,' Jalal told the children, 'our Palestinian mechanics have changed every single thing in it over the years with spare parts from all types of vehicles. The only part of it that is still Mercedes is the badge.'

Khalid and Nada were questioned and teased and joked with by their uncles as we journeyed but once we entered the camp their smiles and giggles faded and were replaced with expressions of incomprehension and anxiety. Rafah is home to more than 95,000 refugees and is one of the most densely populated places on the planet. There were people everywhere, the car moving slowly through the crowds, horn beeping as curious faces pressed against the windows to see who these strangers were.

Stopping outside my mother's house, we had to step over open sewage channels to get to the front door. Khalid and Nada were aghast. These children had been brought up in London and had never known anything but flushing toilets and showers.

The last time I had seen my mother was eight years before at Kamal's house in Saudi Arabia. As she came out to greet us, my heart lurched to see that she was limping, moving her hips awkwardly. She looked older but her smile was radiant on this historic occasion of our family reunion on Palestinian soil. My mother had seen Khalid when he was two but she hadn't met Nada; though she had around forty grandchildren, she longed to see mine, every one of them being so special to her, and she burst into tears of joy as she hugged and kissed them now. But for them, she was a stranger and they accepted her embraces awkwardly, more British than Arab at that moment.

As we entered the tiny house the place erupted with children. Khalid and Nada suddenly discovered that they had dozens of cousins and they were all here to greet them. It was like a whole primary school of ragged urchins speaking to them in a language they could scarcely understand, touching them and marvelling at how well groomed they were. Some were stricken with admiration for their 'Western' cousins, some approached them like pets or dolls, whilst others found them 'spoilt'. Opinion was divided and vocal. Since the house consisted of just three 9-metre square rooms and a courtyard, Khalid and Nada had neither a place to hide nor the possibility of getting away for some 'quiet time'. A situation they were quite unused to.

My mother was critical of the fact that my children didn't speak fluent Arabic, and I agreed with her, pointing out that this was my fault rather than theirs. As time went on, however, they picked up the language and a Gazan accent too. The children's lack of Arabic was not all my mother had to complain about. Although she was delighted with Basima as a daughter-in-law she started a campaign from day one designed to shame her into having more children. 'What is the matter? Is there a problem? No. Well then, why do you only have two children? Are you on birth control? Throw it away! It is not Allah's will ...' Or sometimes is would be, 'Look at Kamal, he has eight, and Ziad has six, Bashir has three already. And I myself, thanks to God, I gave birth to ten.' Poor Basima! She dealt with this onslaught with dignity and tact but privately she was mortified. Basima's family background was more bourgeois than mine and she wasn't used to our peasant-like forthrightness.

Nada and Khalid were holding their own in the moaning department too. They couldn't believe it when the evening meal was brought in on two enormous communal dishes and deposited on the floor on top of sheets of old newspapers. When everyone sat on the ground and dug in with their fingers they frowned in disbelief. The ingredients of the meal were even more disappointing for them, consisting of rice, chickpeas and carrots. They didn't eat a thing.

Bedtime brought further culture shock as mattress after mattress was unrolled on the floor. As guests of honour they were treated to the luxury of sharing with my mother and Basima, which meant they were only four in that room. In the two other rooms at least ten would lie like sardines, mattresses wedged up against each other and the walls. Along with most of the men, I slept outside in the courtyard.

By lunchtime the next day my children were hungry and begging me to organize something they could eat. My mother quizzed them as to what sort of food they liked. 'Burgers,' Nada sobbed.

'Burgers?' My mother asked me. 'What is this burgers?'

'They're like *kofta*,' I did my best to explain. 'Or kebabs.'

'Kebabs!' My mother's eyes widened. 'I myself have had kebab only once, when I visited you in Jordan!' I tried to explain to the children that meat is a rare commodity in the refugee camps and most people there are vegetarian, by force not by choice. My mother, meanwhile, had been racking her brains.

'I can perhaps get hold of some lamb's heads,' she pondered. 'Would that please them?' By now all eyes were on my children and I translated this item from the menu of possibilities. Nada screamed, to the great hilarity of her relatives. 'How about chicken?' Jalal suggested, and Khalid nodded enthusiastically. My mother kept chickens for their eggs but they were rarely slaughtered. Half an hour later Jalal wandered in with two live chickens in his hand, swinging them by their feet. 'Dinner,' he grinned at Khalid and Nada, nodding at the squawking beasts. He put one down and it scuttled across the room; he picked up an enormous kitchen knife and cut the other one's throat then and there. Khalid and Nada gaped in horror. I don't think it had occurred to them that meat comes from live animals before this moment. They ate the chicken but couldn't sleep that night, haunted by the bloody scene and had nightmares about it for months after.

It was difficult to watch the children suffer the deprivations of the refugee camp but, as I reminded them, this was everyday reality for their cousins and back in the comfort of their home in London, they often talk about this situation with sadness. They had stomach upsets throughout the trip and were bitten by every imaginable insect; but with the remarkable adaptability of the young they soon got used to their surroundings, including the sight of rats, cockroaches and ants strolling around in the house. Nobody bothers to kill these pests but treats them instead as friends of the family.

Unused to being surrounded by scores of other children, Nada and Khalid worked out that the only way to get any privacy was to appropriate one of the tiny rooms and barricade the door. They had a good reason to crave this isolation: Nutella. Intending it as a present, they had brought a jar of their favourite chocolate and hazelnut spread from England but now they wanted it for themselves and this became their one treat, smeared on flat Arabic bread. Unfortunately, after a few days one of their cousins discovered their secret stash of Western indulgence and wasted no time alerting the other children. When Khalid and Nada next returned the jar was still there but empty; every last drop had been extracted, and the glass jar licked clean.

I spent a lot of time with the children, telling them about my childhood in this camp and Deir al-Balah. Back in London, I had mentioned the beach where much of my own youth had been played out and in anticipation of this, expecting a holiday resort, they had packed swimming costumes, and snorkels. Now they were agitating for a trip to the sea and had already picked out a posse of cousins to accompany us.

A Day at the Beach

Gaza's beaches are a far cry from the Costa del Sol. The last time a Gazan beach made the news was on 9 June 2006 when an Israeli gunboat opened fire on Beit Lahia, in the north of the Gaza Strip, killing seven members of one family and a friend of theirs as they picnicked on the sand. The beach nearest Rafah was under Israeli military control all the way from Tel Kalifa to the border (an area called the Philadelphi Corridor by Israelis but known as the Saladin Corridor to the Palestinians).

Basima insisted that we smother ourselves with sun cream, to the amazement and amusement of my relatives. Long since blackened by Gaza's fierce sun they had never heard of such a thing. The children were so thoroughly coated in factor 50 sun block that, if anything, they were paler when they came home than when they had left. Burdened with carrier bags containing food and water, rugs to sit on, and buckets and spades, my brothers and I staggered across the sand, surrounded by an over-excited crowd of our offspring.

The beach where I had spent so many days as a boy looked different now. Fenced off with barbed wire, entry was via an Israeli checkpoint presided over by a watchtower where we had to present our passports. The reason for this tight security was the proximity of an illegal Israeli settlement; IDF soldiers on foot and in Jeeps patrolled the beach where a handful of families were endeavouring to enjoy some respite from their claustrophobic living conditions. It was a wild day with high winds and a choppy, violent sea. We pitched our camp and relaxed on the warm sand. The children rushed into the waves, leaping through them and then letting the tide carry them back to the shore. We talked and dozed, recalling the past and filling each other in on the missing details of our present lives.

Suddenly all the children started shouting and screaming. Jalal and I leaped to our feet and ran towards the sea. Two of the boys had got into difficulties in the swell and were struggling some way out, disappearing for long periods under the waves. We raced in and, God knows how because I am no longer a strong swimmer, managed to rescue them.

Settlers

Back in London, some time later, I received reports that even more of the 45-kilometre Gazan coast had been annexed and half of it prohibited to Arabs following a guerrilla attack on one of the illegal Israeli settlements which continued to mushroom near the best beaches and along the most verdant coastal agricultural areas of what was meant to be 'Palestinian territory'.

The settlements had started as early as 1970 and the biggest, Neve Dekalim, had 2,671 residents at its peak. By 2005 when the settlers were forced to withdraw, there were twenty-six such enclaves within Gaza, seventeen of which were either on or by the beach, joined by so-called bypass roads which Palestinians were not allowed to use. Eventually consuming 40 percent of Gaza's meagre 365 square kilometres, just 9,000 Israeli settlers enjoyed the best of Gaza, while 1.5 million Palestinians were crammed together in the remainder with little in the way of resources or employment opportunities.

Often built on hilltops for security purposes these settlements also presented health hazards to the Arab towns and villages nestling in the valleys below; the Israeli settlers didn't have sewage treatment plants but sent their waste downhill to their neighbours whose health and agriculture were seriously affected.

The settlement movement and its illegal land grabs were encouraged by the Israeli government and funded to the tune of $300 million a year even though they were in breach of the fourth Geneva Convention on human rights[1] and were regularly condemned by the UN General Assembly. The Oslo Accords had made no provision for the withdrawal of illegal Israeli settlements and, by 2005, the settler population in both Gaza and West Bank more than doubled from 115,000 to 242,500.[2] The purpose of the settlements was political, as the following extract from the Jewish Virtual Library makes clear:[3]

> The largest group of settlements ... expand the Israeli presence from the city of Ashkelon (inside Israel) to the edges of Gaza City ... strategically located in the heart of the Gaza Strip (along a north-south axis), [they] create a framework for Israeli control of the area and its main transportation route, and facilitate Israel's ability to divide the Gaza Strip into separate areas and isolate each area's inhabitants. In addition, the settlements control prime agricultural land, some of the area's main aquifers, and approximately one-third of the total Gaza coastline.

In July 2005, the Israeli government instructed all settlers to leave Gaza,

1. 'The Occupying Power shall not deport or transfer parts of its own civilian population into the territory it occupies.' Article 49 of the Fourth Geneva Convention of 1949.
2. http://www.fmep.org/settlement_info/stats_data/settler_populations/settler_populations_1972-2004.html
3 www.jewishvirtuallibrary.org/jsource/Peace/gaza_settlements.html

fearing for their lives at the hands of their deprived and increasingly radical neighbours. When Ariel Sharon announced the plan, he was open about the fact that the move was for the benefit of the Israelis, not the Arabs. Each settler family was paid $250,000 compensation for leaving Gaza and was relocated to a new settlement under construction near Jericho inside the West Bank where 235,000 illegal settlers remain undisturbed and settlement expansion continues unabated. The Gaza withdrawal provided a temporary smokescreen for these West Bank settlements and the continuing encroachment onto Palestinian land of the 'West Bank barrier' now known, and internationally condemned, as the Apartheid Wall.

In an interview with the Israeli daily *Haaretz* on 6 October 2004, Dov Weissglas, Sharon's then chief of staff, disclosed another motive for the imminent dismantlement of the Gazan settlements: 'The significance of the disengagement plan is the freezing of the peace process ... When you freeze that process, you prevent the establishment of a Palestinian state and you prevent a discussion on the refugees, the borders, and Jerusalem.'

On leaving Gaza, the settlers and the IDF destroyed everything potentially useful. However, the Palestinian Authority (PA) negotiated the purchase of the settlers' commercial greenhouses, so that the flower-growing industry could continue in an area where there are hardly any employment opportunities. Just a few months later the Israelis closed the border, effectively destroying the industry since the flowers could no longer be exported to their European market.

The demilitarization of Gaza's shoreline had a tragic aftermath: as the last of the settlers reluctantly withdrew, Palestinians flocked to the beaches in their thousands (they hadn't been allowed on them for ten years). Unfortunately, many had no idea how to swim and on the first day alone fourteen Palestinians of various ages drowned.

Fame at Last

In Rafah refugee camp time is meaningless since there is little work available and not much else to do. Used to a stressful and demanding timetable in London, it was a great novelty for me to sleep when I was tired and stay awake as I pleased. Having come from abroad, and being relatively well known in the Arab world, I rapidly became the camp's entertainment. The first half of our stay, an endless stream of visitors came to welcome me and chat for hours. The second half they all came back to say goodbye and wish me a good journey.

My mother was unimpressed by my 'celebrity' status. In fact, she seemed to think there was some mistake –– that is, until Dr Zidan got involved. Dr Zidan was the camp's only private doctor, offering medical advice and treatment in exchange for whatever the refugees had to barter with, even for free if they had nothing. In my mother's case, an examination for a chest infection and a course of antibiotics would be exchanged for a chicken or a duck. She thought he was the most intelligent man on the planet, a complete genius, and hung on his every word. As for me, she had never believed that I was doing well in my career even when I, or my brothers, talked about it. She was still of the opinion that I had wasted my education by not becoming an architect or a doctor, like her hero. One day she came hurrying back home in a state of excitement and found me drinking coffee with Jalal. 'Jalal!' she cried. 'Jalal, your brother Sayeed is a famous man!' This came as no surprise to him and he looked at her blankly. 'He has been doing well in the newspapers,' my mother informed us. 'Yes, Mum, we know,' said Jalal, amused. 'Why have you only discovered this now, when we've been telling you all about it for years!'

'Yes, but now I know it is true because Dr Zidan says so. I just met him in the road and he said Sayeed is a famous journalist and that he has heard him speaking on the BBC World Service. He said, what was it now?' she wrinkled her brow. 'Yes, he said that Sayeed talks "with passion and elegance". Imagine!' And she kissed my forehead. 'I am so proud of you, my dear,' she said. Naturally I was grateful to Dr Zidan for this elevation of my status within the Atwan household. In 2004, I got a call from his son who had a medical fellowship in London and was sad to hear his father had passed away. I wonder who cares for the penniless Gazan refugees when they are sick now.

Fitting in

Meanwhile Khalid and Nada had been making inroads into the world of their Palestinian peers. Their Arabic had improved beyond belief, bubbling up from the subconscious where it had been planted via a combination of Saturday classes, hearing it spoken at home and a genetic predisposition to the language. Nada joined in with the girls playing *hajla*, which is like hopscotch, and with dolls: either of the home-made variety – bits of rags tied around sticks with straw for hair – or second-hand plastic ones which had found their way to Rafah via a charity organization in the West. Khalid, in turn, played with his male cousins, enjoying similar activities to those that had filled my own youth, mostly climbing trees and football.

Both Khalid and Nada had remarked on the posters of 'Martyrs' – young people who had lost their lives fighting the Israelis – that adorned their cousins' walls. Children become politicized at an early age in such harsh circumstances and revere these 'martyrs' in the same way that their Western counterparts idolize film stars or pop musicians. One night we were sitting out in the courtyard and I overheard Khalid and his cousins, up on the flat roof, talking about the First Intifada which had come to an end just two years previously. I had sometimes talked to Khalid about the political situation in Palestine though it seemed to go in one ear and out the other, but now it came alive for him as he listened to his peers.

'These Israeli soldiers with machine guns came marching into the camp,' one boy said. 'Some older boys were trying to stop them going any further.'

'Yes, because they used to come in and shoot people,' another boy explained.

'So they started throwing stones at them,' the first one continued. 'We joined in and – '

'Then they started shooting at us,' I recognized the voice of my nephew Muhammad, Jalal's boy. (He would later become involved in the Second Intifada and Jalal fully expected him to be killed, but in the end he chose to join the Palestinian security forces.) 'We were only about nine years old. They were running at us – bammmm bammm,' he imitated the sound of machine-gun fire. 'I saw my friend Issam fall to the ground. I ran and hid around the side of a house. I could still see Issam lying on the ground, not moving. The soldiers ran on and a group of men and boys went after them showering them with stones. They were getting hit from behind and in front. Imagine, stones against guns!'

'And tanks!' yet another chipped in. 'And helicopters!'

'What happened to Issam?' I recognized Khalid's voice. 'Was he alright?'

'He was taken to hospital in Israel,' one of the boys told him. 'He had to have his leg chopped off and they gave him a false one. First they shoot him, then they give him a false leg.'

'And expect his parents to be grateful,' someone added and they all laughed.

'Wow!' Khalid was impressed. 'I want to fight too. Come on, let's go and throw stones at the soldiers.'

'It's the Oslo Accords now,' said a boy who can't have been more than ten years old judging by his voice. 'It is meant to be peace. But if they come again with tanks and guns we will fight them.'

'And then you can come with us,' said Muhammad. 'You can come over from England and then you will be our brother.'

'Yeah, we'll be brothers!' said Khalid excitedly, and I could hear the sound of the children slapping hands.

Deir al-Balah Refugee Camp

I decided to visit Deir al-Balah, the camp where I had been born, with two of my brothers, Kamal and Jalal. There were checkpoints on every road that passed near an Israeli settlement and we were constantly stopped and searched. More than ever, Gaza resembled a 40-kilometre-long prison.

The first thing that struck me as we entered the camp was how small everything was in comparison with how I remembered it. The roads were so narrow and tiny and the trees that had formed the jungles of my infancy were actually weedy things. We went to the school I had attended and looked around; it had fallen into disrepair and yet this ramshackle place was still the sole source of hope for thousands of Palestinian children who could change the course of their lives through education.

We looked for our house but couldn't find it; the camp had expanded outwards in a mess of improvised dwellings and breeze-block shelters. We went to the beach where I had spent so many happy childhood hours and found it as primitive as ever; the fishermen were still busy eking out a living but now they were clothed in response to the rising tide of Islamic fundamentalism in Gaza, whereas before we had all been naked in the sunshine.

I asked around about my old friends from school days and was delighted when a group of young men told me they knew Ali, who had become an apprentice engineer the last I heard of him. Accompanied by a crowd, I was led to an impoverished dwelling from which a fatter, balder but still recognizable Ali emerged. We embraced, both of us astonished at this spontaneous reunion. As we sat outside his house and drank coffee, Ali gave me some surprising news. 'Abdel Bari, do you remember Hamza?' I nodded. 'Hamza the dreamer who only lived to cross the sea?' I nodded again and told Ali I had met him myself, by chance, a few years back in Shepherd's Bush.

'Well, he's back!' Ali announced. 'Can you imagine, he gets out of here and then chooses to return to this refugee camp?' It turned out that Hamza had left his Maltese wife and had bought a house at the edge of the camp in the town of Deir al-Balah itself. He was happy now, according to Ali, and his son, Yusuf, came to visit him regularly.

'Come, Abdel Bari,' said Ali, getting up. 'I want to show you something.' I followed him down the street to his garage where, he explained, he now ran his own business as a mechanic and second-hand car dealer. He undid the padlock on the rickety iron doors and opened them to reveal a brand new American SUV Jeep. I burst out laughing, 'Where on earth did you get that?' I asked him.

'This is my contribution to the glorious Palestinian resistance,' he explained, stroking the vehicle's sleek black sides and shiny chrome. 'It's stolen, of course. Israeli car thieves bring them to me. They tell the border guards they're visiting the settlements but they drop the vehicle off here and I give them their money. This is the best example of Israeli–Palestinian cooperation that I know of! We dismantle the older ones and use them for spare parts and there's a good black market for luxury vehicles since the PLO boys came back to town.'

'Surely it's not difficult to spot a stolen car here,' I suggested. 'Nobody else in the entire Gaza Strip has a vehicle less than thirty years old.'

'True, my friend,' he conceded. 'But don't forget, Gaza is controlled by the Palestinian Authority now. Israeli cops can't come in anymore and our Palestinian police take a more enlightened view, or you can pay them off if they don't.'

As far as I could see, nothing in Gaza had changed in twenty-seven years except to become older and more run down. The houses were still makeshift, there was no proper sewage system in place, no running water and no services inside the camp. One large electricity generator provided an intermittent supply to more than half the population – even this was destroyed by an Israeli bombardment in June 2006, in 'retaliation' for the abduction of one Israeli soldier.

Despite the appalling conditions people were forced to endure, there was a mood of great optimism, even euphoria, engendered by the Oslo Accords which had been signed on 13 September 1993, with Oslo 2 following on 28 September 1994. I found myself at loggerheads with my family over this issue because of my opposition to the treaty. 'You don't understand what this means to us, here, in Palestine,' my mother complained. 'You have been away too long. We have had enough of death and suffering.'

'Mum is right,' Kamal agreed. 'You are too radical. Arafat did the right thing. Now we have a Palestinian administration, with Palestinian police and a national anthem. Soon we will see an end to the Israeli occupation and Gaza will become a wealthy place with jobs for everyone.'

'Arafat has a fine new office,' my mother added. 'I've been to see it. It's just like a presidential palace with the Palestinian flag flying over it.'

'It might be just like a presidential palace, Mum,' I countered, 'but what actual power does the Palestinian Authority have? Flags and titles and buildings mean nothing, it's just for show – the Israelis could destroy it all with a few shells tomorrow if they felt like it. We need more than token gestures.'

Our conversation went on long into the night. Living abroad, I had a more objective overview than my relatives whom I urged not to concede too much. 'All I want is a roof over my head, my children around me and food on the table,' my mother said. 'I don't hate Jewish people, it's the Israelis that have caused us so much suffering. Oslo will help us live side by side with the Jewish people like we used to long ago.' I realized how the different mindsets and political goals of those who live abroad and those who have remained in Palestine could prove divisive on the road to a just settlement; this is a crucial aspect of the peace process which should not be overlooked.

My family's optimism touched me and I decided to take my brothers to meet Arafat in his new Gaza compound; it was a sprawling building on the beachfront with a helipad for his two, newly acquired, helicopters. My brothers truly believed that this building and Arafat's presence in Palestine constituted a step in the right direction and were keen to talk to the architect of their hopes. I too was glad to see my old friend when he came into the room to greet us, and embraced him with warmth. Arafat was justifiably proud of his new headquarters; he made us very welcome and I enjoyed the moonlit view of the shoreline while he talked with my brothers about the future of Palestine. Unfortunately Arafat's beautiful building, helipad and helicopters were all destroyed in an Israeli bombardment just six years later.

This first trip to Gaza came to an end after ten days and we headed back to Tel Aviv airport. We must have done something to alert the authorities to our presence because now we were stopped and interrogated by both the police and Mossad. They questioned us all, including eight-year-old Nada, and searched every item in our luggage. As the time for our flight grew nearer, I began to worry we would miss it. 'Who did you meet in Gaza?' asked one officer, pulling out my toiletries bag and inspecting the contents at leisure.

'My family,' I said. 'My people.'

'Anyone else?' he persisted.

'Arafat,' I said, wondering what effect this would have. The officer looked shocked, then confused, and then worried. The Israelis still weren't sure what to make of him at this time. Was he a terrorist or a politician; an ally now or still their mortal enemy? The officer put the toiletries bag back in the case and patted it down before snapping the suitcase shut. 'Please continue,' he said and ushered us out of the room.

Gaza, 1997

I returned to Gaza with the family in summer 1997. This time, on leaving Tel Aviv airport, I asked the driver to take us to Jerusalem. I wanted the children, now aged twelve and ten, to see al-Haram al-Sharif (the Noble Sanctuary) in East Jerusalem, the 35-acre complex which houses the al-Aqsa mosque as well as the oldest Muslim building in the world, the Dome of the Rock. It was a glorious day and we were all impressed by the magnificent buildings, with their minarets and domes, as well as the beautifully laid out gardens and fountains. I explained to the children that Jerusalem has been the historical capital of Palestine and a holy Islamic site for fourteen centuries. Khalid and Nada were quick to point out the presence of Israeli soldiers at the entrance to the al-Aqsa mosque, searching people going in.

'What are they doing?' Nada whispered.

'The Israelis occupied Jerusalem after the 1967 war,' I answered. 'But we want it to be our capital again; there's been a lot of argument over this city.'

'Would the Israelis ever try to stop Muslims going into the mosque?' Khalid asked, outraged by the idea.

'They have done in the past,' I said. 'There have even been attempts to burn it down or take it over. There's a group of Zionist extremists called the Temple Mount Faithful who want to build a Jewish temple over the mosque. And then there was a massacre here in 1990,'[1] I continued. 'Israeli soldiers opened fire on worshippers while they were praying, eighteen died and many more were wounded.' Basima looked at me as if to say, 'Don't say so much, they are only children,' but for all I knew we would never set foot again in this sacred location of Muhammad's ascent, the Muslim's first *qibla*.[2] 'It is holy to us Muslims, the Jewish people, and the Christians,' I told them, 'and I believe it should be open to all faiths. That's how it used to be ... '

'That's why your paper's called *al-Quds-al-Arabi*,' Khalid realized. 'Arab Jerusalem!'

We were greeted with tears and embraces in Gaza as before. Little had changed in terms of the infrastructure and the grinding poverty of everyday life in the camps but I was struck by the proliferation of bearded men and veiled women. This time, Hamas's[3] influence in the camps was noticeable; people had started to mistrust the Oslo peace process and those who had

---

1. The reader is referred to the UN report of this tragic event at http://domino.un.org/ UNISPAL.NSF/85255db800470aa485255d8b004e349a/ed4e150d408c987585256 3da006dbfao!OpenDocument
2. *Qibla* is the direction Muslims turn to face when they are praying. Originally this was Jerusalem until Allah ordained that it should change to Mecca.
3. Hamas, the Palestinian Sunni Islamist organisation, was founded at the beginning of the First Intifada by Sheikh Ahmed Yassin in 1987.

signed up to it. They were looking for new, more radical means to achieve justice and a framework which emphasized Islam and the Palestinian national identity. Hamas fitted the bill.

That isn't to say that everyone was turning away from Arafat and his ruling Fatah party. Many remained optimistic about the future under the PA and the Israelis had made some token withdrawals from the cities but there was a general uneasiness about the ostentatious wealth of Fatah leaders who built large villas by the sea and drove around in brand-new cars. All this stood in stark contrast with the widespread poverty of the people and greatly exercised my brother Jalal who took to describing such leaders as 'parasites on our misery'. For my mother, the most shocking thing was the clothes worn by the daughters of PA leaders. 'I don't know what kind of influence these people will have on the youth,' she wondered. 'They allow their daughters to go about in tight trousers.' In contrast with Hamas which had emerged as an Islamist grassroots movement at the beginning of the First Intifada, the Fatah leaders and their families were now viewed as secular outsiders who had fled the hardships endured by the rest of their people. They were outsiders rather than returnees, subtle differences then but a contrast that has brought the Palestinians to the brink of internecine war in recent times.

Rumours were rife about widespread corruption in the Arafat camp. The most notorious scandal to date occurred in 2004 when Egypt provided the PA with large quantities of cheap concrete to be used for rebuilding Palestinian communities devastated by years of war with Israel. The PA middlemen, however, sold it on to Israeli contractors, at a 50 percent profit, and the concrete intended for Palestinian homes was instead turned into kilometres of the infamous Apartheid Wall. 'Thank God we have Hamas,' said Jalal, a view that would later become so popular that it swept them to power in the January 2006 elections.

In 1997, I had a higher profile than at my previous visit, largely due to my interview with Osama bin Laden the previous year which had been syndicated round the world and led to me making countless television appearances. Word of my arrival in Gaza spread like wildfire and I received delegations and dignitaries from all the different parties and organizations, including Hamas and Fatah, each hoping I would take up and endorse their policies. I spoke with them all and listened carefully to what they had to say but I made a point of reaffirming my independence at the end of each exchange. 'I am only a journalist,' I would tell them. 'I can't afford to take sides.'

My new-found celebrity proved to be a useful commodity for friends and relations, however. It was obvious that the only way anybody got one of the few rare jobs in Gaza under the PA was through nepotism and contacts. People used to come to me, not only from Rafah refugee camp but from all over Gaza, asking me to mediate and exert whatever influence I could with people I knew in the PA. 'You have come from abroad,' they'd say, 'Everyone listens to you,' and then they would give me their own or their children's CVs. I did manage to help a few people in this way but it resulted in a deluge of candidates and after a week my mother's house was more like a job centre than a home.

A Close Shave

At the end of this trip, we had first-hand experience of the increasingly violent methods the Israeli settlement movement had been developing since the bellicose Ariel Sharon's stint as housing minister in the 1980s. We were in a Gazan taxi en route to Tel Aviv airport via Jerusalem. As we wound our way around the high mountain road past Ramallah a car appeared coming the other way. It had yellow number plates which identified it as an Israeli car (Gazan plates are green) and it was going recklessly fast, heading straight for us. There was no space to pull over and a precipice yawned beneath us. The children and Basima saw that the Israeli car wasn't going to let us by and started screaming while I was frozen with horror. Fortunately, our driver was cool-headed and held his ground rather than panicking and veering away, which would have sent us to certain death hundreds of feet below. The driver of the other car had to pull over at the last minute and let us by, rather than kill himself in a head-on collision.

Our driver found a place to stop and we got out of the car to recover from this ordeal and comfort the children. 'That was a settler,' the driver explained, drawing on his cigarette. 'They're trying to terrify Palestinians from going anywhere. It's another method of ethnic cleansing.'

'Does it happen often?' asked Basima, incredulously.

'All the time,' said the driver, quite nonchalantly. 'They've already killed dozens of Palestinians this way. We're getting used to it.'

Gaza, 1999

Shortly before my third visit to Palestine in 1999, I had an important meeting at Heathrow airport. I made my way to the VIP lounge where Yasser Arafat sat waiting for me. As usual we embraced warmly but this time I could sense a change in the man. He no longer spoke of a pragmatic solution and didn't mention the Oslo Accords; his answers were terse and brief, he seemed agitated and frustrated. Suddenly he met my eyes and drew out his pen. He tore a tiny scrap of paper from my notebook which lay on the table between us and started to write something on it. I realized he was afraid that the room, or he himself, was bugged. Arafat finished writing and put the piece of paper in front of me. He had written, 'There is no alternative but the Intifada.' When he was sure I had read it, he took the paper, crossed out every word and screwed it up, putting it into the breast pocket of his jacket.

Arafat was right and just a year later, in July 2000, talks at Camp David broke down despite unprecedented Palestinian concessions which would have seen 78 percent of their original land being designated as the Israeli state. When Palestinian negotiators baulked at the Israeli conditions that the remaining 22 percent be divided into four separate cantons, and that a future autonomous Palestinian entity would have no control over its own borders, airspace or water, there was nothing more to be done. The willingness of the Palestinian people to coexist, and their drive towards peace, had failed to satisfy the Israelis who had exploited the Oslo Accords to consolidate their grip on the West Bank and Gaza, where settlements and land grabs had escalated. The al-Aqsa Intifada broke out in September 2000,

The change in mood was obvious during our last trip to Gaza in 1999. All the optimism was gone, battered by worsening living conditions and corruption in the PA. A peaceful existence and an independent Palestinian state were now as remote a dream as they had ever been and negotiations were deadlocked.

The realization that the Oslo Accords had seen the Palestinians cheated and deceived produced a new resolution and a hardening of hearts. Now the rise of Hamas continued unabated, especially after the Israeli assassination of Yahya Ayyash, the Hamas mastermind behind the suicide bombings, or 'human bombs' as they are more often called, which were increasingly common.[1]

It was rather a joyless visit and our last to date. I am again prevented from entering my homeland; the PA mistrusts me because of my criticisms of it and the Israelis refuse most UK passport-holders entry unless they are recognized friends of Israel.

No Chance to Say Goodbye

In August 2003, I was on holiday with my family in Portugal. My deputy, Sanaa al-Oul, was in charge back at the *al-Quds al-Arabi* offices and took the call from my brothers who were trying to track me down with some bad news: my mother had died of cancer. She was seventy-six years old and had outlived my father by thirty-eight years. Sanaa and my brothers came to the conclusion that I would not be allowed into Gaza even at such a time and decided not to tell me the news until I returned from my holiday three days later.

By the time I heard of her death, she was already buried. It was a double blow for me, not only to lose my beloved mother who had sacrificed so much for us and lived such a difficult life but also to be prevented from attending her funeral and mourning her passing in our own land. I received a touching letter of condolence from Yasser Arafat who had read the news of my mother's death in a local Palestinian paper but few others knew about it. My grieving was done in private and this death compounded our sense of isolation and exile.

Besieged

The situation in Gaza continues to deteriorate; the Israelis have blockaded the territory and imposed such devastating sanctions on it since Hamas won the election in January 2006 that it resembles a concentration camp

---

1. I have examined the phenomenon of 'human bombs' at some length in my book, *The Secret History of al-Qa'ida*.

and many international commentators now accuse the Israelis of systematic genocide in Gaza. Meanwhile the Israelis continue building the Apartheid Wall in the West Bank which is twice the height of the Berlin Wall and more than four times longer than it. Encroaching onto land belonging to Palestinians, the construction work, overseen by soldiers, is frequently preceded by the forced eviction of Arabs from their homes and orchards, which are bulldozed and uprooted. Shops, factories, grazing lands, schools and clinics which fall on the 'wrong side' of the wall are no longer accessible to the Palestinians they service. More than 7 percent of Palestinian territory inside the West Bank will be lost to the wall which costs $1 million dollars per kilometre to build.

Ostensibly to protect the Israelis from suicide bombers, there are several purposes for this wall: first, it is a land grab; secondly, it entrenches the illegal settlements in the West Bank and changes the demographics of the Occupied Territories; and finally, it intimidates and contains the Palestinian population within yet another prison. Psychologically, the wall presents its own ironies. The Israelis too are imprisoned by it, physically and morally; its Apartheid ambitions further separate them from the rest of the world. Israel is rapidly becoming the pariah of modern international politics, the new South Africa, a burden on, and embarrassment to, those who support her. Furthermore, the continuing injustices in Palestine fuel the growth and popularity of radical Islamist groups, not least an increasingly globalized al-Qaʻida.

The Israeli persecution of the Palestinians is uncomfortably close to Hitler's treatment of the Jewish people. The Holocaust has long been used to sanction Israeli atrocities but the influence of a younger generation is now emerging who are exercised by more recent historical events and more visible injustices. A Jewish commentator, Norman Finkelstein, the son of Holocaust survivors, noted in his April 2002 article, 'First the Carrot then the Stick' (originally published in *CounterPunch*): 'If the Israelis don't want to stand accused of being Nazis they should simply stop acting like Nazis.'

I will never give up hope that we Palestinians will one day have the right of return. How can the world look on indifferently when a Jewish family from Europe can have a villa, citizenship, and the protection of the international community while I, whose ancestors lived in Palestine for thousands of years, cannot even visit? I am often asked what solution I would offer to the Arab–Israeli conflict and my answer is quite simple: we have to learn to live together in peace and cooperation in a multicultural society in one democratic secular state for two people. We manage it here in London, it is working in South Africa, and there is enough room for everyone in Palestine. I respect the Jewish people and their religion. I do not want to destroy Israel but I do want to end racism and the current Apartheid system.

I long to return to Palestine and will never give up the fight for my people's right to do so. It is my heartfelt desire that Basima and I will be buried in Palestinian soil when our time comes, at rest in our own land, our exile finally over.

Appendix

On 29 October 1956, the day on which Israel launched its assault on Egypt, units of the Israeli frontier guards began at 4.00 PM what they called a tour of the Triangle Villages. They informed the Mukhtars and the rural councils that the curfew in those villages was, from that day onwards, to be observed from 5.00 PM instead of 6.00 PM as was the case before, and that the inhabitants were, therefore, requested to stay at home from that very instant.

One of the villages the frontier guards passed through was Kafr Kassim, a small Arab village situated near the Israeli settlement of Betah Tefka. The villagers there received the alert at 4.45 PM, only 15 minutes before the new curfew time. Kafr Kassim's Mukhtar promptly informed the unit officer that a large number of the villagers, whose work took them outside the village, knew nothing of this new curfew. The officer in charge replied that his soldiers would take care of these. The villagers who were home complied with the newly-imposed curfew and remained indoors. Meanwhile, the armed frontier guards posted themselves at the village gates. Before long, the first batch of villagers came into sight. The first to arrive was a group of four labourers, home-bound, on bicycles. Here is what one of these labourers, Abdullah Samir Bedir by name, said about the incident:

'We reached the village entrance at about 4.55 PM and were suddenly confronted by a frontier unit consisting of twelve men and an officer, all occupying an army truck. We greeted the officer in Hebrew saying "Shalom, katsin" which means "Peace be unto you, officer," to which he gave no reply. He then asked us in Arabic: "Are you happy?" and we said "Yes." The soldiers started stepping down from the truck and the officer ordered us to line up. Then he shouted to his soldiers this order: "Laktasour otem," which means "Reap them!" The soldiers opened fire, but by then I had flung myself on the ground, and started rolling, yelling as I did so. Then I pretended to be dead. Meanwhile, the soldiers had so riddled the bodies of my three friends with bullets that the officer in charge ordered them to cease firing, adding that the bullets were merely being wasted. As he put it, we had more than the necessary dose of those deadly bullets.

'All this occurred while I lay very still, feigning death. Then I saw three labourers approaching on a small horse cart. The soldiers stopped the cart and killed all three of them. Soon after, the soldiers moved a few yards down the road, apparently to take up positions that would enable them to stop a new truckload of home-bound villagers, as well as a bunch of workers returning home on their bicycles. I seized this opportunity and moved as quickly as I could to the nearest house. The soldiers saw me and opened fire. I was safely indoors when they again stopped a truck carrying thirteen olive pickers, all women and girls, and two male labourers and the driver. They were attacked by the same group of frontier guards, who pitilessly butchered all but one of them.'

This is what sixteen-year-old Hanna Soliman Amer, the only survivor, said about this incident:

'The soldiers brought our car to a halt at the entrance of the village and ordered the two workers and the driver to step down. Then they told them they were going to be killed. On hearing this, the women started crying and screaming, begging the soldiers to spare those poor workers' lives. But the soldiers shouted at the women, saying that their turn was coming and that they, too, were going to be killed.

'The soldiers stared at the women for a few moments, as if waiting for their officer to give the order. Then I heard the officer talk over the wireless set, apparently asking his headquarters for instructions regarding the women. The minute the wireless conversation was over, the soldiers took aim at the women and girls, who were thirteen in number, and which included pregnant ones (Fatma Dawoud Sarsour was in her eighth month of pregnancy) as well as an old woman of sixty and two thirteen-year-old girls (Latifa Eissa and Rashika Bedair).'

The number of cars stopped by the Israeli frontier guards was three; the people in all three cars were ordered to get out and were shot by machine-gun fire, killing them instantly.

With the massacre practically over, the soldiers moved around finishing off whoever still showed signs of being alive. Later on, the examination of these bodies indicated that the soldiers had mutilated them, smashing the heads and cutting open the abdomens of some of the wounded women to finish them off, The only survivors were those who for some time lay buried under the corpses of their comrades and thus had their bodies covered with the blood of these victims, giving the impression that they, too, were dead. Those were the only ones who lived to speak of the horrors of the massacre of Kafr Kassim.

The massacre lasted for an hour and a half and the soldiers looted whatever they could find, apparently while going around the bodies ensuring no one was left alive. Thirteen of those wretched people, however, only fainted when they were shot at. These were taken to Bilinson as well as to other hospitals.

One of those wounded was Osman Selim, who was travelling on one of the trucks. He witnessed the massacre, and escaped by pretending to be dead among the pile of corpses. Asaad Selim, a cyclist, was seriously injured. So was Abdel Rahman Yacoub Sarsoura, a youth aged sixteen, who is deaf and dumb. The only one who managed to escape death and reach Kroum El-Zeitoun was Ismail Akab Badeera, aged eighteen, who nursed his wounds until he got there, then climbed up an olive tree despite his suffering. He remained there for two whole days until a passing shepherd came along and carried him to a hospital where one of his legs had to be amputated for gangrene.

The blood bath was not restricted to the entrance or outskirts, but was carried right into the village itself. Talal Shaker Eissa, aged eight, left his home to bring in a flock of goats. He had hardly stepped out of his home when he was murdered by a shot fired by one of the soldiers. When his father ran out to investigate, he was killed by another shot. The mother, dragging in his body, was then shot. Nowa, the remaining child, followed the cries of agony coming from her parents, and was killed on the spot by a hail of bullets. The only survivor of the family, a frail and aged grandfather, hearing the horror and the sounds of death, succumbed to a heart attack and died.

Source: *Kol Haam*, 19 December 1956, 'How 49 inhabitants of Kafr Kassim were Slaughtered' [often cited on the Internet, for example on http://www.ntcsites.com/palestine/statistics/]